MW01157092

# The Elements of Hittite

Hittite is the earliest attested Indo-European language and was the language of a state which flourished in Asia Minor in the second millennium BC. This exciting and accessible new introductory course, which can be used in both trimester and semester systems, offers in ten lessons a comprehensive introduction to the grammar of the Hittite language, with ample exercises both in transliteration and in cuneiform. It includes a separate section of paradigms and a grammatical index, as well as a list of every cuneiform sign used in the book. A full glossary can be found at the back. The book has been designed so that the cuneiform is not essential and can be left out of any course if so desired. The introduction provides the necessary cultural and historical background, with suggestions for further reading, and explains the principles of the cuneiform writing system.

**Theo van den Hout** is Professor of Hittite and Anatolian Languages at the Oriental Institute of the University of Chicago, and editor-in-chief of the *Chicago Hittite Dictionary* (CHD) since 2000. Besides his work on the dictionary, his current personal interests focus on ancient record management and literacy in Hittite society. He has over twenty years of experience teaching Hittite and other Anatolian languages at the Universities of Amsterdam and Chicago.

THE ELEMENTS OF

# Hittite

THEO VAN DEN HOUT
University of Chicago

CAMBRIDGE
UNIVERSITY PRESS

CAMBRIDGE UNIVERSITY PRESS
Cambridge, New York, Melbourne, Madrid, Cape Town,
Singapore, São Paulo, Delhi, Mexico City

Cambridge University Press
The Edinburgh Building, Cambridge CB2 8RU, UK

www.cambridge.org
Information on this title: www.cambridge.org/9780521133005



First published 2011
Reprinted 2012

Printed at MPG Books Group, UK

*A catalogue record for this publication is available from the British Library*

ISBN 978-0-521-11564-3 Hardback
ISBN 978-0-521-13300-5 Paperback

# CONTENTS

# ILLUSTRATIONS

# PREFACE

When I learned Latin and Greek at high school in Amsterdam, we used books called *Tirocinium Latinum* and *Graecum*. *Tirocinium* means "the first military service, the first campaign of a young soldier." The books spread the grammar of the two languages over a number of lessons, each lesson introducing different parts of the language and ending with an exercise. Initially, the individual sentences were very short and elementary, but Lesson 1 already ended with a little story (*Marcus dolorem habet*) that we had to translate and then recite from memory. Learning Hittite and other ancient languages at university, however, was a quite different experience. All pedagogy seemed suddenly thrown overboard: The professor ran through the grammar and we were plunged right into the first real text. Years later, teaching Latin and Greek at my old high school myself, new pedagogical ideals had meanwhile outlawed the use of sentences out of context, and lessons consisted from the very beginning of made-up stories only.

When I started teaching Hittite at the University of Amsterdam in 1990, I wanted to try something different. Writing up stories about a fictional Hittite Marcus was and still is out of the question: We do not yet understand all the intricacies of the Hittite language and cannot claim that we can write flawless classical Muršili-prose. But the *Tirocinium* model with individual sentences might work as long as the sentences come from real texts. My other model here has been the *Lehrbuch des Akkadischen* (Leipzig 1984) of Kaspar K. Riemschneider, who did just that. However, he did not include the cuneiform script in his book. Cuneiform is not just aesthetically pleasing and fun, but is also an integral and essential part of the language as we learn it. Learning ancient Near Eastern languages without it is like learning to fly in a simulator but never really getting off the ground.

The resulting textbook is not a reference grammar. For this we have the excellent *Grammar of the Hittite Language, Part I: Reference Grammar* by H. A. Hoffner and H. C. Melchert (Winona Lake, IN 2008), to which I refer in every section (abbr. [GrHL] with paragraph numbers) in the hope that it will encourage some students to seek more in-depth information. My book does, however, cover the entire grammar and incorporates the Hittite cuneiform script, which most Hittite primers do not do. After a general introduction to the place of Hittite within the Anatolian languages, to Hittite literature, the use of (clay) tablets, the cuneiform writing system and Hittite phonology, ten lessons divide up all morphology and treat all necessary phonological and syntactic phenomena. Each lesson is structured in the same way: Seven sections each discuss a different part of the grammar. The following sections are distinguished:

1. Noun and adjective
2. Pronoun
3. Verb
4. Syntax, semantics, word formation
5. Phonology
6. Sumerian and/or Akkadian; numerals
7. Cuneiform

After ten lessons the basic grammar has been covered, and 134 cuneiform signs have been introduced. The sixth section of the first six lessons contains the barest minimum of what a student should know of Sumerian and Akkadian to be able to read a Hittite text. The same section of Lessons 7, 8, and 9 offers information on Hittite numerals.

Five appendices contain all paradigms given in the preceding lessons (Appendix 1), a source list of all sentences used in the exercises (Appendix 2), an index of syntactic and phonological phenomena discussed in the grammar (Appendix 3), a list of all signs introduced in the lessons supplemented by additional signs attested in KBo 3.4 (Muršili II's *Ten-Year Annals*) (Appendix 4), and a full Glossary of all words in the exercises and in KBo 3.4 (Appendix 5).

I have used this method every year since 1990, tweaking and revising it along the way according to classroom experience. It can be used in a trimester or semester system, although one trimester is almost certainly too short to discuss everything. Once the Introduction and Lesson 1 have been covered, the beginning of each class should be devoted to the homework of the previous lesson. I always take a break after Lesson 5. I give the students some self-made English sentences to be translated into Hittite and have them one by one write their translations on the blackboard. I encourage them to use as many clitics as possible, throwing in the odd sentence particle here and there. This is an excellent exercise to rehearse all the grammar of the preceding lessons before we continue. I have not included the English sentences I usually give my students: Every instructor can make up his or her own using the vocabulary of the first five lessons.

Lesson 6 introduces the relative sentences, in my experience the biggest hurdle for the beginning student. I have tried to include enough examples, but it may be worthwhile for an instructor to collect more examples and devote another break to them.

Another and more general problem is the fact that the sentences in the exercises can be difficult to translate without some knowledge of the wider context.

Although the instructor can and should alleviate this in class, I have tried to counter this in two ways. First of all, I sometimes add brief but general explanatory remarks about a sentence's context.

Secondly, I have cut the entire *Ten-Year Annals* of Muršili II into ten pieces, leaving out only a few very fragmentary passages. Each lesson thus ends with a passage from the *Annals*, beginning with the prologue in Lesson 1 and ending with the epilogue in Lesson 10. Of course, in Lessons 1 and 2 nothing can be translated yet, so a full translation is given, but the cuneiform handcopy can be used to identify the first cuneiform signs, and some forms can be parsed already. In Lessons 3, 4, and 5, increasingly less is rendered into English, until as of Lesson 6 onwards students can be asked to translate everything themselves. The translated parts of Lessons 3–5 provide the maximum context possible for the parts the students have to do themselves, and they lay the groundwork for their complete translation in the last five lessons. Not only is it stimulating for students to read a coherent text, but they will also be able to say after ten lessons that they have read the entire *Ten-Year Annals* of Muršili. Although the sections become quite long in the end, the text is fairly repetitive, and the student quickly gets used to the vocabulary and constructions used by Muršili, as well as to the typical Hittite annalistic style. At the same time, the cuneiform copy provides the most realistic material to practice the signs.

I want to thank Françoise Tjerkstra and Joost Hazenbos for their remarks and criticism of the earliest Dutch versions. I am greatly indebted to my students James Burgin and (especially) Hannah Marcuson, as well as to Ben van Gessel, for their help with this latest version. I also thank Michael Sharp of Cambridge University Press for pushing me to publish this book after so many years and for the pleasant cooperation. A final thanks goes to all my fellow Hittitologists past and present: Being a beginner's grammar, it contains no footnotes referencing secondary Hittitological literature with all its discussions and hard-fought achievements of our roughly century-old discipline. In fact, this *Tirocinium Hethiticum* owes everything to past studies in Hittitology and to all colleagues who will find their contributions in the paragraphs to come without being mentioned.

Theo van den Hout

# ABBREVIATIONS

| | | | |
|---|---|---|---|
| abl. | ablative | Hier. | Hieroglyphic |
| acc. | accusative | Hitt. | Hittite |
| act. | active | HW | *Hethitisches Wörterbuch* |
| adj. | adjective | HZL | *Hethitisches Zeichenlexikon* |
| adv. | adverb | i.e. | id est, that is |
| Akkad. | Akkadian | ind. | indicative |
| all. | allative | inf. | infinitive |
| CHD | *Chicago Hittite Dictionary* | instr. | instrumental |
| com. | common gender | KBo | *Keilschrifttexte aus Boghazköi* |
| conj. | conjunction | KUB | *Keilschrifturkunden aus Boghazköi* |
| CTH | *Catalogue des textes hittites* | lit. | literally |
| Cun. | Cuneiform | loc. | locative |
| dat. | dative | med.-pass. | medio-passive |
| dep. | deponent | neut. | neuter |
| DN | divine name | nom. | nominative |
| e.g. | exempli gratia, for instance | obv. | obverse |
| Engl. | English | part. | participle |
| etc. | et cetera | plur. | plural |
| gen. | genitive | PN | personal name |
| GN | geographical name | postpos. | postposition |
| GrHL | *Grammar of the Hittite Language* | pres. | present |
| HED | *Hittite Etymological Dictionary* | pret. | preterite |
| HEG | *Hethitisches etymologisches Glossar* | rev. | reverse |
| | | sing. | singular |
| | | Sum. | Sumerian |
| | | voc. | vocative |

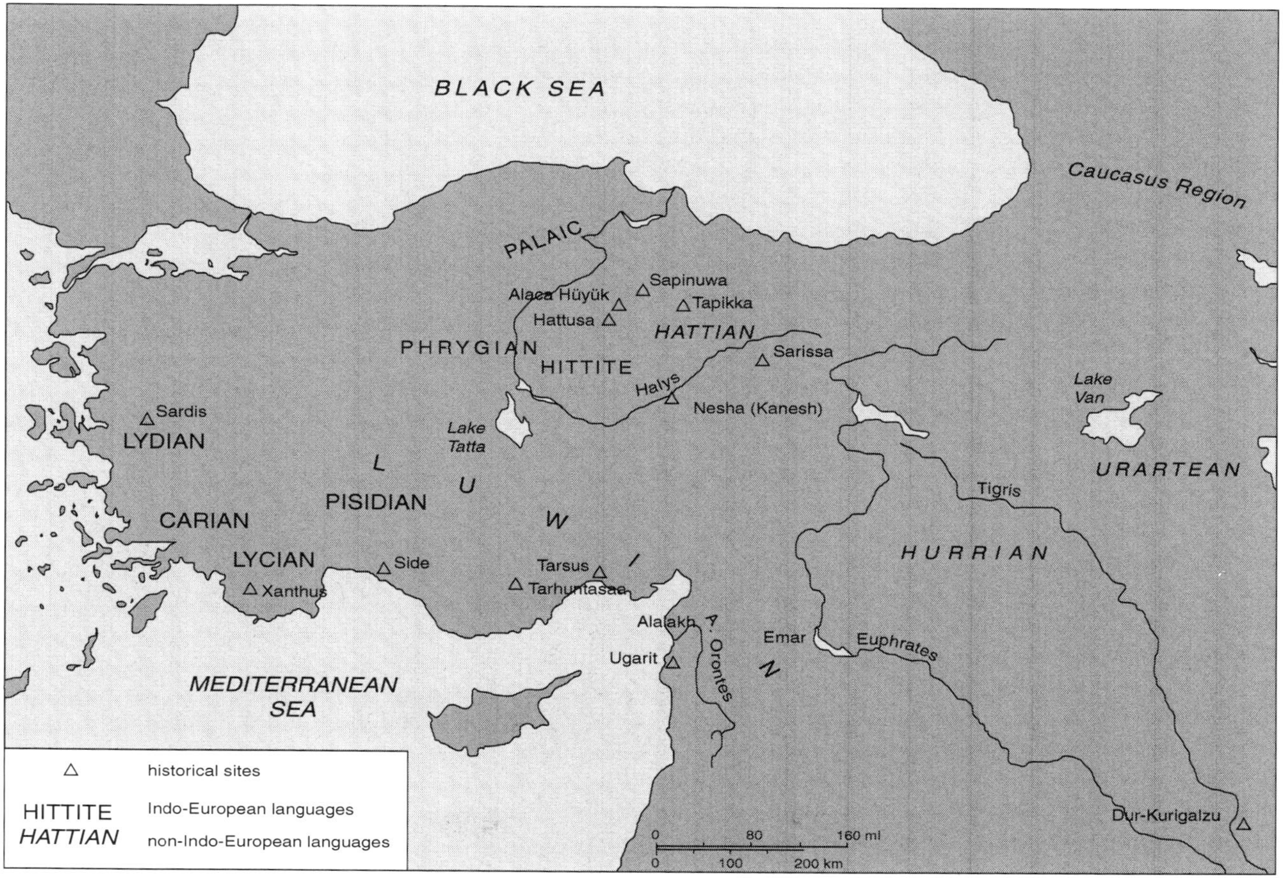
BLACK SEA
Caucasus Region
PALAIC
Sapinuwa
Alaca Hüyük
Tapikka
Hattusa
HATTIAN
PHRYGIAN
HITTITE
Sarissa
Halys
Nesha (Kanesh)
Lake Van
Sardis
LYDIAN
Lake Tatta
L
U
W
I
A
N
URARTEAN
Tigris
PISIDIAN
CARIAN
HURRIAN
LYCIAN
Side
Tarsus
Xanthus
Tarhuntasaa
Alalakh
Oronte
Emar
Euphrates
Ugarit
MEDITERRANEAN SEA
historical sites
HITTITE Indo-European languages
HATTIAN non-Indo-European languages
Dur-Kurigalzu
0 80 160 ml
0 100 200 km

# Introduction

§1. *Hittite* is an Indo-European language; it is related to such languages as (Ancient) Greek, Latin, and Vedic, and also to the Germanic, Slavic, and Celtic languages. Of the entire Indo-European family of languages, Hittite is the oldest attested to date. Within the Indo-European language family, Hittite is only one of the subgroup of *Anatolian languages*, so called after Anatolia, the classical name of the land nowadays known as Turkey. The other members are Palaic, Cuneiform Luwian, Hieroglyphic Luwian, Lydian, Lycian, Carian, Pisidic, and Sidetic (see map, p. xv). Of these, Hittite is by far the best attested, with tens of thousands of texts containing many different genres. The text corpora of the other Anatolian languages are mostly relatively small and fairly restricted in their contents. As a result, our knowledge of these languages is often very limited.

The Anatolian languages span roughly the last two millennia BC and have come down to us in different writing systems, as is shown in the chart below.

| | 2nd millennium BC | | | | 1st millennium BC | | | | |
|---|---|---|---|---|---|---|---|---|---|
| Languages | Hitt. | Palaic | Cun. Luwian | Hier. Luwian | Lydian | Lycian | Carian | Pisidic | Sidetic |
| **Scripts** | | | | | | | | | |
| *Cuneiform* | ✗ | ✗ | ✗ | | | | | | |
| *Hieroglyphic* | | | | ✗ | | | | | |
| *Alphabetic* | | | | | ✗ | ✗ | ✗ | ✗ | ✗ |

Hieroglyphic Luwian is the only one of the above languages attested in both millennia: Its oldest attestations date from about 1400 BC, and they continue until approximately 700 BC. None of the Anatolian languages seem to have survived the Hellenization of Anatolia. Although in rural areas Anatolian languages may have continued to be spoken into the first few centuries AD, no written records have been preserved of them.

§2. Indo-European speakers must have entered Anatolia some time in the third millennium BC and spread over the entire peninsula (see map, p. xv). Hittites and Luwians settled on the Anatolian plateau in the center, and in the mid seventeenth century the Hittites established their capital Ḫattuša (Turkish *Boğazköy*, nowadays *Boğazkale*) some 150 km east of Ankara. Between

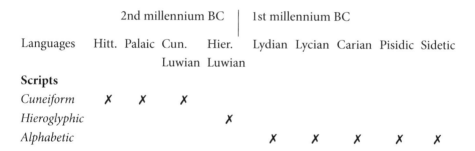

1650 and 1200 BC the Hittites were one of the major powers of the Ancient Near East, alongside the Assyrians, Babylonians, Hurrians, and Egyptians. They also established contacts with the Mycenaean Greeks to the west.

Within Anatolia, Hittites and Luwians partly expelled, partly assimilated with the local inhabitants of the time, the Hattians. These Hattians spoke a non-Indo-European language, of which specimens have been preserved in the Hittite texts, introduced by the term *Ḫattili* "in Hattian." The Hittites named their own language after the city of *Neša* (also known as *Kaneš*, modern *Kültepe*), taken in the eighteenth century BC by the father of Anitta, the man who can be considered the founder of the Hittite royal dynasty. Hittite passages are thus sometimes referred to as *Nešili* "in the language of Neša, in Nesite." Early Hittite scholarship tried to introduce the term "Nesite," but the earlier association with the Biblical Hittites proved too strong, and "Nesite" never caught on. On the other hand, the Hittites did call themselves "men of Ḫatti," borrowing the name of the indigenous Hattians, so our designation is not a complete misnomer.

Writing came relatively late to the Hittites. Anatolians, among whom were Hittite and Luwian speakers, must have been very familiar with the Old Assyrian cuneiform of the merchants from Assur during the first two centuries of the second millennium BC; however, they never took the step of adopting their writing system for internal purposes. It was not until military campaigns brought Ḫattušili I to Syria around 1650 BC that he started employing local Syrian scribes for occasional tasks and missions. Over the following century the volume of writing in the originally Syrian cuneiform was low, but enough to evolve into what we call the typical Hittite cuneiform by about the middle of the sixteenth century. Until 1500 BC, and for some time thereafter, the writing was almost exclusively Akkadian, the language that had come along with the Syrian cuneiform. Hittite text sources began to flow early in the fifteenth century, and by 1400 BC Akkadian was no longer used for internal purposes. The Hittite text tradition came to an end with the fall of the Hittite empire around 1180 BC. No Hittite texts dating after that time have been found.

§3. Although Hittite political history can be described as one continuum from Anitta until the breaking-up of the empire, several chronological stages can be discerned in the time in which the Hittite language has been attested. Most compositions that tell of the early period of Anitta, or of Ḫattušili I and his successors until Telipinu (*c.* 1500 BC), are attested in late thirteenth-century copies or in older manuscripts. Those texts are difficult to date exactly, but were probably written down in the course of the fifteenth century. Both these older texts and the late copies contain all kinds of linguistic elements that allow us to label this entire period up to around 1400 as Old Hittite. After a brief period of transition, "classical" New Hittite starts with Muršili II in the second half of the fourteenth century and continues until the end, with a few developments of its own.

During these stages the language evolved in phonology, morphology, and syntax, but the cuneiform script evolved as well. The older manuscripts from the fifteenth century just mentioned can be identified by looking at certain sign shapes, and we are thus able to determine whether a given tablet was written down in the Old or New Hittite period. This gives us a fairly clear impression of how the language developed over the centuries. Moreover, due to the continuous copying of older texts by Hittite scribes, we can also observe how later, thirteenth-century scribes on the one hand retained older grammatical characteristics of originally Old Hittite compositions, while on the other hand modernizing them. When in the course of this book the terms "Old Hittite" or (more generally) "older language" are used, they refer to the period of Hittite attestation until around 1350 BC.

§4. The main script carrier was the clay tablet, but the texts also mention tablets of gold, silver, bronze, and iron. One bronze tablet has been preserved: a treaty between the Hittite Great King Tutḫaliya IV (*c.* 1240–1220/1210 BC) and his vassal Kuruntiya of Tarḫuntašša in southern Anatolia. We also know that, for instance, one of the copies of the famous peace treaty of the year 1259 between the Egyptian Pharaoh Ramses II and his Hittite counterpart, Ḫattušili III, was made of silver. Such metal tablets seem to have been made for special occasions only. Besides these, there is also mention of wooden tablets, that is, wooden tablets covered with wax on which signs could be written. One such wooden tablet has been recovered from the fourteenth-century BC shipwreck near Ulu Burun, off the south-western coast of Anatolia, although no wax remained on it. It is a matter of some debate whether these tablets were used for cuneiform or hieroglyphic script. The Hittite chancellery, at any rate, seems to have distinguished between simple "scribes" and "wood-scribes."

By far the majority of Hittite texts have been found at the former capital Ḫattuša (modern Boğazköy/Boğazkale). The first real tablet collection to have come to light outside the capital was the small archive of over one hundred tablets, mainly letters, from the site of Maşat Höyük (ancient Tapikka) in the early 1970s. More recently a larger collection has been recovered in Ortaköy, as well as other smaller ones at Kuşaklı (Šarešša) and Kayalıpınar (Šamuḫa?; see map, p. xv). Besides these, there have been incidental finds of Hittite texts in Alaca Höyük, Tel Açana (Alalaḫ), Dur-Kurigalzu, Meskene (Emar), Tarsus, and Ras Shamra (Ugarit). Even the famous Egyptian archive at Tel-el-Amarna (Akhet-aten) contained two letters in Hittite. Found in the late nineteenth century AD, they were the earliest known Hittite tablets.

§5. The total corpus of cuneiform clay tablets and fragments now numbers around 30,000. The following table lists all genres constituting the corpus (the CTH-numbers refer to Emanuel Laroche's standard work, *Catalogue des textes hittites* [Paris 1971], a classification of all texts into genres. This is still maintained online: see www.hethport.uni-wuerzburg.de/hetkonk/).

| **A.** *Texts with duplicates* | **B.** *'unica'* |
|---|---|
| historiography, treaties, edicts (CTH 1–147, 211–216) | letters (CTH 151–210)<br>land deeds (CTH 221–225)<br>administrative texts:<br>– palace and temple administration (CTH 231–250)<br>– cult inventories (CTH 501–530)<br>– tablet inventories (CTH 276–282)<br>– labels (CTH 283) |
| instructions and loyalty oaths (CTH 251–275) | |
| laws (CTH 291–292) | court depositions (CTH 293–297) |
| oracle theory (CTH 531–560) | oracle practice (CTH 561–582) |
| hymns and prayers (CTH 371–389) | vows (CTH 583–590) |
| festival scenarios (CTH 591–721) | |
| ritual scenarios (CTH 390–500) | |
| mythology (Anatolian and non-Anatolian) (CTH 321–370) | |
| Hattic, Palaic, Luwian, Hurrian compositions (CTH 725–791) | |
| Sumerian and Akkadian compositions (CTH 310–316, 792–819) | |
| hippological texts (CTH 284–287) | |
| lexical lists (CTH 299–309) | |

The above table shows a basic distinction between long-term (A) and short-term (B) records. Most of the long-term records were stored, sometimes for several centuries, in the tablet collections, because of their general or potential usefulness. As such, they were often updated, and the royal chancellery often made sure to have more than just one copy in one place. One can easily imagine how the Law collection was regularly consulted, and how the series containing the Royal Funerary Ritual was pulled from the shelf whenever a king or queen had died and the ritual needed to be performed. For similar reasons, treaties and edicts, instructions and loyalty oaths addressing various professional groups in Hittite society, ritual and cultic festival scenarios, hymns, prayers, and the Anatolian myths (which were probably acted out as part of certain rituals) were kept and copied for future use and consultation. Apart from their primary function as legal instruments, the treaties and edicts were also an important historical source for the Hittites themselves, as well as an efficient point of departure whenever new such documents had to be drawn up. It is perhaps for this reason, too, that historiography was stored and kept. This is the most elusive of genres under A, in terms of its *Sitz im Leben*, goal, and audience. It has also sometimes been praised for its lack of all-too-obvious propaganda in comparison with, for instance, Mesopotamian historiography, as well as for its – at times – relatively sophisticated narrative style. There is room for reflection, and for the achievements of people other than the king. Although Hittite historiography can be seen as accounting to the gods, for whom kings administered the land, the texts sometimes contain hints at a worldly public as well. How their dissemination took place, however, remains largely in the realm of speculation.

It is likewise difficult to assign a function to the more "literary" genres of the foreign – Akkadian, Hurrian, and Sumerian – compositions, to the so-called lexical lists or vocabularies, and also to some of the rituals. It has been convincingly shown that several rituals as recorded bear little relation to reality in the sense that they were useless as scenarios for real-life proceedings. These texts may well have been deliberately collected out of some "academic" interest, and as such they come closest to our modern notion of a library. The same may be true of the Hittite versions of foreign myths like the Gilgameš Epic. Based on parallels with Mesopotamia, these texts are often assigned a role in the scribal curriculum, but evidence for this is lacking. The possibility that these texts were (also?) used for entertainment purposes at the royal court cannot be excluded.

Most of the genres under B can be characterized as administrative and of only short-term importance. It is no coincidence that, with a single well-defined exception, all texts belonging to this group date to the last period of the Hittite empire. They have survived only by virtue of the fact that they had not yet been recycled when the ruling class decided to give up the capital Ḫattuša and move elsewhere. As in every administration, there was an ongoing appraisal of records deciding which could be discarded and which should be stored for the time being. Incoming correspondence was kept only as long as it was necessary and relevant for the administration. Outgoing correspondence was likewise sometimes filed for future consultation, and some letters were copied and bundled into dossiers. Similarly, court depositions, oracle reports, and vows are almost exclusively late thirteenth-century documents, whose destruction was pre-empted by the decision to abandon the capital.

The palace and temple administration under B mostly deals with the Hittite system of taxes and the redistribution of goods. The real exception are the charters or land deeds. These form a special group in many respects: shape, language, date, and storage. They record the bestowing of extensive land and properties by the king to members of the royal dynasty. The tablets are thick, pillow-shaped, with a royal seal in the middle; in all probability clay bullae were attached to them by means of strings, embedded in the clay core of the tablet and with the seals of the witnesses impressed on them. The language is Akkadian, written according to a strict formula, and Hittite technical terms are regularly inserted into the text. They were not kept with the other records of Groups A or B, but stored separately along with other documents or objects that were or had been sealed with clay bullae. Finally, there is the chronological anomaly: Unlike all other texts in Group B, these original land deeds were stored and kept for hundreds of years. The oldest ones date to the reign of Telipinu of the late sixteenth century, but were found as an integral part of the tablet collections of the late thirteenth-century residence that was given up by the Hittite ruling class.

§6. Except for specific text genres, such as letters, that are usually fairly small (*c.* 5×10 cm) and the land deeds just mentioned (§5), Hittite tablets mostly measured *c.* 20×30 cm. Needless to say, most of the time they have come down to us in a fragmentary state. It is the job of Hittitologists to restore the tablets to as complete a form as possible from the tens of thousands of fragments preserved. A physical linking of two or more fragments is called a *join.*

Although there are tablets written without any subdivision, or inscribed on only one side, most of them show a layout with two columns on the obverse (abbr. obv., Turkish *önyüz*, abbr. *öy.*, German *Vorderseite*, abbr. *Vs.*, French, Italian *recto*, abbr. *ro.*) and two on the reverse side (abbr. rev., Turkish *arkayüz*, abbr. *ay.*, German *Rückseite*, abbr. *Rs.*, French, Italian *verso*, abbr. *vo.*). Certain tablets, like festival descriptions or administrative texts, may have three columns per side. The columns are usually indicated in our modern editions by Roman numerals, either capital or lower case (as done here: obv. i, ii and rev. iii, iv; see Figure 1).

The direction of the script is always from left to right, and an average tablet contains some 70 lines per column. When changing from the obverse to the reverse on a normal two-column tablet, the scribe would turn the tablet along its shorter *horizontal* axis (so, *not* as we turn the pages of a book, along the longer vertical axis) and would start writing the third column on the right side of the reverse. The bottom side of the obverse thus becomes the upper side of the reverse. As a consequence, the third column on the reverse (rev. iii) corresponds to (i.e., is opposite to) the second column (obv. ii) on the obverse but upside down! The obv. i corresponds with rev. iv in the same way. The lower and upper edges normally remain uninscribed. At the end of the obverse columns a horizontal line (German *Randleiste*) was drawn over the full width of the tablet to mark the lower end, and similar lines were drawn on the upper and lower sides of the reverse (see Figures 1 and 2). Usually there was no such line at the top of the obverse, and neither was there at the sides.

Columns were usually separated by two vertical lines, the so-called *intercolumnium.* Words were often separated by small spaces, just as in our modern script; Old Hittite tablets often show a denser script with fewer word spaces. Words were never broken off at the end of a line. If a word proved too long, a scribe could write the remainder of the word vertically in the intercolumnium (see, for instance, the handcopy of KBo 3.4 i 8 in Lesson 2.8.5) or, if writing in a right-hand column (either obv. ii or rev. iii), on the edge of the tablet. If, however, there was still space left at the end of a line, scribes often shifted the last sign of the last word towards the end, thus filling out (justifying right) the text (for an example, see the placement of UR.SAG in the handcopy of KBo 3.4 i 1–2 in Lesson 1.8.4). The left and right edges were normally not used, but if some text was still left when all four columns were already fully inscribed, and the scribe did not want to start a whole new tablet, the remainder of the composition could be written on the edges. If so, the scribe would start on the left edge, writing from the bottom to the top, as seen from the obverse.

The average tablet is flat on the obverse and curved on the reverse. There are, therefore, several indications to determine the obverse and reverse of a fragment, if the contents do not allow such a decision: the presence or absence of the *Randleiste* on top, the curving of a tablet, and the direction of the script on an edge. But if no edge at all has been preserved and the fragment is too small to show any curvature, it is often difficult to identify the obverse or reverse side of a tablet. "Folded out," a tablet looks like this:

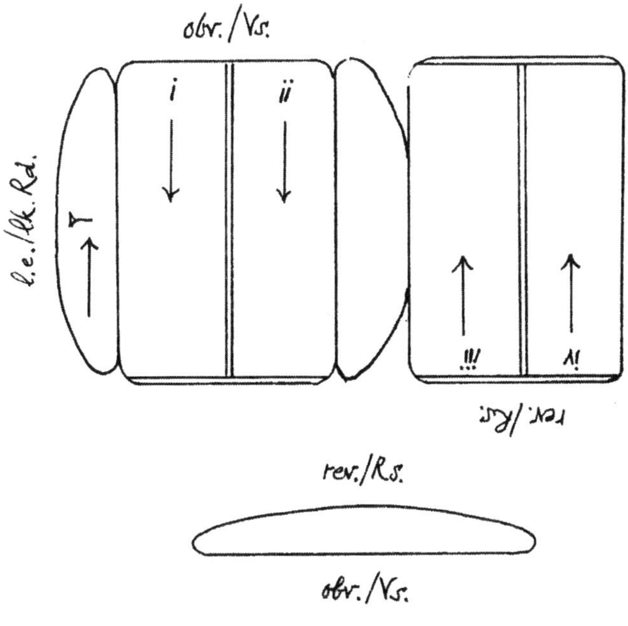


**Figure 1** "Folded-out" tablet and directions of the script. Illustration by the author.

Within a column a scribe divided his text into paragraphs using horizontal lines. A major break – sometimes the beginning of a new composition on a tablet – could be indicated by a double horizontal line. Further punctuation, that is, devices like commas, colons, semicolons, periods, or question marks, did not exist. Neither did the cuneiform script distinguish between capital and small type or between roman and italic. Yet there were certain ways to mark parts of a text for which we use punctuation, capitalization, or different fonts. For instance, proper names, whether personal, geographical, or otherwise, were preceded by specific cuneiform signs indicating that the following word belonged to the category of personal names etc. Such signs are called *determinatives* and can be said to replace our capitalization (see below §9). Similarly, foreign words which we would often italicize were, in the case of Luwian (and rarely Hurrian) words, often preceded by a single (𒑱) or double wedge (𒑲) called *Glossenkeil(e)* (for an example, see Lesson 10.7.2 KBo 3.4 iii 73). The use of our quotation marks (" ") to mark direct speech was taken over by a grammatical element at the beginning of each clause, which was part of the direct speech. Likewise, the beginning and therefore also the end of clauses is in most cases easily recognizable in Hittite because of specific grammatical elements marking clause beginnings. However, the absence of question marks is problematic. Of course, questions introduced by interrogatives (e.g., *kuwat* "why?") are easily recognized, but those without ("Did you do your homework?") are not, since Hittite word order usually does not change.

In case of an error, a scribe could erase the faulty part with the back(?) of his stylus or his fingertip. He would then either write over the erased part or continue after it. Such erasures (Latin *rasura*, German *Rasur*) are usually marked in modern handcopies by dotted lines around the erased area. If a passage was corrupt in any way or illegible to a scribe copying a new text, he could indicate this by putting the relevant part between crossed wedges (✂).

The largest tablet collections are housed in the museums of Ankara and Istanbul in Turkey. What Hittitologists work with are hand-drawn copies made from the originals. An example of such a handcopy, showing the inversion of the script from obverse to reverse and how the edge might be used, is given in Figure 2. The actual size of the fragment is smaller; most copies are enlarged. The average height of a cuneiform line is about 3 to 4 mm.

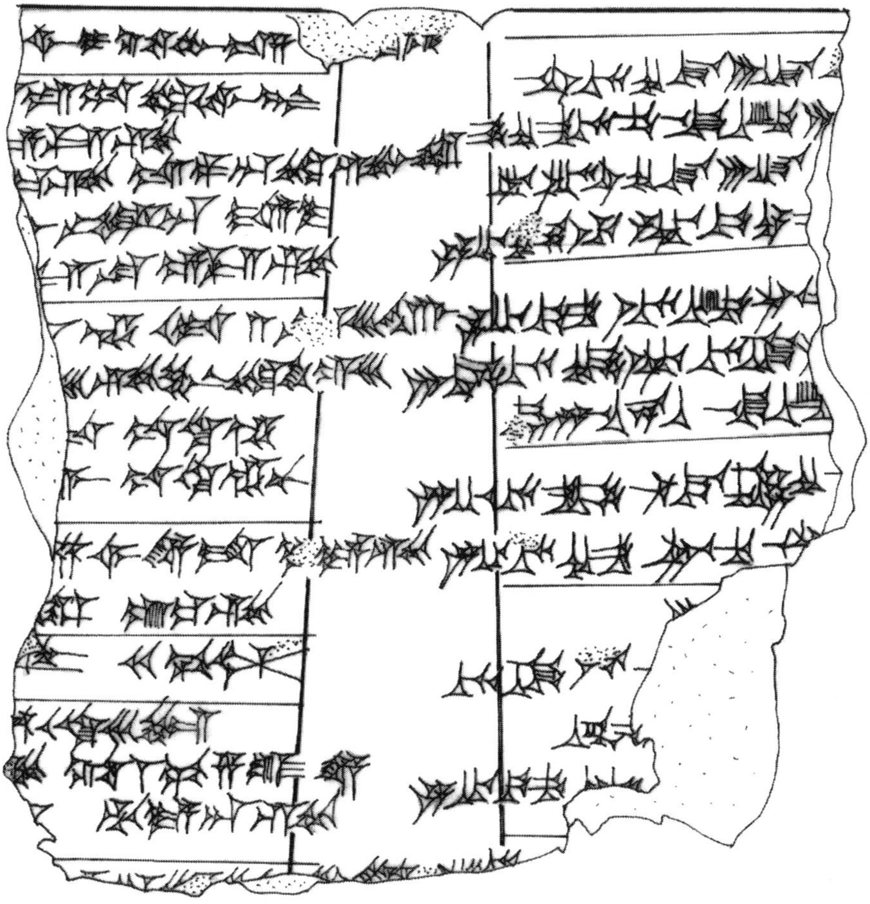

**Figure 2** Handcopy of 842/z with, from left to right, the obv., edge, and rev. (upside down).

§7. The cuneiform script uses the following basic elements: the vertical (𒁹), the horizontal (𒀸), and the diagonal wedge (𒀹, with the head either up or down), and the *Winkelhaken* (𒌋). The heads of the horizontal and diagonal wedges always point to the left. The typical triangular wedge-like form (Latin *cuneus* "wedge") of the head derives from the "pen" or stylus, which had a triangularly cut end. By pressing this end in the soft clay, the scribe left a triangular impression. With light coming in from the left, a shadow appears in the impression, and the sign form characteristic of cuneiform script is the result. By making combinations of the basic elements, a practically endless range of signs can be made. Compare the following series and their readings:

PÍ GU$_4$ GA DUG ŠA TA UL

The cuneiform writing system, as used by the Hittites, was a syllabic script: Each sign represents a syllable, that is, a vowel (A, E, I, U), a vowel + consonant (type VC, e.g., AP, ID, UK), consonant + vowel (type CV, e.g., PA, DI, KU), or consonant + vowel + consonant (type CVC, e.g., TAR, KAT, MIŠ). Taking into account the fact that there is no consistent distinction between the vowels *e* and *i* and that there is no vowel *o*, signs of the type VC and CV can be put into series, as illustrated in the table below.

| | CV | | | VC | | | |
|---|---|---|---|---|---|---|---|
| | *a* | *e/i* | *u* | *a* | *e/i* | *u* | |
| *t* | TA | TE TI | TU | AT/D | ET/D | UT/D | *t* |
| *d* | DA | DE | DU | | | | *d* |
| *p* | PA | PE | P/BU | AP/B | EP/B | UP/B | *p* |
| *b* | BA | | | | | | *b* |
| *k* | KA | KE | KU | AK/G | EK/G | UK/G | *k* |
| *g* | GA | GE | GU | | | | *g* |
| *m* | MA | ME MI | MU | AM | EM | UM | *m* |
| *n* | NA | NE NI | NU | AN | EN IN | UN | *n* |
| *l* | LA | LE | LU | AL | EL IL | UL | *l* |
| *r* | RA | RE | RU | AR | ER | UR | *r* |
| *š* | ŠA | ŠE ŠI | ŠU | AŠ | EŠ IŠ | UŠ | *š* |
| *z* | ZA | ZE ZI | ZU | AZ | EZ | UZ | *z* |
| *ḫ* | ḪA | ḪE ḪI | ḪU | AḪ | EḪ | UḪ | *ḫ* |
| *y* | YA | | | | | | |
| *w* | WA | WI | | | | | |

Whenever in the inventory in this table a sign with the vowel *e* appears alone (e.g., DE), it can also be read with *i* (DE/I). When both values are listed (e.g., TE and TI), two separate signs exist distinguishing *e* and *i*. For signs of the type CV there is an almost complete distinction between voiceless (TA, PA, KA) and voiced (DA, BA, GA) consonants. Signs of the type VC, however, make no distinction between the two. Signs of the type CVC have no apparent system in them, but their use increases over the centuries.

With this sign inventory, practically anything can be written. For instance, the Hittite word for "lord" (as subject of a sentence) was *išḫaš*. If we want to write this, we have to split the word up into syllabic signs, which we separate by hyphens: *iš-ḫa-aš*. More problematic are words which have clusters of consonants in them as, for instance, *walḫta* "he struck." In such a case we have to resort to "graphic" vowels, that is, vowels which were only written, but not pronounced. We find a form like *walḫta* written as *wa-la-aḫ-ta* or *wa-al-aḫ-ta* with an extra inserted *a*, in order to be able to write the cluster *-lḫt-* in the syllabic system.

In taking over the cuneiform system developed in Mesopotamia, the Hittites also adopted Mesopotamian scribal customs. Originally, cuneiform was not syllabic, but a word script, that is, each sign represented a word or a concept, much like our numbers. Such signs are symbols representing a concept without, however, any indication of pronunciation: e.g. □ stands for a square, + means addition, and II or 2 we read as "two." But the latter symbols II and 2 will be read in French as "deux," in German as "zwei," in Turkish as "iki." Gradually this word script evolved into a syllabary, as the need for writing all sorts of texts increased. For common and frequently used words, the use of word signs continued. In Akkadian the word for "lord" was *bēlu(m)*, which usually would be written with three signs as *be-lu-um*; however, it was much more convenient to use the old Sumerian one-word sign, which we read as *en*. We call such originally Sumerian signs *Sumerograms*, and their use in Hittite texts is widespread. It is important to note that this is a purely graphic device: When reading the word sign, the underlying (Hittite) word would be pronounced by the Hittites. Such Sumerograms are so frequently used by scribes that sometimes we do not even know the Hittite reading of highly common words because the scribes wrote them exclusively with Sumerograms! For words like "son" or "woman," for instance, we have no attestations for the word written out syllabically in Hittite, and thus we do not know the Hittite reading.

In a similar way the Hittite scribes also frequently use Akkadian words within a Hittite text: we know that the Hittite negation was *natta* "not," but we encounter it written as *na-at-ta* in the older language only. It is the Akkadian *ul* "not" that we find almost exclusively. Such Akkadian words are called *Akkadograms*.

This means that a normal Hittite text is interspersed with Sumero- and Akkadograms. When reading a cuneiform (Hittite) text or writing about a text we normally use our alphabetic script as a means of notation: We call the process of transferring a cuneiform text to our alphabet *transliteration*. In order to be as precise as possible, different formats are used to distinguish between Hittite words, Sumerograms, and Akkadograms. As already noted above, everything Hittite is in lower case, each individual cuneiform sign separated by hyphens (*iš-ḫa-aš*). Sumerograms are given in roman capitals (in this book in small capitals: EN), and a series of Sumerian word signs is separated by periods (MUNUS.LUGAL "woman.king" › "queen"). Akkadograms are also capitalized, but italicized and hyphenated (*Ú-UL* "not" or *BE-LU* "lord").[1]

As mentioned above, Sumerograms are word signs, and they simply represent

[1] Small caps are used here for the Sumero- and Akkadograms in order to distinguish them from the simple identification of signs. Thus, the Akkadogram *IŠTU* is written with the signs IŠ and TU.

concepts. Sumerian EN means "lord," but its form does not indicate whether it is the subject of a verb ("the lord led the army"), or its object ("she saw the lord"), or indirect object ("he gave something to his lord"). Often the context will be clear enough and leave little room for doubt, but in many cases the need was felt to make the function of the Sumerogram in a particular clause explicit. This was done by adding the Hittite case ending to the Sumerogram: e.g., *išḫaš* is the subject case, *išḫan* the object case, and *išḫi* the indirect object case. These could be written EN-*aš*, EN-*an*, and EN-*i* respectively. Such endings attached to a Sumerogram are known as *phonetic complements.* Sometimes Sumerograms have Akkadian phonetic complements: the Sumerogram for "god" is DINGIR, while the Akkadian word is *ILUM*. The two could be combined to form DINGIR-*LUM*. Occasionally, one even finds a triple combination, DINGIR-*LIM*-*ni* "for/to the god," with two phonetic complements, the first one Akkadian (-*LIM* from *ILIM*) and the second Hittite (from *šiuni*).

Up to now we have seen two ways of representing Hittite words or sign sequences: Besides the sign-by-sign transliteration with hyphens (*iš-ḫa-aš*), we have also cited forms like *išḫaš.* This last way (as for instance used in this book when discussing grammar and giving examples) represents a further step from transliteration to (*bound*) *transcription* or *scriptio continua*, which is an attempt at making "real" words out of the transliterated sign sequences. This is very common in Hittitological scholarly literature. In doing so, we try to render the transliteration as faithfully as possible, retaining, for instance "long" vowels (*ā*, *ē* etc.) and double consonants; for more on this, see Lesson 1.5.2–4 and Lesson 4.5.

In bound transcription we often use the symbol =. It indicates so-called *morpheme boundaries.* Morphemes are the smallest meaningful grammatical elements. Although case endings in nouns, adjectives, and pronouns or verbal endings fall under this heading, in Hittitological publications only the numerous clitic elements (see Lesson 1.2.3, 1.4.2–4) and certain suffixes are separated off from their hosts. Compare the transliteration sequence *ma-aḫ-ḫa-an-ma-wa-du-za-kán* ("but when (for/to) you") with its maximum chain of five clitic elements (-*ma* "but," -*wa* for direct speech, -*du* "for/to you," -*za* reflexive particle, and -*kan* a sentence particle). In bound transcription using the morpheme boundary marker, this becomes *maḫhan=ma=wa=du=za=kan.* However, the grammatical elements do not always coincide so perfectly with the syllabic signs as in the preceding example: compare *nu-wa-at-ták-kán* "and (to/for) you" = *nu=wa=tta=kkan* or *nu-wa-ra-at* "and it" = *nu=war=at.* The subject case *išḫaš* combined with the possessive suffix -*miš* "my" (written *iš-ḫa-aš-mi-iš*) will be broken down into two parts: *išḫaš=miš* "my lord." The Akkadian suffixed possessive pronoun (see Lesson 5.6) is treated in the same way.

§8. Two features characteristic of cuneiform script are *homophony* and *polyphony*. Homophony implies that there are several signs for the same sound value. For instance, the Hittite syllabary uses four signs with a value /u/:

In order to know from a transliteration which of these four signs was used on the tablet, an indexing system is applied using accents and numbers: From left to right, the signs are transliterated as *u* (= u-one), *ú* (= u-two), *ù* (= u-three) and $u_4$ (= u-four). From "four" onwards, subscript numbers are used (e.g. $wi_5$ or ŠE$_{20}$!). In bound transcription such indexing marks (the accents and subscript numbers) are ignored (note the particle -*kán* written with the KÁN sign ["*kan*-two"] rendered as simply =*kan* with no accent in the example for bound transcription given at the end of §7 above).

Polyphony, on the other hand, means that a single cuneiform sign can have more than one sound value: the sign just transliterated as $u_4$ can also be read as *ud/t*, *pir*, or *tam*. Sumerographically, it can be read UD "day," BABBAR "white," or UTU "Sungod." Which of these readings applies in a text depends on the context and is for the reader to determine. Fortunately, the use of polyphony by Hittite scribes was fairly restricted.

§9. Another special use of cuneiform signs is that of the *determinatives* (see already §6). Determinatives are signs mostly preceding, but sometimes also following, a word, marking it as belonging to a certain class of words. On a tablet they are written as any other cuneiform sign, but in transliteration we use a superscript to mark them. Such determinatives exist for male and female personal names, male and female professions, divine names, animals, foodstuffs, geographical names of different sorts, words denoting objects of wood, metal, ceramics, etc. The most important determinatives will be given in Lessons 1 through 5.

§10. The Hittite syllabary, as we already saw (§7), distinguishes four vowels: /a, e, i, u/. The vowels /e/ and /i/ were not systematically kept apart. There is no /o/, but it may well be that the U sign stood for an /o/, whereas Ú represented a real /u/. For further information on vowels and their spellings, see Lesson 1.5.2–4.

For the consonants we have the inventory on p. 14. The affricate transliterated *z* is pronounced /ts/. Although the exact sound value of *s* remains uncertain, and there is only one such sibilant in Hittite, it is traditionally transliterated with a so-called *haček*: *š*. This should not be taken, however, as evidence that it was a palatal sound (as *sh* in *show*). The same is true for the traditional "rocker" under the laryngeal *ḫ*: there is no other *h*-sign, and the diacritic is not strictly necessary. Some scholars will spell *ḫappinešš-* "to become rich" as *happiness-*.

| | | labial | dental | dorsal | laryngeal | sibilant | nasal/ liquid |
|---|---|---|---|---|---|---|---|
| stops | "voiceless" | *p* | *t* | *k* | | | |
| | "voiced" | *b* | *d* | *g* | | | |
| fricative | | | | | *ḫ* | *s* | |
| affricate | | | | | | *z* | |
| sonorant | | | | | | | *m n*<br>*l r*<br>*y w* |

The laryngeal may have sounded like the German *ach*-sound. The sonorants *y* and *w* are also often printed (mostly in German literature) as *i̯* and *u̯*

The distinction in the stops between what is usually described as *voiceless* and *voiced* (or something similar) cannot be based on the use of cuneiform signs (e.g., TA vs. DA). We already saw (§7) that no distinction was made in signs of the type VC (AT/D). Moreover, the signs were not used consistently: Although forms of the verb *dai-* "to put, place" are mostly written with the DA sign (*da-a-i*), the TA sign also occurs. The word for "father" *atta-* may be spelled *at-ta-* or *ad-da-*. Evidence for a difference in articulation, which could be described as something like voiceless vs. voiced, comes from the (more or less) consistent double- vs. single-writing of stops between vowels. The adverb *appa* "behind, later," for instance, is consistently spelled *a-ap-pa* with *-pp-*, as opposed to the pronoun *apa-* "that," which is always written *a-pa-* with single *-p-*; for more on this, see below Lesson 4.5.

Since this opposition can only be observed between vowels within words, and not at their beginning, it is ignored in alphabetizing Hittite words, and *p/b*, *t/d*, and *k/g* are therefore all grouped together under their voiceless variant. Words starting in *r-* or *y-* do not exist. For glossaries and dictionaries this results in the following order of the Hittite alphabet:

*a e ḫ i k/g l m n p/b š t/d u w z*

§11. Further reading: there are some recent and excellent up-to-date reference works that can further guide the interested student into Hittite grammar, history, and culture. The standard grammar for the Hittite language is H. A. Hoffner and H. C. Melchert, *A Grammar of the Hittite Language, Part I: Reference Grammar* (Winona Lake, IN 2008; abbr. GrHL). For Hittite history and culture, see T. R. Bryce, *The Kingdom of the Hittites*, 2nd edn. (Oxford 2005) and *Life and Society in the Hittite World* (Oxford 2002) respectively. Modern general introductions including a history of the field, art, and religion can be found in B. J. Collins, *The Hittites and Their World* (Atlanta, GA 2007; with special reference to the Biblical world) in English and J. Klinger, *Die Hethiter* (Munich 2007) in German. At present there is no overview of Hittite literature written in English, but in German there is available V. Haas, *Die hethitische Literatur* (Berlin, New York 2006). A systematic and up-to-date work on specifically Hittite art and archeology unfortunately does not exist. An overview of Anatolian archeology from the Palaeolithic to the Achaemenid period (including Hittite Anatolia) can be found in A. Sagona and P. Zimansky, *Ancient Turkey* (London, New York 2009).

Single-volume glossaries including lists of Sumero- and Akkadograms exist in German only: the old but still useful J. Friedrich, *Hethitisches Wörterbuch* (reprint Heidelberg 1991) and J. Tischler, *Hethitisches Handwörterbuch* (Innsbruck 2001). In progress are two major dictionary projects: the Hittite–German *Hethitisches Wörterbuch*, 2nd edn. (HW) by J. Friedrich, A. Kammenhuber and I. Hoffmann (Heidelberg 1975–: thus far covering letters A, E–I, and the first part of Ḫ), and the Hittite–English *Chicago Hittite Dictionary* (CHD) by H. G. Güterbock, H. A. Hoffner and Th. P. J. van den Hout (Chicago 1980–: thus far covering letters L, M, N, P, and Š); for an online version go to http://ochre.lib.uchicago.edu/eCHD/

The standard sign list for all cuneiform signs attested in texts from Boğazköy is Chr. Rüster and E. Neu, *Hethitisches Zeichenlexikon* (Wiesbaden 1989). This, too, includes a full listing of Sumerograms in Hittite texts.

There are two ongoing etymological dictionary projects: J. Tischler, *Hethitisches etymologisches Glossar* (HEG, Innsbruck 1977–, with thus far A–U), and J. Puhvel, *Hittite Etymological Dictionary* (HED, Berlin, New York, 1984–, with thus far A–Pa). For words with an Indo-European etymology only, see A. Kloekhorst, *Etymological Dictionary of the Hittite Inherited Lexicon* (Leiden, Boston 2008); its introduction comes closest to a modern historical grammar of Hittite which is otherwise still lacking.

For a website giving a full listing of all Hittite texts and fragments with excavation numbers, findspots, joins, duplicates, and bibliography, as well as many other features, go to www.hethport.uni-wuerzburg.de

# Lesson 1

## 1.1 Case endings of noun and adjective; *a*-stems

### 1.1.1 Noun and adjective [GrHL 3.14]:

Nominal declension concerns the morphology of nouns and adjectives. Within Hittite nominal declension we distinguish **number**, **gender**, and **case**.

There are two basic **numbers**: singular and plural.

There are two **genders**: common gender (*genus commune*, abbreviated: com.) and neuter (*genus neutrum*, abbreviated: neut.). The common gender combines the masculine and feminine of other Indo-European languages into one. Neuter originally means that it is neither masculine nor feminine, and it was originally reserved for inanimate things.

There are nine **cases**: nominative, vocative, accusative, genitive, dative, locative, allative, ablative, and instrumental (for the abbreviations, see the paradigm below). However, these nine cases are fully employed only in Old Hittite and in the singular; the plural is weakly developed, with five case forms at the most (nom. com., acc. com., nom.-acc. neut., gen., and one ending for the remaining cases). In later Hittite the number of case forms in the plural is mostly reduced to four (nom. com., acc. com., nom.-acc. neut., and one "oblique" case form for all remaining functions). With the partial merger of plur. nom. and acc. com. in New Hittite, it may even go down to three cases. The ablative and instrumental never have separate forms for singular and plural: They are indifferent as to number, and a translation as singular or plural depends on the context. In the paradigms they will be given separately in between the singular and the plural.

During the course of the Hittite language some cases became extinct, and their function was taken over by others: The allative and locative disappeared and merged with the dative, while the instrumental disappeared and merged with the ablative. As a result, apart from some exceptions which can be explained as archaisms, New Hittite uses a paradigm with only five cases in the singular: nominative, accusative, genitive, dative-locative, and ablative. For the functions of the cases see Lesson 1.4.1 below.

There are vowel and consonant **stems**; vowel stems can end in °*a*-, °*i*-, °*u*- and in the diphthongs °*ai*- and °*au*-, consonant stems can end in °*l*-, °*n*-, °*r*-, °*r*/*n*-, °*t*-, °*nt*- and °*š*-. All stem classes or declinations use the same case endings. The nominative and accusative neuter are always identical, both in the singular and the plural. Not every declination contains both nouns and adjectives or nouns of both genders. In presenting the various declinations, this information will be given separately in each lesson.

The following table gives the case endings for the older and the later – that is, mostly thirteenth-century – language (V = vowel, C = consonant, Ø = zero ending, i.e., lack of ending leaving the pure stem).

<table>
<tr><th></th><th>Older</th><th>Newer</th></tr>
<tr><td>Sing.</td><td></td><td></td></tr>
<tr><td>nom. com.</td><td>-š, Ø</td><td>-š</td></tr>
<tr><td>voc.</td><td>-Ø, -i</td><td>-Ø, -i/e</td></tr>
<tr><td>acc. com.</td><td>-Vn, -Can</td><td>-Vn, -Can</td></tr>
<tr><td>nom.-acc. neut.</td><td>-n, -Ø</td><td>-n, -Ø</td></tr>
<tr><td>gen.</td><td>-aš (-š)</td><td>-aš (-š)</td></tr>
<tr><td>dat.</td><td>-i</td><td rowspan="3">} -i</td></tr>
<tr><td>loc.</td><td>-i, -Ø</td></tr>
<tr><td>all.</td><td>-a</td></tr>
<tr><td>abl.</td><td colspan="2">-z, -az</td></tr>
<tr><td>instr.</td><td colspan="2">-it, -t(a)</td></tr>
<tr><td>Plur.</td><td></td><td></td></tr>
<tr><td>nom. com.</td><td>-eš, -aš</td><td>-eš, -uš -aš</td></tr>
<tr><td>acc. com.</td><td>-uš</td><td>-uš, -eš, -aš</td></tr>
<tr><td>nom.-acc. neut.</td><td>-a, -i, -Ø</td><td>-a, -i, -Ø</td></tr>
<tr><td>gen.</td><td>-an, -aš</td><td>-aš</td></tr>
<tr><td>dat.-loc.</td><td>-aš</td><td>-aš</td></tr>
</table>

### 1.1.2

In this first lesson the ***a*-stems** [GrHL 4.1–11] will be treated. The *a*-stems comprise both nouns and adjectives; nouns can be of either common or neuter gender. Examples for the nouns: *lala*- com. (Sum. EME) "tongue," *aruna*- com. (Sum. A.AB.BA) "sea," *peda*- neut. "place"; for the adjectives *araḫzena*- "surrounding, neighboring, foreign." There is no fundamental difference between the paradigms of *lala*- and *aruna*-; they only supplement each other because often not all case forms of a noun are attested.

| | | | | |
|---|---|---|---|---|
| **Sing.** | | | | |
| nom. com. | *lalaš* (EME-*aš*) | *arunaš* | | *araḫzenaš* |
| acc. | *lalan* (EME-*an*) | *arunan* | | *araḫzenan* |
| nom.-acc. neut. | | | *pedan* | *araḫzenan* |
| gen. | *lalaš* | *arunaš* | *pedaš* | *araḫzenaš* |
| dat.-loc. | *lali* (EME-*i*) | *aruni* | *pedi*/*pidi* | *araḫzeni* |
| all. | | *aruna* | | *araḫzena* |
| abl. | *lalaz* (EME-*az*/*za*) | *arunaz* (A.AB.BA-*az*) | *pedaz* | *araḫzenaz* |
| instr. | *lalit* | | | |
| **Plur.** | | | | |
| nom. com. | *laleš*, *laluš* | | | *araḫzeneš*/ *araḫzenaš* |
| acc. | *laluš* (EME-*uš*) | *arunuš* | | *araḫzenuš*/ *araḫzenaš* |
| nom.-acc. neut. | | | *peda* | *araḫzena* |
| gen. | | *arunaš* | | *araḫzenaš* |
| dat.-loc. | | | *pedaš* | *araḫzenaš* |

- Note that in several cases the *a* of the stem disappears before the ending: sing. dat.-loc. *lal*(*a*)-*i*, plur. nom. *lal*(*a*)-*eš*.
- The plur. acc. com. (*araḫzenuš*) can be used sometimes as a nom.; this is a particularly strong development in New Hittite *a*-stems.

## 1.2 Pronoun generalities; personal pronoun first person

### 1.2.1 Pronouns [GrHL 5.1–6]:

The Hittite language has personal (I, you, etc.), anaphoric (he, she, it, etc.), demonstrative (this, that), relative (who, which), interrogative (who?, which?, what?), indefinite (somebody etc.), and possessive (mine, your, her, etc.) pronouns.

In many forms, case endings of the nominal declension can be recognized, but there are also case endings or morphemes that are characteristic of a pronominal declension:

- The gen. sing. of all pronouns ends in -*el*.
- In the gen. plur. of several pronouns we find an ending -*enzan*.
- The dat. sing. and plur. and the abl. are further characterized by an element -*eda*(*n*)-.
- The nom.-acc. sg. neut. ends in -*t*.

This lesson will present the personal pronouns of the first person singular and plural. Personal pronouns, however, do not display all of the typical pronominal endings just mentioned.

### 1.2.2

The **personal pronouns** [GrHL 5.7–10] of the **first person** sing. and plur. are *ūk* "I" and *wēš* "we." They are inflected as follows:

| | | |
|---|---|---|
| nom. | *ūk, ammuk* | *wēš, anzaš* |
| acc. | *ammuk* | *anzaš* |
| gen. | *ammel* | *anzel* |
| dat.-loc. | *ammuk* | *anzaš* |
| abl. | *ammedaz* | *anzedaz* |

- The nom. is most often used when the pronoun has to be stressed and stands in contrast with other pronouns ("Not she but *I* did it!").
- For the makron (¯) on the *u* in *ūk* and on the *e* in *wēš*, see Lesson 1.5.2–3 below.
- The nom. can be further stressed by adding *-ila*: *ukila* "I myself/it was me who ...."
- There is no separate allative or instrumental.
- Note that around 1400 BC onwards the acc. (*ammuk, anzaš*) has already started to take over the function of the nom. (*ūk, wēš*). This is a development we will encounter time and again in the pronouns (see already for the nouns and adjectives Lesson 1.1.2 above).

### 1.2.3

Next to the free-standing personal pronoun (Lesson 1.2.2) there also is an **enclitic personal pronoun** [GrHL 5.11–15]. Enclitic means that a certain grammatical form or category cannot stand by itself, but only appears attached to or hanging onto another word. Enclitics (or simply clitics) cannot bear an accent themselves, but form an accentual unit with the word they are appended to.

Except for some elements which we will see in future lessons, such enclitics are always attached to the first word of a clause irrespective of whether it is Hittite or a Sumero- or Akkadogram; compare the sequence of the enclitic elements *-wa*, *-naš*, and *-za* when attached to the connective *nu* "and" in the following clause:

> *nu=wa=naš=za* ÉRIN.MEŠ ANŠE.KUR.RA.ḪI.A *iya*
> ("and make us (=*naš*) your troops and chariots!")

or to an Akkadogram in the following:

BELINI=*wa*=*naš lē ḫarnikti*
("Our Lord, do not destroy us!")

Often a sentence starts with a combination of a Sumero- and Akkadogram – for instance, an Akkadian preposition with a Sumerian word. Such a combination usually hides a single Hittite word, and as a consequence the clitics follow the second element:

*IŠTU* NAM.RA.ḪI.A=*ma* $GU_4$ UDU *anda ēppun*
=Hitt. **arnuwalit*=*ma* $GU_4$ UDU etc.
("... while (=*ma*) I seized the oxen and sheep together with the population")

The wealth of such clitics in Hittite and the other Anatolian languages is one of the most characteristic features of the Anatolian subgroup of Indo-European languages.

For the **first person personal pronoun** we have the following **enclitic** forms:

| | | |
|---|---|---|
| dat.-loc. | *-mu* | *-naš* |
| acc. | *-mu* | *-naš* |

These enclitic forms carry less emphasis than their free-standing counterparts (Lesson 1.2.2).

## 1.3 Verb generalities

### 1.3.1 Verb [GrHL 11.1–9]:

Hittite verbal inflection distinguishes **person**, **number**, **voice**, **tense**, **mode**, and **aspect.**

Within the category **person** there are three persons (1st, 2nd, and 3rd).

Within **number** we have singular and plural.

With **voice** we mean the distinction between active and medio-passive.

Within the category **tense** there are the present-future (henceforth simply present) and preterite (or past tense).

Within **mode** we have indicative, imperative, and infinitive.

Under **aspect** we classify such verbal suffixes that add an extra element to the basic meaning of the verb, modifying its action as starting (inchoative: to begin to do something), as being in a process of change (fientive: to become…), as being repeated regularly (iterative: to regularly do something), as affecting several persons or objects (distributive), or as causing something to happen (causative: to make someone do something). All of these categories will be explained in the following lessons.

Each verb belongs in principle to one of **two conjugations** or inflection types. These conjugations are named after the ending of the first person singular present indicative active of each conjugation: the *mi*- ("I") and the *ḫi*-conjugation ("II"). Many verbs, however, change conjugation during the history of the Hittite language: Original *mi*-verbs take on endings of the *ḫi*-conjugation, and vice versa. Some of these irregularities can be explained by certain influences and become regular in a sense, whereas others seem to have developed more at random.

Within the -*mi*- and -*ḫi*-conjugations various stem classes can be discerned. There are two basic groups: verbal stems that never change, and those that show certain alternations within the same paradigm. Some of these changes concern vowels and are known as *Ablaut*: compare, e.g., the change between the two stem forms *kuen*- and *kun*- "to kill" in the 3. sing. *kuenzi* "he/she kills" vs. the 3. plur. *kunanzi* "they kill." In others, consonantal changes can be observed: compare 3. sing. *šaḫzi* "he/she seeks" vs. the 3. plur. *šanḫanzi* "they seek." In the first three lessons we will learn the present and preterite, active and medio-passive of verbs of unchanging stem. In the subsequent lessons verbs showing Ablaut or other changes will be presented.

The endings for the **present indicative active** are as follows:

| | -mi (I) | -ḫi (II) |
|---|---|---|
| **Sing.** 1 | *-mi* | *-ḫi* |
| 2 | *-ši* | *-ti* |
| 3 | *-zi* | *-i* |
| **Plur.** 1 | *-weni, -meni (-wani)* | |
| 2 | *-teni (-tani),* | *-šteni* |
| 3 | *-anzi* | |

- These endings are the same for all stem classes, but, as we will see, the combination of certain stems and endings may cause specific (morpho)phonological changes (see, for instance, Lesson 1.5.1 below).
- Sometimes verbs of the *mi*-conjugation take the *ḫi*-conjugation's 2. sing. in *-ti*; this is especially the case with verbal stems in °*š*-, e.g., *ištamašti* instead of regular *ištamašši* "you hear/listen."
- In the plural the ending *-šteni* seems restricted to the *ḫi*-conjugation.
- The variant endings *-wani* and *-tani* for the 1. and 2. plur. are characteristic of the older language and occur next to *-weni* and *-teni.*
- The ending *-meni* is a variant of *-weni* after stems ending in °*u*-: e.g., *waḫnuweni* › *waḫnumeni* "we turn (something) over" (on this, see Lesson 2.5).

## 1.3.2

As examples of **verbs with an unchanging stem** [GrHL 12.8–9 (*-mi*), 13.3–7 (*-ḫi*), 1.37–44 (logograms)] here are the verbs *walḫ-* (Ia) "to strike, attack" and *šipand-* (IIa) "to libate, bring an offering" for the *mi-* and *ḫi*-conjugation respectively. The latter is supplemented by forms of *maniyaḫḫ-* (IIa) "to assign, govern, show."

| | -mi | -ḫi |
|---|---|---|
| **Sing.** | | |
| 1 | *walḫmi* | *išpantḫi* |
| 2 | *walḫši* | *(maniyaḫti)* |
| 3 | *walḫzi* | *išpanti/šipanti* |
| **Plur.** | | |
| 1 | *walḫuweni* | *šipanduweni* |
| 2 | *walḫteni* | *šipanzašteni (maniyaḫteni)* |
| 3 | *walḫanzi* | *šipandanzi* |

- In the case of verbs like *walḫ-* and *šipand-* various clusters of consonants arise (*-lḫm-*, *-lḫš-*, *-lḫz-*, *-lḫt-*, and *-ntḫ-*) which have to be split up in the syllabic cuneiform system. This problem is solved by inserting a (purely orthographic) vowel *-a-* into the cluster [GrHL 1.11–12], resulting in spellings like *wa-al-aḫ-te-ni* or *wa-la-aḫ-te-ni* "you (plur.) strike" for /*walḫteni*/ or *ši-pa-an-ta-aḫ-ḫi* for /*šipantḫi*/ "I bring an offering" (see Introduction §7). For the 2. plur. *šipanzašteni*, see below Lesson 1.5.1.
- The change between *šipand-*/*išpand-* reflects the inability of the Hittites to pronounce a cluster of consonants of the type /sC-/ (i.e., *šḫ-*, *šk*, *šm-* etc.) at the beginning of a word.

- Very often these and other verbs will be written Sumerographically with a phonetic complement. For *walḫ-* we find the Sumerogram GUL (in oracle texts also RA); for *šipant-/išpant-* we have BAL. Compare the following attested forms:

| | | |
|---|---|---|
| **Sing.** | | |
| 1 | GUL-*aḫmi*, RA-*mi* | BAL-*ḫi*, BAL-*antaḫḫi* |
| 2 | | BAL-*atti* |
| 3 | GUL-*aḫzi*, RA-*zi* | BAL-*anti*, BAL-*ti*, BAL-*i* |
| **Plur.** | | |
| 3 | GUL-*aḫḫanzi* | BAL-*anzi*, BAL-*andanzi* |

## 1.4 Syntax

### 1.4.1 Syntax [GrHL 16]:

Each **case** ending has its own **functions**, the most important of which are listed here.

The **nominative** indicates the subject or the nominal predicate of a sentence:

> *nu* LUGAL-*uš apāš kišaru* "may that one (*apāš*) become king!"

The nominative is also used for the vocative since the latter occurs only rarely; examples of the vocative are: *išḫa* "O lord", $^{d}$UTU-*i* "O Sundeity."

The direct object stands in the **accusative**, the indirect object in the **dative**:

> $^{LÚ}$*šankunniš zerin* LUGAL-*i pāi*
> "The priest gives the cup (*zerin*) to the king (LUGAL-*i*)"

In general, the dative indicates to whose advantage or disadvantage an action happens. In the previous example, the king is the recipient or beneficiary of the act of giving. But something can also be taken *from* him:

> LUGAL-*i ayin wāyin dāḫḫun*
> "from the king I have taken (*dāḫḫun*) pain and woe"

Here, too, the "king" is in the dative, and while this action is in his favor, something else might be taken from him that is detrimental to him. Mostly, this dative indicates animate beings; for "from" with inanimates, see the ablative immediately below. Another important function of the dative is to indicate possession (to me there is a house › I have a house).

The accusative is sometimes attested as a directional case (ḪUR.SAG-*an* "to the mountain") and as an accusative of respect ("concerning …" e.g., I have pain concerning my head > I have a headache).

The **(dative-)locative** indicates the place where or the moment at which something happens (URU*Ḫattuši* "in Ḫattuša," *ḫamešḫanti* "in the spring").

The **allative** is productive in Old Hittite only and answers the question: where to?, towards what? (*parna paizzi* "he/she goes home").

The **ablative** has several functions. It answers the questions:

- where from? (*Ḫattušaz* "from/out of Ḫattuša")
- whence? (*nepišaz* "from heaven")
- why?, because of what? (*kez memiaz* "through this deed", *ermanaz* "because of an illness")
- through what? (*aškaz* "through the door")
- by whom? (DINGIR.MEŠ-*za* "by the gods")
- when? (UD-*az* "by day")
- on which side? (ZAG-*az* "on/to the right").

The **instrumental** answers the question: with what? (*wetenit* "with water [he cleanses]") or with whom? ("together with his sons he was killed").

Note that, as will be explained in Lesson 1.6.3, case functions can also be expressed by way of Akkadian prepositions.

### 1.4.2

Hittite has several **connectives** [GrHL 29.3–22]. Most clauses are introduced by ***nu***. Often – but not by any means always – it can be translated "and." Sometimes it is best left untranslated. One of its most important functions is being the "carrier" of the many clitics present in the Hittite language, e.g., *nu=mu walḫzi* "(and) he beats me," *nu=naš šipandanzi* "(and) to us they bring an offering." The connective *nu* links both main and subordinate clauses, but never individual words (see Lesson 1.4.3).

The older language has two more connectives, ***ta*** and ***šu***, with basically the same functions as *nu*. The old connective *ta* sometimes appears in New Hittite, but only as an archaizing feature in certain festival texts. In spite of its having more connectives, it is also characteristic of Old Hittite not to use any connectives at all: This absence of connectives is called *asyndeton*.

For the enclitic conjunction *-a/-ya* connecting clauses, see Lesson 1.4.3.

### 1.4.3

Individual words can be linked ("A and B") by way of the clitic **conjunction** ***-a/-ya*** [GrHL 29.38–45]. The conjunction is attached to the second word: A B=*ya* = "A *and* B." If a word ends in a consonant, the *y* of *-ya* assimilates to the preceding consonant, which is doubled while the *y* itself disappears: *nepiš tekann=a* (‹ *tekan=ya*) "heaven and earth," LUGAL-*uš* MUNUS.LUGAL-*ašš=a* (‹ MUNUS.LUGAL-*aš=ya*) "king and queen," [LÚ]A.ZU *ugg=a* "the physician and I." After a Hittite word ending in a vowel or after a Sumero- or Akkadogram (without a phonetic complement), *-ya* appears: *ḫarganna tepnummanzi=ya* "to destroy and to diminish," LUGAL MUNUS.LUGAL=*ya* "king and queen." The conjunction *-a/-ya* can also mean "too, also, even." As a consequence of its function, *-a/-ya* is not restricted to the first word of a sentence, but can appear in any position. The conjunction *-a/-ya* can also link clauses.

### 1.4.4

A special group of clitics is that of the so-called **sentence particles** [GrHL 28.43–114], whose exact function is not yet known. They seem to be closely related to the verb and especially to movements expressed by the verb. In general there can be only one such particle per clause, although there are occasional exceptions to this rule. In the chain of enclitic elements they always fill the last slot (for more on this, see Lesson 3.4.3). Since the system behind these particles remains largely unknown, they are usually left untranslated. This does not mean, however, that one should simply ignore them. Their presence or absence with certain verbs influences the translation of the verb: e.g., *-kan* ... *šanḫ-* "to search through something (for something else)" vs. *šanḫ-* "to search for something," *-kan* ... *parā epp-* "to touch, afflict(?)" vs. *parā epp-* "to hold out to (somebody), present." Since some verbs take certain particles and some do not, the presence or absence of a sentence particle may also reduce the number of the possible verbs when restoring a broken text.

The following particles are found:

| | |
|---|---|
| *-an* (rare and only in Old Hittite) | (direction inwards) |
| *-apa* (only in the older language) | (direction from outside inwards?) |
| *-ašta* | (separation?) |
| *-kan* | (?) |
| *-šan* | (movement downwards from above?) |

- In the case of particles starting with a vowel, the *u* of the connective *nu* disappears, e.g., *nu + ašta › n=ašta.*
- In other cases the beginning *a* of the particles *-an*, *-ašta*, and *-apa* merges with the preceding vowel and disappears: e.g., *nu=ši + ašta › nu=ši=šta*, *n(u)=an=ši + apa › n(u)=an=ši=pa.*
- In the oldest Hittite texts these particles were still used only sparingly, but during the fifteenth to fourteenth centuries the system reached its widest extension. During the New Hittite period *-kan* gradually took over the functions of the other particles, until in late New Hittite only *-kan* was left.

1.4.5

Hittite has no separate **future tense** [GrHL 22.2–13]; present forms may always be translated as futures if the context so requires: LUGAL-*uš* *ANA* DINGIR-*LIM* *šipanti* "the king brings an offering/will bring an offering to the deity" (for *ANA*, see below, Lesson 1.6.3).

1.4.6

Hittite has no **article**.

## 1.5 Phonology

1.5.1

If within a paradigm two **dentals** (*t/d*) come to stand immediately next to one another, a sibilant emerges to ease the pronunciation [GrHL 1.125]: ***-TT- › -TsT.** Compare, for instance, the 2. plur. pres. act. of the verb *šipand/išpand-* (Lesson 1.3.2) where we expect **šipand-teni*, which then regularly becomes */šipand-s-teni/*. Since the Hittite /z/ was an affricate and pronounced as [ts], the resulting clusters could be spelled by using the signs ZA, IZ, AZ: e.g., *ši-pa-an-za-aš-te-ni* (cf. also Lesson 2.3.2) with a graphic *a* in *-zaš-* to write the cluster /-ndst/.

### 1.5.2

The cuneiform writing system makes no systematic distinction between the **vowels** *e* and *i* (see Introduction §7) [GrHL 1.49–65]. For instance, there are separate signs for the syllables MI and ME and IŠ and EŠ, but there is only a single sign for LI/LE or IR/ER. In order to indicate the exact vowel quality, a scribe could add an extra I or E respectively: e.g., LI-E = /le/ "not" (prohibitive), *ú*-E-IR = /uer/ "they came." Such spellings are called *plene writing* or *plene spelling*. Nowadays we usually adjust the coloring of the adjacent sign to the plene written vowel: *le-e* (instead of *li-e*), *ú-e-er*. Such plene spellings should be indicated in bound transcription or **scriptio continua** (see Introduction §7) using a macron: *lē*, *uēr*. They do not, however, necessarily imply lengthening of the spoken vowel or some kind of accent.

Comparable is the case of the vowel signs U and Ú. Given the general consistency of their appearance within paradigms or words, they are likely to indicate two different vowels or vowel qualities, perhaps [o] and [u] respectively. Yet this distinction does not exist for signs of the structure VC (e.g., UP, UK, UD) and CV (e.g., PU, TU, RU) that contain the vowel /*u*/. So here, too, in a spelling like *u-up-zi* (*ūpzi*) "he/she rises," the particular use of the sign U may be due simply to the need to indicate the exact quality of the following sign UP.

### 1.5.3

**Plene spellings** also occur in cases where there are separate signs for *e* and *i* available (e.g., IŠ vs. EŠ) as well as with the vowel *a*; compare, for instance, *ma-a-an* "as, if, when" or *e-eš-zi* "he/she is." In a case like *ma-a-an*, the almost systematically plene written A is functional in that it distinguishes the conjunction *mān* "if, when" from the modal particle *ma-an* = *man* (see Lesson 7.4.3). Here the plene spelling might indicate length, accent, or both.

The same may be true for consistent spellings like in the verb *eš-* "to be," where almost without exception all forms are written with a plene E (*e-eš-*), the more so, since the sign EŠ (next to a separate IŠ) does not need the extra E to determine its *e*-quality.

Sometimes a plene spelled I or U can indicate a glide *y* or *w*: *ši-i-e-eš-sar* "beer" thus probably stands for /siyēssar/ and *ku-ut-ru-u-e-eš* "witnesses" for /kutruwēs/ (see more on glides in Lesson 2.5).

How difficult it is, however, to detect a system behind all plene writings can be illustrated by looking at the various spellings of the 3. sing. pres. act. of the verb *laḫuwai-* "to pour": *la-ḫu-wa-i, la-a-ḫu-wa-i, la-ḫu-u-wa-i, la-ḫu-wa-a-i, la-a-ḫu-u-wa-i, la-ḫu-u-wa-a-i, la-a-ḫu-wa-a-i,* and *la-a-ḫu-u-wa-a-i.*

1.5.4
The adjustment of the vowels *e* and *i* in a transliteration mentioned above in Lesson 1.5.2 (*le-e* instead of *li-e*) is also used in the case of consonants in signs of the structure VC. Whereas there are individual signs for TA and DA, KA and GA, PA and BA, etc., VC-signs do not exist in similar pairs of voiced and voiceless variants: There are no separate signs for AT and AD, but only undifferentiated AD/T, AK/G, or AP/B etc. (see Introduction §7). Therefore, depending on a following CV-sign we adjust the matching consonant: AD/T-TA-*aš* becomes *at-ta-aš* "father" and UD/T-DA-*ni* becomes *ud-da-ni* "in the matter (of ...)." In **bound transcription** (see Introduction §7) both the double consonant and their quality are preserved: *attaš* and *uddani.*

## 1.6 Sumerian and Akkadian

1.6.1
To express the plural in Sumero- and Akkadograms, the **Sumerian plural** endings MEŠ and ḪI.A (as well as occasionally DIDLI [written AŠ.AŠ] or DIDLI.ḪI.A) are used: LUGAL "king" and LUGAL.MEŠ "kings," $\text{GU}_4$ "ox" and $\text{GU}_4$.ḪI.A "oxen," URU "town, city" and URU.(DIDLI.)ḪI.A "towns," DINGIR.DIDLI "gods." Sometimes a double Sumerogram is used: KUR.KUR "lands" next to KUR "land."

Note, however, that behind a Sumerian plural there can be a Hittite singular noun. This is often the case with collectives like ÉRIN.MEŠ "army," which usually renders a Hittite singular, as is evident through singular agreement either on the verb (if it is the subject of the sentence) or on an adjective or pronoun. Sometimes this is clear when the Sumerian plural is followed by a singular Hittite phonetic complement: A.ŠÀ.ḪI.A-*ni* "in a field."

1.6.2
A **genitival relation** ("of") can be expressed in Sumerian by way of a simple juxtaposition of Sumerograms: $\text{GU}_4$ LUGAL "the ox of the king, the king's ox," LUGAL KUR URU*Ḫatti* "the king of Ḫatti-land."

1.6.3
Besides the possibility of phonetic complements (see Introduction §7) to express a genitive, dative-locative, ablative, or instrumental with a Sumero- or

Akkadogram (see above Lesson 1.1.2 EME-*i*, EME-*az*), one frequently finds the **Akkadian prepositions**:

| | | |
|---|---|---|
| *ANA* | to, for, in, at | = dat.-loc. |
| *INA* | in, at, towards | = dat.-loc. |
| *IŠTU* | by, through, with, from | = abl.-instr. |
| *ITTI* | together with | = abl.-instr. |
| *PANI* | before, for, to | = dat.-loc. |
| *QADU* | (together) with | = abl.-instr. |
| *ŠA* | of | = gen. |

- According to Akkadian grammar, these prepositions are followed by the Akkadian oblique or genitive case (see below, Lesson 2.6), which can often be recognized in an Akkadian phonetic complement: *INA* URU-*LIM* "in/to the town," *ANA* DINGIR-*LIM* "to/for the deity."
- Often there is no phonetic complement at all: *ANA* LUGAL "to/for the king."
- One also finds Hittite phonetic complements: *ANA* LUGAL-*i* "to/for the king," *IŠTU* URU-*az* "from/out of the town."
- Occasionally a Sumerogram occurs in a sentence without any indication of its function: Compare the word $^{\text{GIŠ}}$ŠÚ.A "throne" in *n(u)=aš=z=šan ŠA* $^{\text{d}}$IŠKUR $^{\text{GIŠ}}$ŠÚ.A *ešari* "(and) he sits down (*ešari*) on the throne of (ŠA) the Stormgod ($^{\text{d}}$IŠKUR)." The interpretation of $^{\text{GIŠ}}$ŠÚ.A as a locative ("*on* the throne") is required by the context but not indicated in any formal way.
- It is always important to remember that although such **Sumero- and Akkadographic combinations** were written this way, they were spoken or read in Hittite and **they are only another way of indicating a Hittite case ending on a Hittite word.**

## 1.7 Cuneiform signs

### 1.7.1

For a complete listing of all cuneiform signs used in this book, see Appendix 4. The meaning of Sumerograms can be found in the Glossary (Appendix 5).

a  e  i  u  ú 

aš  pát/BE  nu 

ḫal  tar 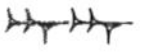 an/DINGIR 

### Determinatives

| | | |
|---|---|---|
| $^{\text{m}}$□ |  | for names of men (pronounced "m" or "Mr.") |
| $^{\text{LÚ}}$□ |  | for male gender |
| $^{\text{f/ MUNUS}}$□ |  | for names of women and female gender |
| $^{\text{d}}$□ |  | for names of deities or deified objects (pronounced "dingir") |
| $^{\text{KUR}}$□ |  | for names of lands, areas, regions, etc. |
| $^{\text{URU}}$□ | 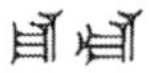 | for names of cities, towns, and settlements |
| $^{\text{É}}$□ |  | for houses and general architectural units |

## 1.8 Exercises; KBo 3.4 1–7

### 1.8.1 Translate:

A note on translating Hittite sentences and texts: Hittite is a strong verb-final language, that is, the verb of a sentence almost always comes last. Also, since many sentences begin with *nu* and/or have one or more clitics that are by definition attached to the first word of a sentence, sentence boundaries are fairly easy to recognize. This can help you translate texts. Try the following five steps:

(1) Determine where sentences begin and end.
(2) Starting with the first sentence, identify the verb and translate it (e.g., "he/she/it hears"); then ask yourself the following questions:
(3) Is there an explicit subject (e.g., "the king hears")? If not, stay with the person indicated by the verbal ending ("he/she/it hears").
(4) Then follow the questions that a verb naturally brings up: e.g., a verb like "to hear" only supposes something or someone heard (e.g., "the king hears the message/messenger"), "to give" supposes a direct object that someone gives ("the king gives an order," so look for an acc.) and an indirect object to whom the subject gives it ("the king gives an order to the servant," so look for a dat.-loc.). A verb like "to take" will let you ask "what" (acc.) and perhaps also "from whom" or "from where" (abl.).
(5) You are then mostly left with, for instance, genitives that depend on nouns or adverbial expressions in a dat.-loc., all., abl., or instr.

1. *nu-mu* Ú-UL *iš-dam-ma-aš-zi*
2. (omen) *ma-a-an* I-NA UD.15.KAM $^{\text{d}}$SÎN-*aš a-ki* (i.e., eclipses) LUGAL.GAL *a-ki*
3. *ta* KÁ.GAL *ḫa-at-ki*
4. (omen, protasis:) *ma-a-an-kán* $^{\text{d}}$SÎN *na-a-ú-i u-up-zi* (followed by apodosis: "then …")

5. (omen, protasis:) *ma-a-an an-tu-uḫ-ša-an* SAG.DU-*ZU* (-*ZU* = "his") *iš-tar-ak-zi* (followed by apodosis: "then ...")
6. *nu-kán* *A-NA* ᵈ*IŠTAR* *an-na-al-li an-na-al-la-an* SISKUR *ḫa-pu-ša-an-zi*
7. ᴳᴵˢIG-*an-na ḫa-at-ki*
8. *ma-a-an-mu* DINGIR.MEŠ *ka-ne-eš-ša-an-zi* LUGAL-*iz-zi-aḫ-ḫa-ri* ("then I will become king")
9. UGULA ᴸᵁ́.ᴹᴱˢMUḪALDIM *ḫa-aš-ši-i* 1-*šu ši-pa-an-ti*
10. (ritual:) *ma-a-an* UN-*an* ᵈ*Iš-ḫa-ra-az* GIG-*zi* (followed by apodosis: "then they act thus ...")
11. *nu* ᴸᵁ́Ú.ḪUB ᴳᴵˢAB.ḪI.A *an-da iš-ta-a-pí*
12. *a-ra-aš a-ra-an* *Ú-UL* *ka-ni-e-eš-zi*
13. *nu-kán tu-u-ru-up-pa-an* GEŠTIN-*it ši-pa-an-ti*
14. *nu-kán* *A-NA* DINGIR-*LIM* 1 $\text{GU}_4$ 48 UDU BAL-*aḫ-ḫi*
15. *na-aš-ta* 1 UDU *ad-da-aš* DINGIR.MEŠ-*aš ši-pa-an-da-an-zi*

## 1.8.2

Analyze the following verb forms according to person and number, and translate:

1. *pa-aḫ-ḫa-aš-te-ni*
2. *pár-aḫ-ši*
3. *ḫa-at-ku-e-ni*
4. *pa-aḫ-ḫa-aš-mi*
5. *pár-aḫ-mi*
6. *pár-ḫa-an-zi*
7. *na-aḫ-ti*
8. *iš-dam-ma-aš-te-ni*
9. *ši-ip-pa-an-da-an-zi*
10. *pu-nu-uš-šu-u-e-ni*

## Words for Lesson 1

| | | | |
|---|---|---|---|
| *ak-* (IIa) | to die | ᴳᴵˢAB | window |
| *annalla-* | old, former | DINGIR | god, goddess |
| *antuḫša-* (UN), com. | person, human being | GEŠTIN(-*a*) | wine |
| | | GIG | = *ištark-* |
| *ara-*, com. | comrade, friend | ᴳᴵˢIG(-*a*) | door |
| *ara- ... ara-* | one ... the other ... | KÁ.GAL | gate |
| *araḫzena-* | surrounding, neighboring, foreign | LUGAL.GAL | Great King |
| *atta-*, com. | father | ᴸᵁ́MUḪALDIM | cook |
| | | SAG.DU | head |

| | |
|---|---|
| *gulš-* (Ia) | to carve, record |
| *ḫapuš-* (Ia) | to make up for, resume |
| *ḫašša-*, com. | hearth |
| *ḫatk-* (IIa) | to close (transitive) |
| *ištamašš-* (Ia) | to hear, listen |
| *anda ištap-* (IIa) | to close |
| *ištark-* + acc. (GIG) | to fall/be ill, have pain in (with acc. or dat. of person and body part) |
| *kaneš-* (Ia) | to recognize, choose |
| *mān* | 1. as, like<br>2. if<br>3. when |
| *naḫḫ-* (Ia) | to be afraid of, fear |
| *nawi* | not yet |
| *nu* | (connective) |
| *paḫš-* (I/IIa) | to protect |
| *parḫ-* (Ia) | to chase away |
| *punuš-* (Ia) | to question |
| *šipant-/išpant-* (IIa) | to bring an offering, libate, offer |
| *ta* | (connective) |
| *turuppa-* | turuppa (= a kind of pastry) |
| *up-* (Ia) | to rise |
| *walḫ-* (Ia; GUL) | to beat, strike, attack |

| | |
|---|---|
| SISKUR/SÍSKUR (= SISKUR.SISKUR) | offering, ritual |
| UD.KAM,<br>UD. (number).KAM | day<br>the ...-th day, ... days |
| UDU | sheep |
| UGULA | chief, overseer |
| $^{LÚ}$Ú.ḪUB | deaf (man/person) |
| UN | = *antuḫša-* |
| *ANA*(*PĀNI*) | = Hitt. dat.-loc. |
| *INA* | = Hitt. dat.-loc. and all. |
| *UL* | not, no(ne) (negation) |
| number-*šu* | x-time(s) (cf. Lesson 7.6) |

**DN**

| | |
|---|---|
| $^{d}$*Išḫara* | (goddess) Išḫara |
| $^{d}$*IŠTAR* | (goddess) Ištar |
| $^{d}$*SÎN*(-*a*-) | Moon God (Hitt. *Arma*) |

### 1.8.3 *The Ten-Year Annals* of the Hittite King Muršili II

*The Ten-Year Annals* of Muršili (*c.*1318–1295 BC) is one of several historical works by that king. He wrote a biography of his father, Šuppiluliuma, known as the *Deeds of Šuppiluliuma* as well as a full account of his entire reign, the so-called *Extensive Annals.* Several copies of the *Ten-Year Annals* exist, the best of which, KBo 3.4 joining the small fragment KUB 23.125 (see Lesson 8.7.2), is given here. Breaks are largely restored through duplicates or through parallel passages describing the same events in the *Extensive Annals.*

The transliteration below and in subsequent lessons follows Hittitological conventions as already partially laid out in the Introduction. Note the following additional markings:

| | |
|---|---|
| ⌜ ⌝ | half brackets indicate (a) damaged but still legible sign(s) |
| [ ] | square brackets indicate a break on the tablet |
| ‹ › | mark a sign or signs that the ancient scribe inadvertently left out |
| « » | mark a sign or signs that the ancient scribe inadvertently wrote, but that should not be there |
| ^ | marks space per sign in a break |
| ! | marks sign with deviating shape |

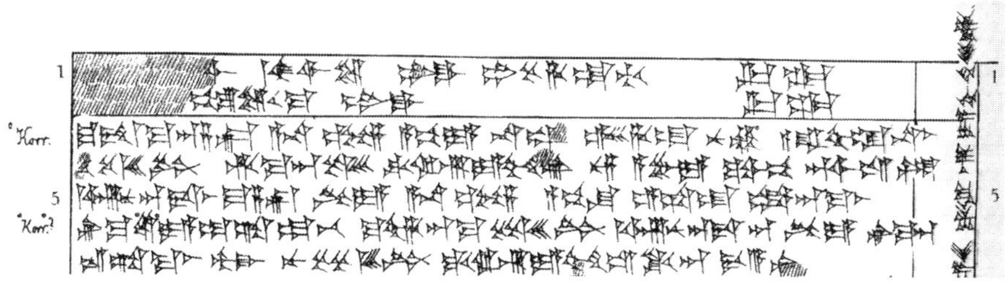

Figure 3a

KBo 3.4 + KUB 23.125 i

1. [UM-*MA* $^{\text{d}}$UTU]-*ŠI* $^{\text{m}}$*Mur-ši-li* LUGAL.GAL LUGAL KUR *Ḫa-at-ti* UR.SAG
2. [DUMU $^{\text{m}}$*Šu-up-*]*pí-lu-li-u-ma* LUGAL.GAL UR.SAG

---

3. *ku-it-ma-an-za-kán* *A-NA* $^{\text{GIŠ}}$GU.ZA *A-BI-IA* *na-*⌜*wi*$_5$⌝ *e-eš-ḫa-at nu-mu*[1] <u>*a-ra-aḫ-zé-na-aš*</u>
4. KUR.KUR.MEŠ LÚ.KÚR *ḫu-u-ma-an-te-eš ku-u-ru-ri-ia-aḫ-ḫe-er nu-za* *A-BU-IA* *ku-wa-pí* DINGIR-*LIM*-*iš* DÙ-*at*
5. $^{\text{m}}$<u>*Ar-nu-an-da-aš*</u>*-ma-za-kán* ŠEŠ-*IA* *A-NA* $^{\text{GIŠ}}$GU.ZA *A-BI-ŠU* *e-ša-at* EGIR-*an-ma-aš*
6. *ir-ma-li-ia-at-ta-at-pát ma-aḫ-ḫa-an-ma* KUR.KUR.MEŠ LÚ.KÚR $^{\text{m}}$<u>*Ar-nu-an-da-an*</u> ŠEŠ-IA <u>*ir-ma-an*</u>
7. *iš-ta-ma-aš-šer nu* KUR.KUR.MEŠ LÚ.KÚR *ku-u-ru-ri-ia-aḫ-ḫi-iš-ke-u-an da-a-*⌜*er*⌝

---

[1] MU written over erasure.

¡ 1–2 [Thus (speaks) His Maje]sty Muršili, Great King, King of Ḫatti-Land, Hero, [son of Šup]piluliuma, Great King, Hero.

3–7 Before I sat down on the throne of my father, all neighboring enemy countries were hostile to me. When my father became a god (i.e., died), Arnuwanda, my brother, sat down on the throne of his father. Afterwards, however, he became ill as well, and when the enemy countries heard of Arnuwanda, (that is,) my brother's illness, the enemy countries began to be hostile.

## Questions

1. Identify in the handcopy the cuneiform signs given in this Lesson (1.7).
2. Parse the underlined nominal *a*-stem forms.

## Words

5. $^{m}$*Arnuwanda* Muršili II's brother and predecessor on the throne
6. *irma*-, com. illness

# Lesson 2

## 2.1 *i*-stem nouns and adjectives

### 2.1.1

Like the *a*-stems, the class of ***i*-stems** contains both **nouns** and **adjectives**, and there are common as well as neuter gender nouns. But most adjectival *i*-stems (Lesson 2.1.2) are declined differently from the nominal *i*-stems.

For the **nouns** [GrHL 4.23–24] the following paradigms are given: *ḫalki-* com. "grain," supplemented by *ḫalḫaltumari-* com. "corner" and *luli-* com. "pond, basin," and ⁽ᴰᵁᴳ⁾*išpanduzzi-* neut. "wine ration," supplemented by ᴺᴬ⁴*ḫuwaši-* "*ḫuwaši*-stone" (a kind of stone monument). There is no fundamental difference between the paradigms of *ḫalki-* and *luli-*: they just supplement each other.

| | | | |
|---|---|---|---|
| **Sing.** | | | |
| nom. com. | *ḫalkiš* | *luliš* | |
| acc. com. | *ḫalkin* | *lulin* | |
| nom.-acc. neut. | | | *išpanduzzi* |
| gen. | *ḫalkiyaš* | *luliyaš* | *išpanduzziyaš* |
| dat.-loc. | (*halḫaltumari*) | *luli, luliya* | *išpanduzzi* |
| all. | | *luliya* | *išpanduzziya* |
| abl. | *ḫalkiyaz* | *luliyaz* | *išpanduzziyaz* |
| instr. | *ḫalkit* | *lulit* | *išpanduzit* |
| **Plur.** | | | |
| nom. com. | *ḫalkeš* | *luliyaš* | |
| acc. com. | *ḫalkiuš, ḫalkeš* | | |
| nom.-acc. neut. | | | (ᴺᴬ⁴*ḫuwaši*ᴴᴵ·ᴬ) |
| gen., dat.-loc. | (*ḫalḫaltumariyaš*) | | |

- As is clear from the above paradigms, the same endings that we already saw in the *a*-stem inflection come immediately after the °*i-*: *-i+š*, *-i+n* etc.
- If a case ending starts with a vowel (like the gen. *-aš*, abl. *-az*), a *y* usually appears between the stem vowel and the ending, functioning as a glide (e.g., gen. *-iyaš*, abl. *-iyaz*): see below, Lesson 2.5. In older Hittite especially such glides are often not written (e.g., gen. *-i-aš* or abl. *-i-az*).
- The original all. ending *-iya* continued to be used as a variant of the dat.-loc.

- Some nouns show a mixed *a*- and *i*-inflection: Compare $^{\text{GIŠ}}$*ḫuluganna/i*- (a wheeled vehicle) with an abl. $^{\text{GIŠ}}$*ḫulugannaz* (instead of -*iyaz*) and a gen. sing. $^{\text{GIŠ}}$*ḫulugannaš* (instead of -*iyaš*).
- The nom. and acc. sing. com. of the *i*-stems can sometimes be spelled -*eš* and -*en*: compare *ḫal-ke-en*.
- The nom.-acc. plur. neut. is endingless; it cannot be distinguished from the singular in writing, except for the often-added Sumerographic plural marker ḪI.A (see Lesson 1.6.1).

2.1.2

Among the *i*-stem **adjectives** [GrHL 4.36–38] we have to distinguish between those that inflect just like the nouns (Lesson 2.1.1) and those that do not. For the first we give here *nakki*- "weighty, important, hard." Characteristic of the second group is a change (*Ablaut*) within the paradigm: the nom. and acc. sing. com. have the simple stem vowel -*i*- (-*iš*/-*in*), whereas the oblique cases and the nom. and acc. plur. com. and neut. have an extended stem in -*ai*-/-*ay*- (e.g., gen. sing. -*ayaš*). Examples for the second group are *šalli*- "great, big" (supplemented by *šuppi*- "sacred, holy") and *mekki*- "many, numerous."

| | | | |
|---|---|---|---|
| **Sing.** | | | |
| nom. com. | *nakkiš* | *šalliš* | *mekkiš* |
| acc. com. | *nakkin* | *šallin* | *(mekkan)* |
| nom.-acc. neut. | *nakki* | *šalli* | *mekki* |
| gen. | | *šallayaš, šallaš* | |
| dat.-loc. | *nakkiya* | *šallai* | |
| abl. | *nakkiyaz* | *šallayaz* | *mekkayaz* |
| instr. | *nakkit* | *(šuppit)* | |
| **Plur.** | | | |
| nom. com. | *nakkiyaeš* | *šallaeš* *(šuppeš)* | *mekkaeš,* *mekkauš* |
| acc. com. | *nakkiuš* | *šallauš* | *mekkauš* |
| nom.-acc. neut. | *nakki* | *šalla, šalli* | *mekkaya* |
| gen., dat.-loc. | *nakkiyaš* | *šallayaš* | *mekkayaš* |

- Contraction of -*aya*- to -*a*- resulted in apparent *a*-stem forms like the gen. sing. *šallaš* or the nom.-acc. plur. neut. *šalla*.
- In the paradigm of *mekki*- some forms of a consonant stem *mekk*- are attested: acc. sing. com. *mekkan*, nom.-acc. sing. neut. *mēk* and the nom. and acc. plur. com. *mekkeš* and *mekkuš*.
- A form like the nom. plur. com. *nakkiyaeš* developed in analogy to forms like *šallaeš*.

- The regular nom.-acc. sing. neut. *mekki* can be used as an adverb meaning "very."

## 2.2 Third person enclitic pronoun

### 2.2.1

The most frequently used pronoun in the Hittite language is no doubt the **enclitic anaphoric** (i.e., referring back within a text to a person or object already mentioned) **pronoun of the third person** "he, she, it, they" [GrHL 5.11–15 (form), 18.1 (use)]. Two stems can be distinguished: *-a-* and *-š-/-šm-*. Other case forms than those given here are not available.

| | Sing. | Plur. |
|---|---|---|
| nom. com. | *-aš* | *-e, -at* |
| acc. com. | *-an* | *-uš, -aš* |
| nom.-acc. neut. | *-at* | *-e, -at* |
| dat.-loc. | *-ši* | *-šmaš* |

- These clitics are attached to the first word of the sentence, mostly the connective *nu*, in the older language *ta* and *šu* (see Lesson 1.4.2). The connectives *nu*, *ta*, and *šu* lose their *-u* or *-a* if the pronoun starts with a vowel: e.g., *na-aš* = *n=aš* (‹ *nu+aš*) "(and) he/she," *te* = *t=e* (‹ *ta+e*), "(and) they" as opposed to *nu-uš-ši* = *nu=šši* (for the necessity to express the double *-šš-* in bound transcription, see Introduction §7 and Lesson 4.5 below), or *nu-uš-ma-aš* = *nu=šmaš*.
- In Older Hittite the dat.-loc. can be written as *-še*.
- The sequence *=ma* (see Lesson 2.4.4)*=šmaš* "but to them" may appear as *-ma-aš* through haplography: *-ma-aš-ma-aš* › *-ma-aš*.
- The nom. sing. com. *-aš* and its plural are used only in sentences governed by certain classes of intransitive verbs like "to go": *n=aš paizzi* "he/she goes"; for more on this, see Lesson 2.4.1.
- The plural forms *-e* and *-uš* are typical of the older language. There are a few examples in Old Hittite of a non-enclitic use of this pronoun: e.g., *e-eš-ta* = *e=(a)šta* "they ..." (for the particle *-(a)šta*, see Lesson 1.4.4).

## 2.3 Preterite indicative active

### 2.3.1

Like in the present tense, the endings for the **preterite indicative active** [GrHL 11.1–9] are the same for all verbal stem classes, but there may be certain (morpho)phonological changes due, for instance, if a verbal stem ending in a consonant is immediately followed by a verbal ending beginning with a consonant.

| | -mi (I) | -ḫi (II) |
|---|---|---|
| **Sing.** ind. pret. 1 | -C*un*, -V*nun* | -*ḫun* |
| 2 | -Vš, -C*ta*, -*šta*, -V*t* | -*ta* |
| 3 | -V*t*, C*ta*, -*šta* | -*š*, -*ta*, -*šta* |
| **Plur.** ind. pret. 1 | -*wen*, -*men* | |
| 2 | -*ten* | -*šten* |
| 3 | -*er* | |

- The ending -*šta* developed in the later language.
- Just like the 2. plur. pres. -*šteni*, the ending -*šten* seems again (see Lesson 1.3.1) restricted to the *ḫi*-conjugation.
- The variant 1. plur. -*men* occurs with the causative verbs in -*nu*- (see Lesson 2.4.2) as well as with some others (see Lesson 1.3.1, 1.3.5).
- The 3. plur. pret. ending is here given as -*er*, but is also often transliterated -*ir*.

## 2.3.2

For the verbs of unchanging stem (see Lesson 1.3.1–2; [GrHL 12.8–9 (-*mi*), 13.3–7 (-*ḫi*)]) we get the following paradigms:

| | -mi (Ia) | -ḫi (IIa) |
|---|---|---|
| **Sing.** 1 | *walḫun*, GUL-*(aḫ)ḫun*, GUL-*un* | *šipandaḫḫun*, BAL-*aḫḫun* |
| 2 | *walḫta* | *(maniaḫta)* |
| 3 | *walḫta*, GUL-*aḫta* | *šipandaš*, *šipanzašta* |
| **Plur.** 1 | *walḫuwen* | *šipanduwen* |
| 2 | *walḫten* | |
| 3 | *walḫer*, GUL-*(aḫ)ḫer* | *šipanter*, BAL-*er* |

- The 3. sing. *šipanzašta* is another attempt at writing /sipand-s-ta/ (see Lesson 1.5.1).

## 2.3.3

The *mi*-verb *mauš*- "to fall" may be considered to belong to the class of verbs of unchanging stem, but is slightly irregular with its 1. sing. pres. *muḫḫi* "I fall/will fall" and pret. *muḫḫun* "I fell," and 3. plur. pret. *mauer* "they fell" [GrHL 13.32–33].

## 2.4 Syntax and word formation

### 2.4.1

The nom. sing. com. ***-aš*** of the enclitic personal pronoun (see Lesson 2.2) and its plural are used only in sentences governed by certain classes of intransitive verbs like "to go": *n=aš paizzi* "he goes." It can never occur with a **transitive verb**. In a sentence like *n=aš walḫzi* the *-aš* can therefore only be the acc. plur. com. "he beats them" (and not *"he beats").

### 2.4.2

Important groups of verbs of unchanging stem are the **causatives** in ***-nu-*** and ***-aḫḫ-*** ("to make something happen, to turn something into ..."), the **fientives** ("to become ... /to turn ..."), and the **statives** ("to be ...") in ***-ešš-*** [GrHL 10.6–18]. Those in *-nu-* and *-ešš-* follow the *mi*-conjugation, those in *-aḫḫ-* the *ḫi*-conjugation. Mostly they are derived from adjectives that lose their stem vowel: Compare *šalli-* "big" › *šallanu-* "to make big, to raise," *šallešš-* "to be(come) big," *marša-* "profane, treacherous" › *maršanu-/maršaḫḫ-* "to make treacherous, betray," *maršešš-* "to be(come) treacherous."

### 2.4.3

It is important to realize that in spite of its very limited formal repertoire (present – preterite), the Hitt. **verbal tense system** was very flexible, and in an English translation we can use everything from pluperfect through future as needed. The tenses do not have a fixed meaning, and they are always to be translated relative to one another. The present tense not only expresses what happens now, but also what will happen in the future (see already Lesson 1.4.5). In addition, it can occur in narratives about the past to indicate an ongoing action without a specific beginning or end ("I was walking (pres.) in the park, the birds were singing (pres.), when suddenly a man jumped (pret.) from behind a tree"). The status of an historical present ("I was walking (pret.) in the park, the birds were singing (pret.), when suddenly a man jumps (pres.) from behind a tree") is more difficult to prove for Hittite.

The preterite, on the other hand, can cover any action in the past. If it comes prior to another action in the past ("when I had finished my work, I drank tea") it is best to translate a pluperfect ("had finished"). In a similar way, the first of two subsequent actions in the future can be expressed through a preterite, that is, a future perfect ("when I (will) have done my work, I will drink tea").

### 2.4.4

We already saw the **connectives** *nu*, *ta*, and *šu*, as well as the clitic conjunction *-a/-ya* (Lesson 1.4.2–3). Another very common **clitic conjunction** is ***-ma*** (see already briefly Lesson 2.2). With very rare exceptions all these conjunctions are mutually exclusive. The basic function of *-ma* is to establish a relation with the preceding clause or context. The traditional adversative rendering "but, however" can be appropriate, but is certainly not always applicable. It can join a main clause to a preceding subordinate one where one might translate "then" or leave it untranslated ("If the old king dies, then his son will succeed," "If the old king dies, his son succeeds"). As in these examples, it often marks a change of person. When connecting two main sentences, often Engl. "while" works very well ("she drank coffee, while I had tea"). The clitic *-ma* may also mark the beginning of new, larger text units or paragraphs. In that case it is best left untranslated.

If a sentence starts with *mān* "if, when," *-ma* can often be delayed to the second word (for an example see Lesson 4.8.1 sentence 10).

In older Hittite we find a **clitic conjunction *-a***, different from *-a/-ya* "and, too" (see Lesson 1.4.3), which performed the same functions as *-ma*. Because it does not cause doubling of a preceding consonant, it is also known as the "Old Hittite non-geminating *-a*." With, for instance, *kinun* "now," one can thus find both *ki-nu-un-na* = *kinunn=a* (‹ **kinun=ya*) "and now" and *ki-nu-na* = *kinun=a* "but now." Fairly soon this non-geminating *-a* went out of use and was replaced by *-ma*.

2.4.5
Personal or topographic names often appear uninflected in the so-called **stem form** [GrHL 16.3]. Country names preceded by the Sumerogram KUR almost never show case endings. Compare, e.g., KUR URU*Piggainarešša walḫta* "he attacked the country of Piggainarešša" but *nu* dUTU-*ŠI* URU*Katḫaidduwan* GUL-*un* (= *walḫun*) "I, my Majesty, attacked the town of Katḫaidduwa"; *ANA* d*Telipinu šipanti* "he brings an offering to (the deity) Telipinu" vs. the real dative(-locative) in *n=ašta* d*Telipinui … dāḫḫun* "from Telipinu I took" (note the separative *-(a)šta*, see Lesson 1.4.4).

## 2.5 Phonology

### 2.5.1

For the contraction of ***-aya-*** to ***-a-*** see Lesson 2.1.2. If a consonant is followed by the **sonorants** *y* or *w* plus a vowel, often the vowel matching the sonorant is inserted between the consonant and the sonorant to ease pronunciation: C*y*V › C*iy*V and C*w*V › C*uw*V; e.g., /šipandwen/ "we offered" › *šipanduwen* [GrHL 1.80–83].

Conversely, a sonant may be inserted in order to avoid hiatus: e.g., *nakkiaš* › *nakkiyaš*. Such an inserted, secondary sonant is called a **glide**. Such a glide may be written using the sign IA or the sign WA (and sometimes $WI_5$): *na-ak-ki-ya-aš*, *wa-al-ḫu-wa-ni*. In other cases plene written vowels *i* and *u* can be used: see Lesson 1.5.3. Forms written without a glide are usually typical of the older language (see Lesson 2.1.1).

## 2.6 Akkadian

### 2.6.1

Akkadian nominal inflection has three **cases**: nominative, accusative, and a genitive or oblique case. There are two genders: masculine and feminine. For the **masculine noun**, the paradigms of *ŠARRU* "king" and *BĒLU* "lord" are given (within an Akkadian context forms can be given in lower case):

| | | | |
|---|---|---|---|
| **Sing.** | nom. | *ŠARRU* | *BĒLU* |
| | gen. | *ŠARRI* | *BĒLI* |
| | acc. | *ŠARRA* | *BĒLA* |
| **Plur.** | nom. | *ŠARRŪ* | *BĒLŪ* |
| | gen.-acc. | *ŠARRĪ* | *BĒLĪ* |

In the plural the acc. and gen. have merged. Originally, the singular ended in *-m* (*ŠARRUM*, *ŠARRIM*, *ŠARRAM*), but this *-m* was largely dropped. Nevertheless, it is often written in Hittite texts. Fully spelled out Akkadian nominal forms are relatively rare. The Akkadian case endings are mostly used as phonetic complements to Sumerograms: e.g., DINGIR-*LUM*, DINGIR-*LAM*, DINGIR-*LIM*. The gen. is used after the Akkadian prepositions *ANA*, *INA*, *IŠTU*, *PĀNI*, *QADU*, and *ŠA* (see Lesson 1.6.3): *ANA* DINGIR-*LIM* "to/for the deity." It is, however, apparent that in many cases the Hittites' knowledge of Akkadian grammar was only superficial and many forms are incorrect from an Akkadian point of view (e.g., *ANA* DINGIR-*LUM*).

## 2.7 Cuneiform Signs

| | | | |
|---|---|---|---|
| $ka_4$/qa  | pár/maš  | iz/GIŠ  | pa/ḫat  |
| ti  | en/EN 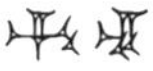 | na  | ARAD/ÌR  |
| ni  | DÙ  | ir  | |

Determinatives

| | | |
|---|---|---|
| ḪUR.SAG □ |  | for mountains |
| ÍD □ |  | for rivers |
| PÚ □ |  | for springs and wells |
| GIŠ □ |  | for wooden objects |
| NA4 □ |  | for stone objects |
| URUDU □ |  | for bronze objects |
| DUG □ |  | for containers |

## 2.8 Exercises; KBo 3.4 i 8–18

### 2.8.1 Translate:

1. *ma-aḫ-ḫa-an-ma* I-NA $^{\text{URU}}$*Tar-ku-ma a-ar-aḫ-ḫu-un* ("I arrived") *nu* $^{\text{URU}}$*Tar-ku-ma-an ar-ḫa wa-ar-nu-nu-un*
2. *nu-kán* LÚ.KÚR Ú-UL *pár-aš-ta*
3. *na-aš-mu-kán pé-ra-an ar-ḫa pár-aš-ta*
4. $^{\text{URU}}$*Ku-zu-ru-ú-i ka-ak-ka*$_4$*-pu-uš ma-ra-ak-ta*
5. *na-aš-kán* $^{\text{URU}}$*Ma-ra-aš-ša-an-ti-ia-za ar-ḫa pár-aš-ta*
6. (from a mythological text) ÍD*-pa mu-u-uḫ-ḫi lu-li-ia mu-uḫ-ḫi*
7. I-NA KUR $^{\text{URU}}$*Ḫa-at-ti-ya-aš-ma-aš* KASKAL*-an* Ú-UL *ma-ni-ya-aḫ-ti*
8. *nu-uš* $^{\text{m}}$*Te-li-pí-nu-uš ar-ḫa pár-aḫ-ta*
9. LUGAL*-uš-ša* GU$_4$.MAḪ *ši-pa-an-ti* $^{\text{LÚ}}$SANGA*-ša* GU$_4$.MAḪ *ši-pa-an-ti ta-an* AN.BAR*-aš* $^{\text{GIŠ}}$GIDRU*-it* GUL*-aḫ-zi*
10. *na-aš ka-a-ša pu-nu-uš-šu-un*
11. *na-aš-mu-kán na-aḫ-ta*
12. $^{\text{d}}$UTU*-*ŠI*-ma* $^{\text{m}}$*Kal-lu-un* $^{\text{LÚ}}$BE-EL ANŠE.KUR.RA ("chief charioteer") *wa-tar-na-aḫ-ta*
13. EGIR*-an-ma* LÚ.KÚR $^{\text{URU}}$*Zi-ik-kat-ta-an wa-al-aḫ-ta*
14. (from a parable with talking mountains and deer, in which a deer has just cursed a mountain) ḪUR.SAG*-aš-ša ma-aḫ-ḫa-an iš-ta-ma-aš-ta nu-uš-ši-kán* ŠÀ*-*ŠU ("his heart") *an-da iš-tar-ak-ki-at* (3. sing. pret. of *ištark-*) *nu* ḪUR.SAG*-aš a-li-ia-na-an a-ap-pa hu-wa-ar-za-aš-ta*
15. *še a-ker*
16. *te-eš-šu-mi-in* $^{\text{LÚ}}$SIMUG *wa-al-li-ia-an-ni* ("for fame") *la-a-ḫu-uš*

### 2.8.2

Write the sentences 1 through 6 in bound transcription (using the morpheme boundary marker =, marking plene written vowels with a macron, and maintaining double written consonants; see Introduction §7 and Lesson 1.5.2–4). Compare as an example sentence 10: *n(u)=aš kāša punuššun.*

## 2.8.3

Analyze the following forms as to either person, number, and tense, or case, number, and gender:

1. *ma-ni-ia-aḫ-ḫi-iš*
2. *ma-ni-ia-aḫ-ḫi*
3. *iš-pa-an-du-uz-zi*
4. *mar-ak-zi*
5. *da-šu-wa-aḫ-ḫu-u-en*
6. *ma-uš-ta*
7. *pár-ḫe-er*
8. *la-li-it*
9. *mar-ak-te-ni*
10. *ḫal-ki-it*

## 2.8.4

Read and transliterate the following sign combinations:

## Words for Lesson 2

| | | | |
|---|---|---|---|
| *aliyana-*, com. | deer | AN.BAR | iron |
| *anda* | in(to), inside | ANŠE.KUR.RA | horse, chariot |
| *appa* (EGIR-*pa*) | afterwards, back | EGIR-*an* (*appan*) | afterwards, behind, back, later |
| *arḫa* | away from; in compounds also reinforcing | $^{\text{GIŠ}}$GIDRU | staff, stick |
| | | GIM-*an* | = *maḫḫan* |
| *dašuwaḫḫ-* (IIa) | to (make) blind | | |
| *ḫalki-*, com. | grain | GU$_4$.MAḪ | bull |
| *ḫapa-* (ÍD), com. | river | ḪUR.SAG | mountain |
| *ḫuwart-* (IIa) | to curse | ÍD | = *ḫapa-* |
| *išpanduzzi-*, neut. | libation, offering | KASKAL | = *palša-* |
| *kakkapa-*, com. | (an animal) | LUGAL | king |
| *kāša* (adv.) | (just) now, behold | LÚ.KÚR (or $^{\text{LÚ}}$KÚR) | enemy |
| *laḫu-* (IIa) | to pour, cast | $^{\text{LÚ}}$SANGA | priest |
| *lala-*, com. | tongue | $^{\text{LÚ}}$SIMUG | smith |
| *luli-*, com. | pool, basin | ŠÀ | heart |
| *maḫḫan* | 1. just as, like | | |
| | 2. how | *BĒLU*(*M*) | lord, master, chief |
| | 3. when | | |
| *maniyaḫḫ-* (IIa) | to govern, assign, show | **GN** | |
| | | KUR $^{\text{URU}}$*Ḫatti* | Ḫatti-Land, Ḫattuša |

| | | | |
|---|---|---|---|
| *mark-* (Ia) | to cut (into pieces), appropriate | $^{URU}$*Kapapaḫšuwa* | |
| | | $^{URU}$*Kuzuruwa* | |
| *mauš-* (Ia) | to fall | $^{URU}$*Marašantiya* | |
| *mekki-* | many, numerous | $^{URU}$*Tarkuma* | |
| *namma* (adv.) | then, further, again | $^{URU}$*Zikkatta* | |
| *palša-*, com. | 1. road, trip<br>2. the…-th time | | |
| *parḫ-* (Ia) | to chase (away) | **PN** | |
| *parš-* (Ia) | to escape, flee | $^{d}$UTU-*ŠI* | His Majesty (title of the Hittite Great King, lit. "My Sun") |
| *peran* | before, in front of | | |
| *punuš-* (Ia) | to question | | |
| *šu* | (connective) | | |
| *teššummi-*, com. | cup | $^{m}$*Kallu* | |
| *warnu-* (Ia) | to set on fire, burn | $^{m}$*Telipinu* | |
| *watarnaḫḫ-* (IIa) | to order, send on a mission | | |

## 2.8.5 *The Ten-Year Annals* of the Hittite King Muršili II

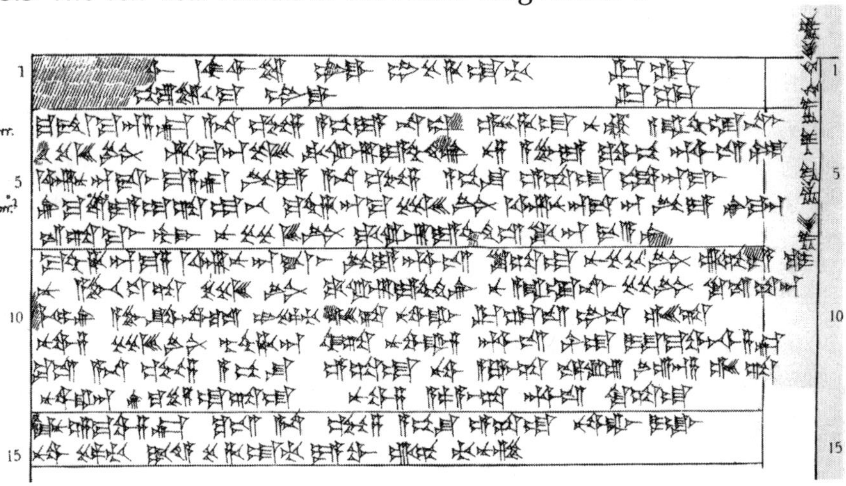

**Figure 3*b***

(Lines i 1–7 of the handcopy are repeated here because line 8 is written vertically in the intercolumnium.)

8. *ma-aḫ-ḫa-an-ma-za* $^{m}$*Ar-nu-an-da-aš* ŠEŠ-*IA* DINGIR-*LIM*-*iš* *ki-ša-at nu* KUR.KUR LÚ.KÚR *Ú-UL*-⌈*ia*⌉ *ku-i-e-eš ku-u-ri-ia-aḫ-ḫe-eš-ker*
9. *nu a-pu-u-uš-ša* KUR.KUR.MEŠ LÚ.KÚR *ku-u-ru-ri-ia-aḫ-ḫe-er nu a-ra‹-aḫ›-zé-na-aš* KUR.KUR LÚ.KÚR *ki-iš-ša-an*

10. *me-mi-er* A-*BU*-*ŠU*-*wa-aš-ši!*[1] *ku-iš* LUGAL KUR *Ḫat-ti* ⌈*e*⌉-*eš-ta nu-wa-ra-aš* UR.SAG-*iš* LUGAL-*uš e-eš-ta*
11. *nu-wa-za* KUR.KUR.MEŠ LÚ.KÚR *tar-uḫ-ḫa-an ḫar-ta nu-wa-ra-aš-za* DINGIR-*LIM*-*iš* DÙ-*at* DUMU-*ŠU*-*ma-wa-aš-ši-za-kán*
12. *ku-iš* A-*NA* [GIŠ]GU.ZA A-*BI*-*ŠU* *e-ša-at nu-wa a-pa-a-aš-ša ka-ru-ú* [LÚ]GURUŠ-*an-za e-eš-ta*
13. *nu-wa-ra-an ir-ma-li-at-ta-at nu-wa-za a-pa-a-aš-ša* DINGIR-*LIM*-*iš ki-ša-at*

---

14. *ki-nu-un-ma-wa-za-kán ku-iš* A-*NA* [GIŠ]GU.ZA A-*BI*-*ŠU* *e-ša-at nu-wa-ra-aš* DUMU-*la-aš*
15. *nu-wa* KUR *Ḫat-ti* ZAG.ḪI.A KUR *ḫa-at-ti-ia*‹‹-wa›› *Ú*-*UL* TI-*nu-zi*

---

i 8–13 When Arnuwanda, my brother, became a god, even the enemy countries who had not been hostile, those enemy countries, too, turned hostile and the neighboring enemy countries spoke as follows: "His father (lit. for him, his father), who was King of Ḫatti-Land, he was a heroic king. He held the enemy countries subdued but he became a god. His son (lit. for him, his son), who sat down on the throne of his father, he too was formerly a man in the prime of his life, but illness befell him and he, too, became a god.

14–15 But he who now has sat down on the throne of his father, he is a child, and he will not save Ḫatti-Land and the borders of Ḫatti-Land."

## Questions

1. Identify in the handcopy the cuneiform signs given in this and the previous Lesson.
2. Parse the underlined forms (with the help of the translation).
3. Identify as many sentence boundaries as possible by looking for connectives and clitics.

## Words

| | |
|---|---|
| 8. DINGIR-*LIM*-*i*- | god, deity |
| 10. UR.SAG-*i*- | hero |
| 14. DUMU-*la*- | child, son |
| 15. TI-*nu*- (Ia) | to cause to live, to save |

[1] Tablet has WA.

# Lesson 3

## 3.1 *u*-stem nouns and adjectives

### 3.1.1

The ***u*-stem nouns** [GrHL 4.42–52] contain words of both genders and behave similarly to the *i*-stems of the preceding lesson. Like most adjectival *i*-stems, the *u*-stem adjectives (3.1.2) inflect somewhat differently from the nouns.

Examples for *u*-stem nouns are: *wellu-* (Ú.SAL-*it*) "meadow, pasture," and the ubiquitous LUGAL "king," behind which **ḫaššu-* has to be read, both common gender; for the neuter are given here ^É^*ḫalentu-* (É.GAL/É.LUGAL) "palace (complex)," supplemented by *išḫaḫru-* "tear" and *genu-* "knee."

| | Common | (LUGAL) | Neuter |
|---|---|---|---|
| **Sing.** | | | |
| nom. com. | *welluš* | LUGAL-*uš* | |
| acc. | *wellun* | LUGAL-*un* | |
| nom.-acc. neut. | | | *ḫalentu* |
| gen. | *welluwaš* | LUGAL-*waš* | *ḫalentuwaš* |
| dat.-loc. | *wellui* | LUGAL-*i/e* | *ḫalentūi* |
| all. | *welluwa* | | *ḫalentuwa* |
| abl. | *welluwaz* | LUGAL-*waz* | *ḫalentuwaz* |
| instr. | Ú.SAL-*it* | | *išḫaḫruit* |
| **Plur.** | | | |
| nom. com. | | LUGAL-*ueš* | |
| acc. com. | | LUGAL.MEŠ-*uš* | |
| nom.-acc. neut. | | | *genuwa, išḫaḫruwa* |
| gen. | | LUGAL-(*w*)*an* (**ḫaššuwan*), LUGAL.MEŠ-*aš* | |
| dat.-loc. | *wellu*(*w*)*aš* | LUGAL.MEŠ-*aš* | *genuwaš* |

- For the glides in the paradigms (e.g., *ḫalentuaz* › *ḫalentuwaz*), see Lesson 2.1.1, 2.5. Besides *ḫalentu-* there are also forms of a stem *ḫalentiu-*.
- A separate vocative is well attested for the *u*-stems: LUGAL-*ui*/LUGAL-*ue* "O lord/king," ^d^UTU-*i*/^d^UTU-*e* (= *Ištanui/e*) "O Sun deity."
- In Old Hittite there may be evidence for a rare gen. sing. in *-š*: ^m^*Nunnuš* ^LÚ^*kainan ēpper* "they took/arrested (*ēpper*) Nunnu's relative (*kainan*)."

- The gen. plur. LUGAL-(*w*)*an* "of the kings" is one of the rare examples of the archaic gen. plur. ending in *-an* (see Lesson 1.1.1).
- Irregular is the Hittite word behind DINGIR "god, deity," *šiu-*. In the nom. and acc. sing. and plur. it is a *u*-stem (*šiu-*), but the oblique cases show an *n*-stem (*šiun-*). From this *n*-stem developed a mixed *a-/i-*stem (*šiuna/i-*):

| | Sing. | Plur. |
|---|---|---|
| nom. | *šiuš*, DINGIR-(*LIM*-)*uš/iš* | DINGIR.MEŠ-*eš* |
| acc. | *šiun*, *šiunan*, DINGIR-*LAM*-*an*/-*LIM*-*in* | *šimuš*, DINGIR.MEŠ-(*m*)*uš* |
| gen. | *šiunaš*, DINGIR-*LIM*-(*n*)*aš* | *šiunan*, DINGIR.MEŠ-(*n*)*aš* |
| dat.-loc. | *šiuni*, DINGIR-*LIM*-*ni* | *šiunaš*, DINGIR.MEŠ-(*n*)*aš* |
| abl. | *šiunaz*, DINGIR-*LIM*-*za* | |
| instr. | *šiunit*, DINGIR-*LIM*-*it* | |

- The acc. plur. *šimuš* comes from **šiwuš*, for which see Lesson 3.5. The gen. plur. *šiunan* "of the gods" contains again the archaic *-an* ending (compare above LUGAL-(*w*)*an*).

### 3.1.2

Comparable to what we saw for the *i*-stems, the ***u*-stem adjective**'s [GrHL 4.55–57] declension is characterized by the insertion of an *-a-* in the oblique cases and in the nom. and acc. plur., as opposed to the nom. and acc. sing. com.: *aššuš/aššun* vs. gen. *aššawaš* etc.

Examples are: *aššu-* "dear to, pleasant, good" and *idalu-* "bad, evil."

| | | |
|---|---|---|
| **Sing.** | | |
| nom. com. | *aššuš* | *idaluš* |
| acc. com. | *aššun* | *idalun* |
| nom.-acc. neut. | *aššu* | *idalu* |
| gen. | *aššawaš* | *idalawaš* |
| dat.-loc. | *aššawi* | *idalawi* |
| abl. | *aššawaz* | *idalawaz* |
| instr. | *aššawit* | *idalawit* |
| **Plur.** | | |
| nom. com. | *aššaweš* | *idalaweš* |
| acc. com. | *aššamuš*, *aššaweš* | *idalamuš* |
| nom.-acc. neut. | *aššawa*, *aššū* | *idalawa* |
| gen., dat.-loc. | *aššawaš* | *idalawaš* |

- The *w* can be spelled in different ways: for *idalawaš* we find *i-da-la-u-aš*, *i-da-la-wa-aš* and *i-da-la-u-wa-aš*.
- For the *m* in *aššamuš* and *idalamuš*, see Lesson 3.5 below.
- Note that the nom.-acc. plur. neut. of *aššu-* shows both *-aw-* (*aššawa*) and *-u* (*aššū*).

## 3.2 Second person personal pronoun

### 3.2.1

The **free-standing personal pronoun** of the second person [GrHL 5.7–10] is: *zik* "you" and *šumeš* "you (plur.)":

| | | |
|---|---|---|
| nom. | *zik, tuk* | *šumeš* |
| acc. | *tuk* | *šumaš, šumeš* |
| gen. | *tuel* | *šumel, šumenzan* |
| dat.-loc. | *tuk* | *šumaš* |
| abl. | *tuedaz* | *šumedaz* |

- For the pronominal characteristics *-el* and *-eda-*, see already Lesson 1.2.1.
- For the use of the acc. *tuk* in subject function, see already Lesson 1.2.2.
- Like *uk*, the nom. *zik* and the acc. *šumaš* can be extended to *zikila* and *šumašila* "you yourself" for reasons of emphasis.

### 3.2.2

Like for the first person pronoun (see Lesson 1.2.3), there also is an **enclitic pronoun** for the **second person** [GrHL 5.11–15, 18.1]. There is one single form for both the dat.-loc. and the acc.:

| | | |
|---|---|---|
| dat.-loc. | *-ta* | *-šmaš* |
| acc. | *-ta* | *-šmaš* |

- The clitic *-ta* "you" changes to *-du* before the particle *=za*, for which see Lesson 3.4.1 below: e.g., **nu=ta=za* › *nu=ddu=za* (usually written *nu-ud-du-za*).
- Note that *-šmaš* can also be the dat.-loc. of the third person enclitic pronoun "to/for them" (Lesson 2.2)!

## 3.3 Present and preterite indicative medio-passive

### 3.3.1

Previously, we saw the present and past tenses of the active of the Hittite verb. Besides these, there is also a **medio-passive** [GrHL 11.7].

In general the medio-passive indicates that the subject is performing an action on him- or herself (e.g., *weštari* "she dresses herself") or is subjected to an action by someone else (e.g., *walḫtari* "he is beaten").

However, there is not always a clear difference between the active and medio-passive forms of the same verb: e.g., 3. sing. pres. act. *paḫšzi* and 3. sing. pres. med.-pass. *paḫšari* can both be used for "he/she protects" with an expressed object, but *paḫšari* can also be a real passive, "he/she is protected." The interpretation of the medio-passive in such cases will depend upon the context.

Other verbs have only medio-passive forms, even though their meaning is not necessarily medio-passive, e.g., *ešari* "he/she sits down" or *kišat* "it happened." These verbs are called *deponent* verbs or deponents (abbreviated dep.).

In the medio-passive inflection there is also a distinction between the *mi*- and *ḫi*-conjugation, but it is restricted to the 3. sing. Here are the pres. and pret. paradigms:

| | | -mi (I) | | -ḫi (II) |
|---|---|---|---|---|
| **Sing.** ind. pres. | 1 | | *-ḫa, -ḫari, -ḫaḫari* | |
| | 2 | | *-ta, -tari (-tati)* | |
| | 3 | *-ta, -tari* | | *-a, -ari* |
| **Plur.** | 1 | | *-wašta, -waštari (-waštati)* | |
| | 2 | | *-duma, -dumari* | |
| | 3 | | *-anta, -antari* | |
| **Sing.** ind. pret. | 1 | | *-ḫati, -ḫaḫati, -ḫat, -ḫaḫat* | |
| | 2 | | *-tati, -tat* | |
| | 3 | *-tati, -tat* | | *-ati, -at* |
| **Plur.** | 1 | | *-waštati, -waštat* | |
| | 2 | | *-dumati, -dumat* | |
| | 3 | | *-antati, -antat* | |

Just like in the active paradigm (see Lesson 1.3.1), there are sometimes cross-overs from *-mi* to *-ḫi*-conjugation and vice versa: cf. *kišat* ("he/she/it became/happened," *-ḫi*) next to *kištat* (*-mi*).

In general it can be said that, in the present tense, forms without *-ri* are the original ones, and forms with *-ri* spread rapidly throughout the paradigm starting from certain 3. sing. med.-pass. forms of the *ḫi*-conjugation, which are practically the only *ri*-forms attested in Old Hittite (e.g., *kišari*). In the preterite the development of *-ti* forms, as opposed to forms without *-ti*, seems to be the other way around: Over time the final *-i* is dropped. Therefore, the most frequent set of endings is:

| | Present | Preterite |
|---|---|---|
| **Sing.** 1 | *-ḫari* | *-ḫat* |
| 2 | *-tari* | *-tat* |
| 3 | *-tari, -ari* | *-tat, -at* |
| **Plur.** 1 | *-waštari* | *-waštat* |
| 2 | *-dumari* | *-dumat* |
| 3 | *-antari* | *-antat* |

### 3.3.2

As examples of verbs of unchanging stem (like *walḫ-* and *šipand-* for the active verbs), the verbs *ar-* (Ia, dep.) "to stand" and *eš-* (IIa, dep.) "to sit down" are given here. Except for some mainly Old Hittite active forms, the latter verb can be considered a deponent.

| | Ia | IIa |
|---|---|---|
| **Pres.** | | |
| **Sing.** ind. 1 | *arḫa(ri)* | *ešḫa(ri)* |
| 2 | *arta(ri), (artati)* | *ešta(ri)* |
| 3 | *arta(ri)* | *eša(ri)* |
| **Plur.** ind. 1 | *arwašta(ri)* | *ešuwašta(ri)* |
| 2 | | *ešduma(ri)* |
| 3 | *aranta(ri)* | *ešanta(ri)* |
| **Pret.** | | |
| **Sing.** ind. 1 | *arḫat(i)* | *ešḫaḫat(i)* |
| 2 | *artat(i)* | *eštat(i)* |
| 3 | *artat(i)* | *ešat(i)* |
| **Plur.** ind. 1 | *arwaštat(i)* | *ešuwaštat(i)* |
| 2 | | *ešdumat(i)* |
| 3 | *arantat(i)* | *ešantat(i)* |

As usual, the cuneiform script has to find ways to write certain consonant clusters. For a verb like *paḫš-* "to protect" one usually finds the spelling *pa-aḫ-ḫa-aš*-CV-.

## 3.4 Syntax and semantics

### 3.4.1

In Lesson 1.4.4 the enclitic particles *-an*, *-apa*, *-ašta*, *-kan*, and *-šan* were introduced. Three more particles are the ones known as *-za*, *-wa*(*r-*) (Lesson 3.4.2) and *-pat* (Lesson 3.4.4).

The **particle *-za*** [GrHL 28.16–42] is also written *-az*, which means it was probably /-z/ (or /ts/, see Introduction §10). The overall function of *-za* is to indicate a close relation between the action described in the clause and its subject. The two clearest expressions of that relation are reflexivity and possession: e.g., *na=aš=za warpzi* "he washes himself" or *n=an=za* DUMU*-an iyami* "I will make him my son." Some verbs, like *taruḫ-* "to conquer, defeat," are almost always accompanied by *-za*, although it is difficult for us to appreciate its function there. Another important function of the particle *-za* will be discussed in Lesson 4.4.2. Note that reflexivity can also be expressed in the medio-passive voice (see Lesson 3.3.1).

As an enclitic particle, *-za* is attached to the first word of a sentence and always precedes any of the particles *-an*, *-apa*, *-ašta*, *-kan*, or *-šan* if they are present (e.g., *maḫḫan=ma=du=za=kan*); on this, see more at Lesson 3.4.3. As illustrated by the last example, the enclitic personal pronoun *-ta* "you" becomes *-du* if followed by *-za* (see Lesson 3.2.2 above).

### 3.4.2 *Direct speech* [GrHL 28.2–15]:

This can be recognized by the enclitic **particle *-wa(-)/-war-***, which is usually attached to the first word of each clause of the direct speech quotation. If this quotative particle *-wa*(-) is followed by other clitics starting with a vowel, the *-r-* emerges.

In the chain of enclitic elements *-wa*(-)/*-war-* comes in second place, in between the conjunctions *-a*/*-ya* and *-ma* and the personal pronoun *-a-*/*-naš*/*-šmaš*; if *-a*/*-ya* or *-ma* are not present, it is directly attached to *nu* or whatever is the first word of the sentence. Compare:

- *maḫḫan=ma=wa=du=za=kan* "when, however (*-ma*), (to) you"
- *nu=war=aš=mu=ššan* "and he/she (to) me."

In principle, every clause that is part of direct speech should have the particle at the beginning, but scribes were not always consistent in this; certainly in Old Hittite its use was not always mandatory.

Direct speech is often introduced by verbs of speaking or asking (e.g., *mema-*, *te-*/*tar-* "speak, say" [see Lesson 9.3.2–3], *punušš-* "to ask, question" or forms of the Akkadian verb QABÛ "to speak," see, for instance, AQBI Lesson 3.8.5 line 23 below, and Lesson 6.6 for some examples); it can also follow a clause implying the use of speech (e.g., *link-/lik-* "to swear an oath"):

- *nu=šši kiššan memaḫḫun mān=wa=mu* DINGIR.MEŠ *kaniššanzi* LUGAL-*izziaḫḫari=wa tuk=ma=wa ammedaz* $\text{SIG}_5$-*ešzi* "and I said to him as follows: 'If the gods choose me and I become king, then you will profit by me'"
- *nu=nnaš lenkiyaš ešūen* 1-*aš=wa* 1-*an paḫšaru* "and we were (men) of the oath (i.e., sworn comrades) (saying): 'One shall protect the other!'"

### 3.4.3

Most of the **clitics** discussed so far (Lesson 1.4.3 *-a/-ya*, Lesson 2.4.2 *-ma* and non-geminating *-a*, Lesson 1.2.3 *-mu*, *-naš*, Lesson 3.2.2 *-ta*, *-šmaš*, Lesson 2.2 *-aš/-an/-ši* etc., Lesson 2.4.3 *-an*, *-apa*, *-ašta*, *-kan*, or *-šan*, Lesson 3.4.1 *-za*, and 3.4.2 *-wa(r-)*) can and often will appear next to each other in a series or **chain** [GrHL 30.15–21]. While *-a/-ya* and *-ma* exclude each other, as do the members of the series *-an*, *-apa*, *-ašta*, *-kan*, and *-šan*, all other combinations are possible. There is, however, a strict rule for the positions in which they can occur. Six slots can be distinguished, as given in the following table (*-a-* stands for the 3. sing. and plur. personal pronoun (see Lesson 2.2) without the forms *-ši* and *-šmaš*):

| 1 | 2 | 3 | 4 | 5 | 6 |
|---|---|---|---|---|---|
| | | | | | *-an* |
| *-a/-ya* | *-wa(r-)* | *-naš/-šmaš* | *-a-* | *-za* | *-apa* |
| *-ma* | | *-a-* | *-mu/-ta/-ši* | | *-ašta* |
| | | | | | *-kan* |
| | | | | | *-šan* |

- Note how the position of *-a-* "he, she, it, they" changes if it is combined with other personal pronouns (including the dat.-loc. *-ši* and *-šmaš*): if it is combined with a singular pronoun (*-mu*, *-ta*, *-ši*) it precedes; if it is combined with a plural pronoun (*-naš*, *-šmaš*) it follows. E.g., *nu=naš=at pāi* "she gives it (*-at*) to us (*-naš*), but *n=at=ši pāi* "he gives it (*-at*) to her (*-ši*)."
- With *-ši* "to/for him/her" *-a-* can be doubled, i.e., appear both before and after *-ši*: *n=at=ši=at.*
- The same is true for the combination with the particle *-za* (Lesson 3.4.1): *n=an=za=an.*

### 3.4.4

The **particle** ***-pat*** (always written with the PÁT sign) [GrHL 28.115–140] can be attached to any word in the sentence, as opposed to *-za* and the group of *-an*, *-apa*, *-ašta*, *-kan*, and *-šan*. Its function is to stress or emphasize the word to which it is attached: e.g., *nu išḫaš* ÌR=*pat punušzi* "The master asks th servant=*pat.*" Such stress can be brought out in the translation in various ways and should always be judged by the context: "The master asks even/only the servant/It is the servant whom the master asks."

The cuneiform sign PÁT with which this particle is written can also be read as *pìt* or *pè*. Nowadays *pát* is the accepted reading, but in older Hittitological literature one may encounter *pìt*.

3.4.5
If the subject of a clause is a **neuter plural**, the verb always appears in the **singular** [GrHL 15.15–16]: e.g., *nu=šmaš=kan išḫaḫruwa ... āršta* "their (-*šmaš*, lit. for/to them) tears flowed." Here we have the 3. sing. pret. *āršta* instead of a 3. plur. *aršer*. This phenomenon is due to the original – and still very present – function of the neuter plural as indicating a collective: The example just given is not about individual tears but about a steady *stream* of them.

Starting already in Old Hittite, even a nominal predicate agreeing with the neuter plural subject could be singular: e.g., *n=e=ššan* NA4*pēruni wetan* "it (was) built on rock" (*wetan* is the nom.-acc. sing. neut. of the participle of *wete-* "to build"; for the ending, see Lesson 5.1.1). The enclitic nom. plur. neut. -*e* (see Lesson 2.2) refers to a palace *complex*, and the nominal predicate (*wetan*) stands in the singular. Although several examples still attest to the original situation, where the nominal predicate agrees with the neuter plural subject (*šakuwa=šmet išḫaškanta* "their eyes (are) blood-shot" (plur. neut. *išḫaškanta*), the singular became the rule.

This same collective value of the neuter plural in -*a* is also responsible for what often have been taken as mistakes in gender. Regularly, otherwise common gender nouns like *alpa-* "cloud," plur. *alpeš* "clouds" will also have a collective ("neuter") plural *alpa* "cloud mass," cf. *mena-* "cheek," plur. *meneš* "cheeks" and *mena* "face." These are not mistakes but a special case of the category number in Hittite.

## 3.5 Phonology

3.5.1
In the combinations -***uw***- and -***wu***- the *w* dissimilates to *m* so that -***um***- and -***mu***- emerge [GrHL 1.126–127]; compare the acc. plur. com. of the *u*-stem *idalu-*: **idalawuš* › *idalamuš*, or the 1. plur. pres. and pret. of causative verbs in -*nu*-: *-*nuweni*/-*nuwen* › -*numeni*/-*numen*.

## 3.6 Akkadian

### 3.6.1

The declension of **feminine nouns** in Akkadian shows the same endings as the masculine, except that it is mostly characterized by a *-t-*. Examples: *ŠARRATU* "queen" and *BĒLTU* "lady" (cf. *ŠARRU* "king" and *BĒLU* "lord," Lesson 2.6):

| | | | |
|---|---|---|---|
| **Sing.** | nom. | *ŠARRATU* | *BĒLTU* |
| | gen. | *ŠARRATI* | *BĒLTI* |
| | acc. | *ŠARRATA* | *BĒLTA* |
| **Plur.** | nom. | *ŠARRĀTU* | *BĒLĒTU* |
| | gen.-acc. | *ŠARRĀTI* | *BĒLĒTI* |

Here too the final *-m* may appear in writing (see Lesson 2.6).

## 3.7 Cuneiform signs

| | | | |
|---|---|---|---|
| LÚ  | ŠEŠ  | LUGAL  | |
| up  | pí/KAŠ  | $GU_4$  | ga  |
| DUG  | ša  | ta  | |
| ap 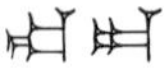 | at  | la  | |

### Determinatives

| | | |
|---|---|---|
| TÚG □ |  | for pieces of clothing and textiles |
| SÍG □ |  | for things of wool |
| GADA □ |  | for things of linen |
| KUŠ □ |  | for things of leather |
| IM □ |  | for things of clay |

## 3.8 Exercises; KBo 3.4 i 16–35

### 3.8.1 Translate:

1. (from a ritual for the renewal of kingship) LUGAL-*e-mu* DINGIR.MEŠ *me-ek-ku-uš* MU.KAM.ḪI.A-*uš ma-ni-ia-aḫ-ḫe-er*
2. (from a condolence letter) *nu-ut-ta* d*Gul-ša-aš* ḪUL-*aḫ-da*
3. LUGAL-*uš-ša-an* GIŠ*ḫu-lu-ga-an-ni e-ša*
4. *na-aš-kán* TA dU *za-aḫ-ta-ri*

5. LUGAL-*uš-za šu-up-pí-a-aḫ-ḫa-ti*
6. *kat-ta-ma tu-el* DUMU.MEŠ-*KA* (-*KA* = "your") *am-me-el* DUMU-*IA* (-*IA* = "my") *pa-aḫ-ša-ri*
7. *nu-kán da-aš-šu-uš* $^{\text{NA4}}$*ku-un-ku-nu-uz-zi-iš ne-pí-ša-az* ("from heaven") *kat-ta ma-uš-ta-at*
8. (omen, protasis:) *ma-a-an-kán an-tu-uḫ-ša-aš la-ga-a-ri na-aš-ma-aš-kán* $^{\text{GIŠ}}$GIGIR-*az kat-ta ma-a-uš-zi* (followed by an apodosis: "then ...")
9. *zi-ik* UR.BAR.RA-*aš ki-iš-ta-at*
10. *ma-aḫ-ḫa-an-ma-za A-BU-IA* (-*IA* = "my") $^{\text{m}}$*Mur-ši-li-iš* DINGIR-*LIM*-*iš ki-ša-at* ŠEŠ-*IA*(-*IA* = "my")-*ma-za-kán* $^{\text{m}}$NIR.GÁL *A-NA* $^{\text{GIŠ}}$GU.ZA *A-BI-ŠU* (-*ŠU* = "his") *e-ša-at am-mu-uk-ma-za A-NA PA-NI* ŠEŠ-*IA* EN.KARAŠ *ki-iš-ḫa-ḫa-at*
11. *nu-wa-ra-at-kán* GÌR.MEŠ *ar-ḫa kar-ša-an-ta-at*
12. *na-aš iš-dam-ma-aš-ta-ri*
13. *nu-za* NIN.DINGIR-*aš* $^{\text{É}}$*ḫi-i-li* $^{\text{DUG}}$*iš-nu-ra-aš kat-ta-an e-ša-ri*
14. *nu* DINGIR.MEŠ-*aš A-NA* EZEN$_4$.ḪI.A EGIR-*an-pát ar-wa-aš-ta*
15. *nu* $^{\text{d}}$U EN-*IA* ("my") *a-aš-ša-u-e-eš* UN.MEŠ-*uš ka-ne-eš-zi*
16. *nu-za* $^{\text{URU}}$*Pal-ḫu-iš-ša-an-na tar-uḫ-ḫu-un nu* URU-*an ar-ḫa wa-ar-nu-nu-un*
17. *ma-a-an-mu* DINGIR.MEŠ *ka-ni-iš-ša-an-zi* LUGAL-*iz-zi-aḫ-ḫa-ri* ("I will be king") *tu-uk-ma am-me-ta-az* SIG$_5$-*iš-zi*
18. *nu-uš-ma-aš-kán* ḪUR.SAG-*an pár-ḫa-an-zi*
19. *nu-za* $^{\text{MUŠ}}$*Il-lu-ia-an-ka-aš* $^{\text{d}}$IM-*an tar-uḫ-ta*
20. *am-mu-uk-ma-az* ŠÀ-*az la-aḫ-la-aḫ-ḫi-ma-an Ú-UL tar-uḫ-mi* NÍ.TE-*az-ma-za pít-tu-li-ia-an nam-ma Ú-UL tar-uḫ-mi*

### 3.8.2

Rewrite sentences 1–6 in bound transcription.

### 3.8.3

Analyze the following verb forms according to person, number, and tense, and nominal forms according to case and number, and translate:

1. *ki-iš-du-um-ma-at*
2. *pa-aḫ-šu-wa-aš-ta*
3. *iš-ḫa-aḫ-ru-it*
4. *tar-uḫ-ta*
5. *ti-it-ta-nu-um-me-en*
6. *la-a-ki*
7. *da-aš-ša-u-i*
8. *e-šu-aš-ta*

3.8.4

Read and transliterate the following sign combinations:

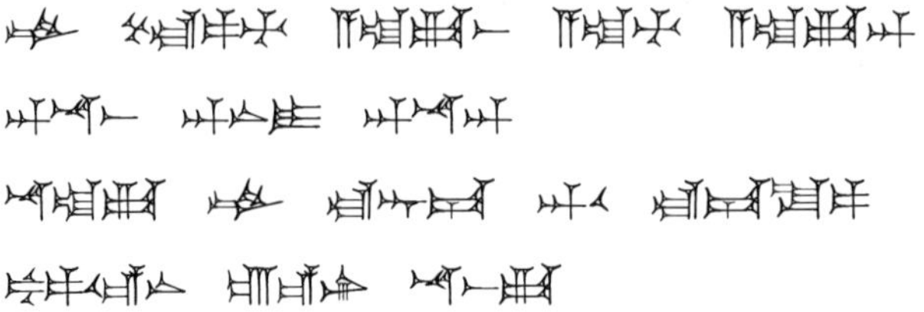

## Words for Lesson 3

| | | | |
|---|---|---|---|
| *ar-* (Ia, dep.) | to stand | DUMU | child, son |
| EGIR-*an ar-* + dat.-loc. | to stand behind, take care of | EN | lord, master |
| | | $EZEN_4$ | festival |
| *aššu-* | beloved, good | $^{\text{GIŠ}}$GIGIR | wagon, cart |
| *daššu-* | mighty, powerful | | |
| *eš-* (IIa, dep.) | to sit down | GÌR | foot |
| $^{\text{É}}$*ḫila-*, com. | court | $^{\text{GIŠ}}$GU.ZA | throne, chair |
| $^{\text{GIŠ}}$*ḫuluganni-*, com. | wagon, cart | ḪUL-*aḫḫ-* | = *idalawaḫḫ-* |
| *idalawaḫḫ-* (IIa) | bowl | KARAŠ | army, troops |
| *idalu-* | to treat badly | MU(.KAM) | year |
| $^{\text{DUG}}$*išnura-*, com. | evil, bad | NÍ.TE | body |
| *kanešš-* (Ia) | to recognize, choose | NIN.DINGIR | (a priestess) |
| | | $SIG_5$-*eš-* | to get better |
| *karš-* (Ia) | to cut | ŠÀ | heart |
| *katta* (sometimes postpos. + gen. or dat.-loc.) | 1. down (to) 2. next to 3. later | ŠEŠ | brother |
| | | TA | by, through |
| | | UN | = *antuḫša-* |
| *kattan* (ditto) | down, below, next to | UR.BAR.RA | wolf |
| *kiš-* (IIa, dep.) | to become, happen | *ABU(M)*, *ABI* | father |
| DINGIR-*LIM*-*iš kiš-* | to become a god = to die (said of kings and queens) | *ANA PANI* | for, in front of |
| | | **DN** | |
| $^{\text{NA4}}$*kunkunuzzi-*, com. | (a stone) | $^{\text{d}}$*Gulša-* | goddess of Fate |
| | | $^{\text{d}}$U/IM | Storm God |
| | anguish | | |
| *lag-* (IIa) | to lean, fall (also med.-pass.) | **PN** | |
| *laḫlaḫḫima-*, com. | | $^{\text{m}}$*Muršili-* | Hittite Great King (*c.* 1318–1295 BC) |
| *mekki-* | many, numerous | | |
| *namma* UL/UL *namma* | no longer | $^{\text{m}}$NIR.GÁL = $^{\text{m}}$*Muwatalli-* | Hittite Great King (*c.* 1295–1274 BC) |

| | | | |
|---|---|---|---|
| *našma* | or | | |
| *pittuliya-*, com. | worry, fear | **GN** | |
| *šuppiyaḫḫ-* (IIa) | to cleanse, purify | $^{\text{URU}}$*Palḫuišša-* | |
| *taruḫ-* (Ia) | to conquer | | |
| *tittanu-* (Ia) | to place, install | $^{\text{MUŠ}}$*Illuyanka* | (a dragon or snake-like monster) |
| *zaḫḫ-* (Ia) | to hit | | |

## 3.8.5 *The Ten-Year Annals* of the Hittite King Muršili II

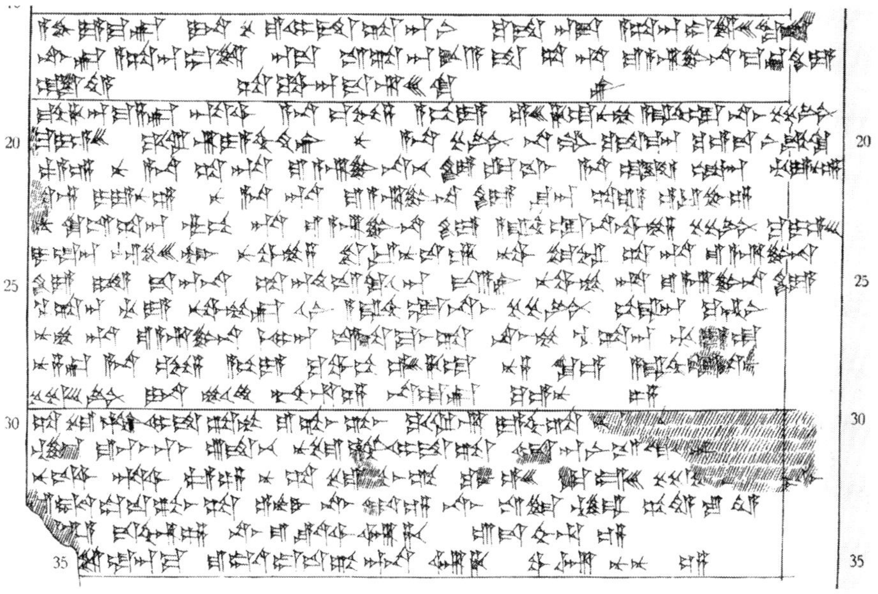

Figure 4

i 16. A-BU-IA-*ma-kán* I-NA KUR $^{\text{URU}}$*Mi-it-ta-an-ni ku-it an-da a-ša-an-du-le-eš-ke-*⌈*et*⌉

17. *na-aš-kán a-ša-an-du-li an-da iš-ta-an-da-a-it* ŠA $^{\text{d}}$UTU $^{\text{URU}}$*A-ri-in-na-ma-kán* $^{\text{d}}$GAŠAN-IA

18. EZEN$_4$.ḪI.A *ša-ku-wa-an-da-re-eš-ke-er*

---

19. *ma-aḫ-ḫa-an-ma-za-kán* $^{\text{d}}$UTU-ŠI A-NA $^{\text{GIŠ}}$GU.ZA A-BI-IA *e-eš-ḫa-at nu-mu a-ra-aḫ-zé-na-aš* KUR.KUR LÚ.KÚR

20. *ku-i-e-eš ku-u-ru-ri-ia-aḫ-ḫe-er nu* A-NA KUR LÚ.KÚR *na-wi*$_5$ *ku-it-ma-an ku-e-da-ni-ik-ki*

21. *pa-a-un nu* «a-na» ŠA $^{\text{d}}$UTU $^{\text{URU}}$*A-ri-in-na-pát* GAŠAN-IA SAG.UŠ-*aš* A-NA EZEN$_4$.ḪI.A EGIR-*an ti-ia-nu-un*

22. [*n*]*a-aš-za i-ia-nu-un nu* A-NA $^{d}$UTU $^{URU}$*A-ri-in-na* GAŠAN-IA ŠU-*an ša-ra-a e-ep-pu-un*
23. [*n*]*u ki-iš-ša-an* AQ-BI $^{d}$UTU $^{URU}$*A-ri-in-na* GAŠAN-IA *a-ra-aḫ-zé-na-aš-wa-mu-za* KUR.KUR LÚ.KÚR *ku-i-e-eš*
24. DUMU-*la-an ḫal!*[1]*-zi-eš-šer nu-wa-mu-za te-ep-nu-uš-ker nu-wa tu-el* ŠA $^{d}$UTU $^{URU}$*A-ri-in-na*
25. GAŠAN-IA ZAG.ḪI.A *da-an-na ša-an-ḫi-iš-ke-u-an da-a-er nu-wa-mu* $^{d}$UTU $^{URU}$*A-ri-in-na* GAŠAN-IA
26. *kat-ta-an ti-ia nu-wa-mu-kán u-ni a-ra-aḫ-zé-na-aš* KUR.KUR LÚ.KÚR *pé-ra-an ku-en-ni*
27. *nu-mu* $^{d}$UTU $^{URU}$*A-ri-in-na me-mi-an iš-ta-ma-aš-ta na-aš-mu kat-ta-an ti-*⸢*ia*⸣*-at*
28. *nu-za-kán* A-NA $^{GIŠ}$GU.ZA A-BI-IA *ku-wa-pí e-eš-ḫa-at nu-za ke-e a-ra-aḫ-*⸢*zé-na-aš*⸣
29. KUR.KUR.MEŠ LÚ.KÚR I-NA MU.10.KAM *tar-uḫ-ḫu-un na-at-kán ku-e-nu-un*

---

30. ŠA KUR $^{URU}$*Dur-mi-it-ta-mu* $^{URU}$*Ga-aš-ga-aš ku-u-ru-ri-ia-aḫ-ta nu*[*-mu za-*] *a*[*ḫ-ḫi-ia*]
31. *nam-*⸢*ma*⸣ $^{URU}$*Qa-aš-qa-aš ú-it-pát nu* KUR $^{URU}$⸢*Dur*⸣*-mi-it-ta* ⸢GUL⸣*-an-ni-iš-*⸢*ke-u-an*⸣ [*da-a-iš*]
32. *nu-uš-ši* $^{d}$UTU-ŠI *pa-a-un nu* ŠA KUR $^{URU}$[*G*]*a-aš-ga ku-*⸢*i*⸣*-e-eš* ⸢SAG⸣.DU.MEŠ KUR.KUR.ME[Š $^{UR}$]$^{U}$[*Ḫa-li-l*]*a-aš*
33. [$^{U}$]$^{RU}$*Du-ud-du-uš-ga-aš-ša e-šer na-aš* ⸢GUL⸣*-un na-aš* IŠ-TU NAM.RA GU$_{4}$.ḪI.A UDU.ḪI.A
34. [*š*]*a-*⸢*ra*⸣*-a da-aḫ-ḫu-un na-aš* $^{URU}$KÙ.BABBAR-*ši ar-ḫa ú-da-aḫ-ḫu-un*
35. [$^{URU}$*Ḫa-*]*li-la-an-ma* $^{URU}$*Du-ud-du-uš-ga-an-na ar-ḫa wa-ar-nu-nu-un*

---

i 16–18. Since my father had been garrisoning in Mittani-Land and had been held up in the garrison, the cultic celebrations of the Sun goddess of Arinna, My Lady, had been left uncelebrated.

19–29. … (19: *maḫḫanmazakan … ēšḫat*), before I went against any of the enemy countries who had turned hostile towards me, I took care of the regular cultic celebrations only for the Sun goddess of Arinna, My Lady. I performed them and held up (my) hand to the Sun goddess of Arinna, My Lady, [a]nd spoke as follows: "O Sun goddess of Arinna, My Lady, the neighboring enemy countries that called me a child and

---

[1] Tablet has AŠ.

humiliated me have begun to try to take the territories of you, O Sun goddess of Arinna, My Lady. Sun goddess of Arinna, My Lady, stand by me and destroy for me those neighboring enemy countries!" … (27: *numu … ištamašta*) and stood by me: … (28–29: *nuzakan … kuenun*).

30–35. … (30: ŠA … *kūruriyaḫta*) and then the Gašgaean indeed came [to me for b]a[ttle] and [began] to attack Durmitta. I, My Majesty, went to it/him, and [Ḫalil]a and Duddušga, which were the main regions of [G]ašga-Land, … (33: *naš* GUL-*un*). I captured them with (their) inhabitants, cattle, (and) sheep and carried them off to Ḫattuša … (35: $^{\mathrm{URU}}$*Ḫalilanma … warnunun*).

## Questions

1. Identify in the handcopy the cuneiform signs given in this and the previous Lessons.
2. Parse the underlined forms.
3. Identify as many sentence boundaries as possible by looking for clitics and connectives.
4. Translate the sentences that are left untranslated (marked by …, the first and last word and/or line number(s)).

## Words

| | | |
|---|---|---|
| 19. | $^{\mathrm{GIŠ}}$GU.ZA | throne |
| 21. | $^{\mathrm{d}}$UTU | Sun deity |
| | $^{\mathrm{URU}}$*Arinna* | one of the most important cult places in Hittite religion, of uncertain location, home of the Sun goddess of Arinna |
| 27. | *memian* | "prayer" (lit. word) |
| 28. | *kē* | "these" |
| 29. | *taruḫ-* (Ia) | to defeat, conquer, subject |
| | *kuenun* | "I destroyed" |
| 30. | $^{\mathrm{URU}}$*Gašga-*, com. | Gašgaean (adj.), the Gašgaean (noun) |
| | *kururiyaḫḫ-* (Ia) | to be/turn hostile, wage war |

# Lesson 4

## 4.1 *ai*- and *au*-noun diphthong stems

### 4.1.1

Besides the *i*- and *u*-stems there are so-called **diphthong stems** in ***ai***- [GrHL 4.32–35] and ***au***- [GrHL 4.53–54]. They contain nouns only; nouns can be either common or neuter gender.

Originally the *ai*- and *au*-stems showed an Ablaut -*ai*-/-*i*- and -*au*-/-*u*- respectively (e.g., nom. sing. *lingaiš* ~ gen. *linkiyaš*, nom. sing. *ḫarnauš* ~ gen. *ḫarnuwaš*), but over time the system was obscured by the spreading of -*ai*- and -*au*- from the nom. and acc. into the oblique cases (e.g., gen. *lingayaš* = *lingai-aš* instead of the original *linkiyaš* = *linki-aš*).

Examples here are: *lingai*- com. "oath," *ḫaštai*- neut. "bone" (supplemented by ᴳᴵŠ*luttai*- neut. "window") for the *ai*-stems, and *ḫarnau*- com. "birth stool," *išḫunau*- neut. "upper arm, strength" for the *au*-stems.

| | -ai- | -ai- | -au- | -au- |
|---|---|---|---|---|
| **Sing.** | com. | neut. | com. | neut. |
| nom. com. | *lingaiš* | | *ḫarnāuš* | |
| acc. com. | *lingain* | | *ḫarnaun* | |
| nom.-acc. neut. | | *ḫaštai* | | *išḫunāu* |
| gen. | *linkiyaš*, *lingayaš* | *ḫaštiyaš* | *ḫarnuwaš*, *ḫarnauwaš* | *išḫunauwaš* |
| dat.-loc. | *linkiya* (= all.), *linkai* | *ḫaštai* | *ḫarnui* *ḫarnāuwi* | *išḫunaui* |
| abl. | *linkiyaz* | (ᴳᴵŠ*luttiyaz*) | | |
| instr. | | *ḫaštit* | | |
| **Plur.** | | | | |
| nom. com. | | | *ḫarnaueš* | |
| acc. com. | *lingauš* | | | |
| nom.-acc. neut. | | | | |
| gen., dat.-loc. | | (ᴳᴵŠ*luttiyaš*) | | |

This concludes the nominal vowel stems.

## 4.2 Demonstrative pronoun *kā*-; *tamai*-

### 4.2.1

Hittite had a three-tiered deictic system, that is, one **demonstrative pronoun** referring to things in the speaker's immediate surroundings ("*this* here with me"), another one for anything referring to things near the addressee ("*that* there with you"), and a third one for anything elsewhere ("*that* over there").

This lesson presents the demonstrative pronoun referring to someone or something in the speaker's immediate surroundings, which is ***kā***- "this (here)" [GrHL 7.3–9 (forms), 18.20–32 (use)].

| | **Sing.** | **Plur.** |
|---|---|---|
| nom. com. | *kāš* | *kē, kūš* |
| acc. com. | *kūn* | *kūš, kē* |
| nom.-acc. neut. | *kī* | *kē* |
| gen. | *kēl* | *kenzan, kēl, kedaš* |
| dat.-loc. | *kēdani* | *kedaš* |
| abl. | *kēz, kezza* | |
| instr. | *kēdanda* | |

- Besides the familiar pronominal characteristics (gen. in *-el* and the element *-eda-*), we see again the tendency in the nom. and acc. plur. com. to interchange.
- Note also how, alongside the original plur. gen. *kenzan*, both the sing. *kēl* and the oblique plur. *kedaš* are also sometimes used as a plur. gen.
- An old form *ket/kit* survives in the frozen expression *kit(-)pantalaz* "as of this moment, from now on." *ket/kit* is also found adverbially used in the sense of "hither, on this side."
- The abl. *kēz* is often found used in a pair: *kēz* … *kēz* … "on this side … on the other …"
- From the same demonstrative stem *kā*- are also derived the adverbs:
  - *kā* "here"
  - *kāša* and *kāšma* "(just) now" or "behold"
  - *kiššan* "thus, in this/the following way."

### 4.2.2

The word ***tamai***- "other" can be considered "semi-pronominal" [GrHL 8.10 (forms), 18.37–38 (use)]: Although the meaning is not that normally associated with a pronoun, it does show several of the pronominal characteristics in its inflection. It is spelled with both TA and DA at the beginning. Surprising forms are the (isolated) dat.-loc. *damēte* next to a more familiar *tamēdani* and an old all. *dameda* "to another place, elsewhere," which is used only adverbially.

| | **Sing.** | **Plur.** |
|---|---|---|
| nom. com. | *tamaiš* | *tamaēš* |
| acc. com. | *tamain* | *tamāuš* |
| nom.-acc. neut. | *tamai* | *tamāe* |
| gen. | *damēl* | *damedaš* |
| dat.-loc. | *tamēdani* (*damēte*) | *damedaš* |
| all. | *tameda* | |
| abl. | *tamēdaz* | |

## 4.3 Ablauting verbs Ib (type *epp-/app-*)

### 4.3.1

Now that all the verbal endings have been illustrated by verbs of unchanging stem (Ia and IIa), we can proceed with verbs that do change within a paradigm. A small but important class of such verbs is the *mi*-conjugation class showing an ***e/a*-Ablaut** (Ib) [GrHL 12.2–4]. The *e*-grade was originally restricted to the singular, changing to *-a-* in the present plural. However, over time the *-e-* can be seen invading there as well.

Examples are: *epp-/app-* "to take, seize," *eš-/aš-* "to be," and *ed-/ad-* "to eat" for the active, and *epp-/app-* and *weḫ-/waḫ-* "to turn" for the medio-passive.

**Active**

| | | | |
|---|---|---|---|
| **Pres. sing.** 1 | *ēpmi* | *ēšmi* | *ēdmi* |
| 2 | *ēpši* | *ēšši* | *ēzši, ezzatti* |
| 3 | *ēpzi* | *ēšzi* | *ezzazzi* |
| **plur.** 1 | *appuweni, eppuweni* | *ešuwani* | *aduweni, eduweni* |
| 2 | *apteni, epteni* | | *azzašteni, ezzatteni* |
| 3 | *appanzi* | *ašanzi* | *adanzi* |
| **Pret. sing.** 1 | *ēppun* | *ešun* | *edun* |
| 2 | *ēpta* | *ēšta* | *ezatta* |
| 3 | *ēpta* | *ēšta* | *ēzta, ezzatta, ezzaš, ezzašta* |
| **plur.** 1 | *ēppuen, appuen* | *ešuwen* | *eduwen* |
| 2 | *ēpten* | *ēšten* | |
| 3 | *ēpper* | *ešer* | *eter* |

The medio-passive is only poorly attested:

| Medio-passive | | |
|---|---|---|
| **Pres. sing.** 1 | | *weḫaḫḫa* |
| 3 | | *weḫari,* *weḫatta(ri)* |
| **plur.** 3 | | *weḫanta(ri)* |
| **Pret. sing.** 1 | | *weḫḫaḫat* |
| 3 | *appattat* | *weḫtat,* *weḫattat* |
| **plur.** 3 | *appandat* | *weḫandat* |

For the forms of *ed-/ad-* spelled with *ezz*° (e.g., *ezzatti* with *-ti* of the *ḫi*-conjugation!; see also *ezzaš*) and *azz*°, see Lesson 1.5.1 (-TT- › -T*s*T-).

## 4.4 Syntax

### 4.4.1

The verb ***eš-/aš-*** **"to be"** as a **copula** is usually not expressed in the present tense, but only in the preterite or imperative (for the imperative, see Lesson 8.3.3) [GrHL 22.3]: e.g., *nu tān pēdaš* DUMU-*RU* "he (is) a son of second (*tān*) rank (lit. place)," but $^{m}$*Pappaš* $^{LÚ}$*uriyanniš ēšta* "Mr. Pappa was an *uriyanni*-man." Present tense forms usually mean "to exist, to be in a certain place, sit": *nu=ššan nepiši ešši* "You (O god) are (residing)/sit in heaven."

### 4.4.2

If the subject of a **nominal sentence** [GrHL 28.32–42], i.e., a sentence with the verb *eš-/aš-* "to be" whether expressed or not (see Lesson 4.4.1), is a first or second person sing. or plur., then Hittite uses:

1 the particle *-za* (see Lesson 3.4.1)
2 or a form of the encl. personal pronoun (see Lesson 1.2.3, 3.2.2) corresponding to the subject.

- For *-za* compare: *nu=mu=za zik* EN-*aš ammuk=ma=ddu=za* ARAD-*iš* "You (will be) master to me (*=mu*) while I (will be) servant to you (*=ddu*)" —› "You will be my master while I will be your servant." Here the pronouns *zik* and *ammuk* make clear who the subject is in both sentences, but often no subject is expressed and only the context can help determine this.
- For the corresponding personal pronoun instead of *-za* compare: *šummeš=<u>šmaš</u>* … $^{LÚ.MEŠ}$SAG "you … (are) SAG-men."
- Almost all exceptions to this rule stem from the Old Hittite period.

4.4.3

The verb *eš-/aš-* is also frequently used in the so-called **possessive dative construction** [GrHL 16.67]: "to me is a house" —› "I have a house." E.g., *mān=ši* DUMU *UL ēšzi* lit. "If to him there is not a son" —› "If he has no son."

A possessive dat. can also be expressed by the Akkadian preposition *ANA*: *ANA* ŠEŠ=*IA* DUMU.MEŠ *mekkaeš* "to my brother (there are) many sons" —› "my brother has many sons." As is clear from the last example, in this construction, too, *eš-/aš-* can be left out.

4.4.4

Sometimes possession can also be expressed by using the **genitive** [GrHL 16.35–40]: e.g., *nu=za* ŠA [d]UTU-*ŠI Ù* ŠA KUR [URU]*Ḫatti ešši* "you will be (a subject) of His Majesty and of Ḫatti-land." For the particle *-za* in this example, see Lesson 4.4.2. For the particle *-za* as sometimes indicating a possessive relation, see Lesson 3.4.1.

## 4.5 Phonology

4.5.1

Comparing the paradigms of the verbs *epp-/app-* and *ed-/ad-*, one notices the systematic **doubling** of the labial in *epp-/app-* as opposed to the consistently **single** dental in *ed-/ad-* in intervocalic position: e.g., *appanzi* "they take" vs. *adanzi* "they eat." This is an attempt by the Hittite scribes to indicate a phonological opposition which is often described as one between *voiced* vs. *voiceless* or something similar [GrHL 1.84–86]:

- a single written consonant for a voiced one (/b, d, g/)
- a double written consonant for a voiceless one (/p, t, k/).

That such a distinction is indeed phonemic, i.e., functional to distinguish one word from another, can be seen when comparing the adverb *appa* "back, after" and the pronoun *apa-* "that (one)": The former is consistently written with double *-pp-*, the latter with single *-p-*. Whether *adanzi* is spelled with a TA-sign (*a-ta-an-zi*) or a DA-sign (*a-da-an-zi*) is irrelevant; important is the fact that the forms are written with a *single* dental. This phenomenon is known as **Sturtevant's Law**, after the American Indo-Europeanist Edgar Sturtevant.

The interpretation of this phonemic opposition as one of voice (/p/ vs. /b/ etc.) is based on a comparison with etymologically related stems in other Indo-European languages. Hittite *epp-/app-* is considered to be related to the Sanskrit root *āp-* "to reach, obtain" pointing to a voiceless labial /p/, whereas Hittite *ed-/ad-* can be compared to Latin *edo* "to eat" with a voiced dental /d/. For the adverb *appa* just mentioned, Greek *opisthen* "behind" with the voiceless *p* can be adduced; for *apa-*, Lycian *ebe-* ("this, that") points to a voiced labial. Others have pleaded for an opposition of aspirated for the double-written consonants (/p$^h$/) vs. unaspirated for the single-written ones (/p/), or an opposition of "long" (pp = /p:/, like in Italian) vs. short consonants (p = /p/).

The opposition described above can only be realized in intervocalic position. What about consonants at the beginning or end of words? There is good evidence to suggest that at the beginning of words all or most consonants sounded like the voiceless or "long" consonants, whereas consonants at the end of a word had more of a voiced or "short" quality. Normally, however, Hittitologists pronounce Hittite as it is written in transliteration or transcription without really attempting to approximate how it might originally have sounded.

## 4.6 Akkadian

### 4.6.1

If an Akkadian noun is combined with an Akkadian gen. (or with an Akkadian possessive pronoun, see Lesson 5.6) or with a Sumerogram, the noun governing the gen. (or the possessive pronoun) appears in a special form, the so-called **status constructus**:

- This status constructus is in most cases identical to the stem, i.e., the nom. minus the ending *-U(M)*. E.g., *UMMĀNU(M)* "army" + *ŠARRU(M)* "king" › *UMMĀN ŠARRI(M)* "the army of the king."
- As a consequence, the case ending of the governing noun (the *regens*) is not visible any more: e.g., *ANA BĒL ALI(M)* (or *ANA BĒL* URU-*LIM*) "to/for the lord of the city."
- Some nouns have an irregular status constructus, like *ABI* from *ABU* "father."

## 4.7 Cuneiform Signs

am  ne 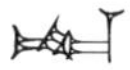

e  kal/dan  un/UN 

ma  ku  ba  URU 

i  ia 

Determinatives

| | | |
|---|---|---|
| $^{NINDA}$□ |  | for dough products (“bread”) |
| $^{UZU}$□ |  | for meats |
| $^{TU7}$□ |  | for stews |
| $^{Ú}$□ |  | for vegetation (grass, crops) |
| $^{GI}$□ |  | for things made of reed |

## 4.8 Exercises; KBo 3.4 i 36–ii 6

### 4.8.1 Translate:

1. *nu* NINDA-*an e-ez-za-at-te-ni wa-a-tar*(“water”)-*ma e-ku-ut-te-ni*
2. (from a treaty) *na-at-ša-an ke-e-da-ni li-in-ki-ia-aš tup-pí-ia ú-ul ki-it-ta-ri* (*kittari* = “is laid down in writing”)
3. $^{d}$*Ku-mar-pí-iš* DINGIR.MEŠ-*aš ad-da-aš e-eš-zi*
4. *nu-un-na-aš an-ni-ša-an-pát na-ak-ki-e-eš a-aš-ša-u-e-eš e-šu-u-en nu-un-na-aš le-en-ki-ia-aš* (add: “men (of ) …”) *e-šu-u-en*
5. (title/incipit of the Hittite royal funerary ritual) *ma-a-an* $^{URU}$*Ḫa-at-tu-ši šal-li-iš wa-aš-ta-a-iš ki-ša-ri na-aš-šu-za* LUGAL-*uš na-aš-ma* MUNUS.LUGAL-*aš* DINGIR-*LIM*-*iš ki-ša-ri* (text continues: “then they do as follows: …”)
6. (from a prayer to the Sun deity) $^{d}$UTU-*uš dam-me-iš-ḫa-an-da-aš* (passive part., “oppressed”) *ku-ri-im-ma-aš-ša an-tu-uḫ-ḫa-aš at-ta-aš an-na-aš zi-ik*
7. *nu-ut-ta ar-ḫa e-et-mi*
8. *ki-nu-un-za e-et-mi e-ku-mi*
9. *I-NA* $^{URU}$*Ka$_4$-aš-ka$_4$-ma ḫal-ki*$^{ḪI.A}$-*uš* BURU$_5$.ḪI.A *e-ez-za-aš-ta*
10. *ma-a-an ke-e-el-ma tup-pí-aš ud-da-a-ar* (“words”) *pa-aḫ-ḫa-aš-ti* (text continues: “then … ”)
11. *ku-wa-at-za* Ú-UL *e-za-at-ti* Ú-UL *e-ku-ut-ti*
12. (from a ritual to free a person from evil curses) *i-da-la-u-e-eš-wa-kán ḫur-da-a-uš pa-ra-a al-la-pa-aḫ-tén*
13. (omen apodosis) *nu* LUGAL-*uš a-ki* *I-NA* $^{GIŠ}$GU.ZA-*ŠU*(“his”)-*ma-za-kán ta-ma-iš ku-iš-ki* (“someone” nom. sing. com.) *e-ša-ri*
14. LÚ $^{GIŠ}$BANŠUR-*aš* ŠE *ša-ra-a e-ep-zi* UGULA $^{LÚ.MEŠ}$MUḪALDIM $^{d}$*Iš-tu-uš-ta-ia-aš pé-ra-an* 3-*šu* $^{d}$*Pa-a-pa-ia-aš pé-ra-an* 3-*šu* $^{d}$*Ḫa-ša-am-mi-li pé-ra-an* 1-*šu* *PA-NI* $^{d}$U.GUR 1-*šu ši-pa-an-ti*

### 4.8.2

Read and transliterate the following sign combinations:

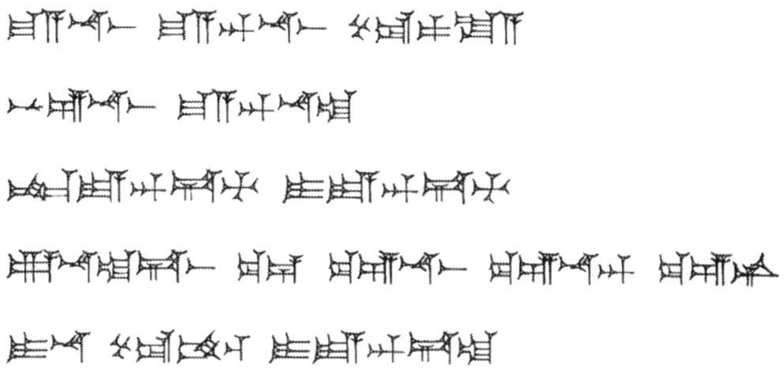

## Words for Lesson 4

| | |
|---|---|
| *allapaḫḫ-* (IIa) | to spit |
| *anna-*, com. | mother |
| *annišan* (adv.) | formerly |
| *antuḫḫa-*, *antuḫša-*, com. | human being, person |
| *aššu-* | beloved, good |
| *atta-*, com. | father |
| *eku-/aku-* (Ib) | to drink |
| *epp-/app-* (Ib) | to take, seize |
| *ed-/ad-* (Ib) | to eat |
| *eš-/aš-* (Ib) | to be |
| *ḫalki-*, com. | grain |
| *ḫurdai-*, com. | curse |
| *ki-* (IIa, dep.) | to lie, be laid |
| *kinun* | now |
| *kuitman* | when, as long as |
| *kurimma-*, com. | orphan (noun), orphaned (adj.) |
| *kuwat* | why? |
| *lingai-*, com. | oath |
| $^{\text{GIŠ}}$*luttai-*, com. | window |
| *nakki-* | important, weighty, important, hard, close |
| *naššu … našma …* | either … or … |
| *parā* | forth (from), forward, further |

| | |
|---|---|
| *tuppi-*, neut. | tablet |
| *waštai-*, com. | sin, error, lack, loss |
| *weḫ-/waḫ-* (Ib) | to turn |
| $^{\text{GIŠ}}$AB | = *luttai-* |
| $^{\text{A.ŠÀ}}$A.GÀR | field, meadow |
| $^{\text{GIŠ}}$BANŠUR, $^{\text{GIŠ}}$BANŠUR(*-a-*) | table |
| BURU$_5$ | locust |
| LÚ(*-a-*) | man |
| LÚ | table man, waiter |
| MUNUS.LUGAL | queen |
| NINDA | bread |
| ŠE | grain |
| UGULA | overseer, chief |

**DN**

| | |
|---|---|
| $^{\text{d}}$*Ḫašammili* | |
| $^{\text{d}}$*Ištuštaya* | |
| $^{\text{d}}$*Kumarbi* | |
| $^{\text{d}}$*Papaya* | |
| $^{\text{d}}$U.GUR | god of the Netherworld |
| $^{\text{d}}$UTU | Sun god(dess), Sun deity |

**GN**

| | |
|---|---|
| $^{\text{URU}}$*Ḫattuša* | (name of Hittite capital) |

| | | | |
|---|---|---|---|
| *peran* (sometimes with preceding gen. or dat.) | before, in front of | | |
| *šalli-* | big, large | $^{URU}$*K/Gaška* | (area north of Ḫattuša on the Black Sea coast) |
| *šarā* | up(wards), over, above | | |
| *tamai-* | other | | |

## 4.8.3 *The Ten-Year Annals* of the Hittite King Muršili II

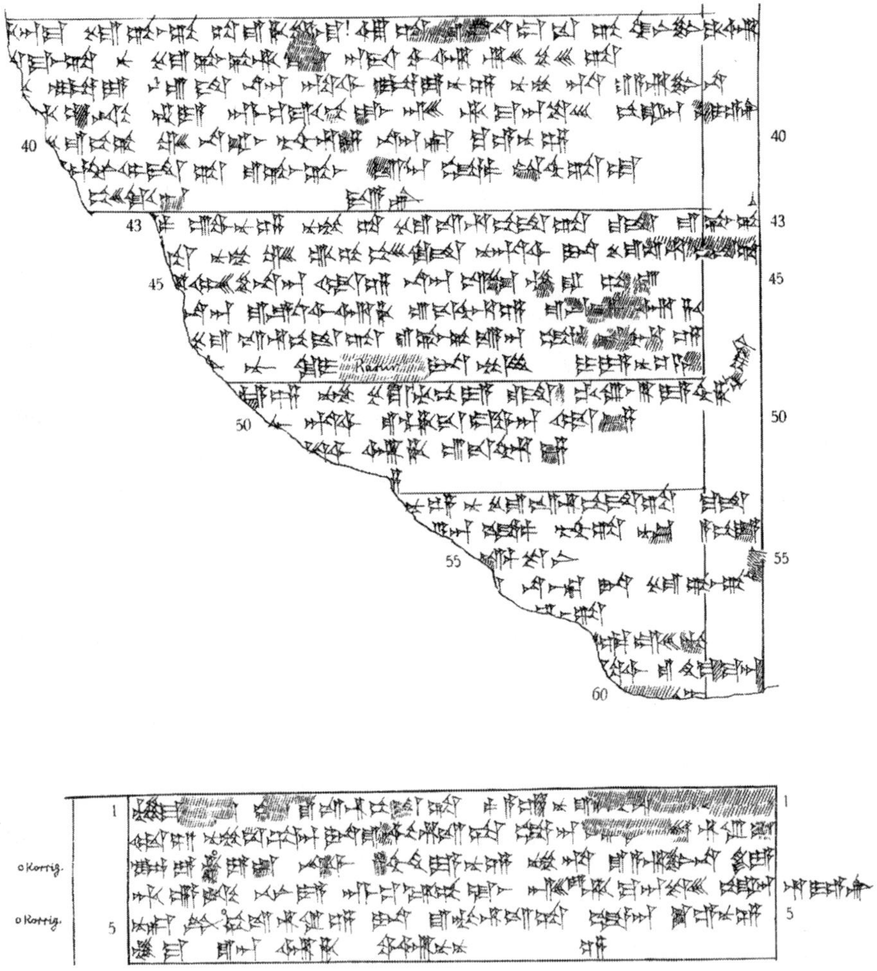

Figure 5

i

36. [*ma-aḫ-ḫ*]*a-an-ma* KUR [URU]*Ga-aš-ga* *ŠA* [URU]*Ḫa-li-la* Ù *ŠA* ⌜[URU]*Du*⌝-*ud-du-uš-ga ḫar-ni-in-ku-u-ar*
37. [*iš-t*]*a-ma-aš-ta nu* KUR [URU]*Ga-aš-ga ḫu-u-*⌜*ma-an*⌝ *an-da* *wa-ar-re-eš-še-eš-ta*
38. [*na-aš-m*]*u* MÈ-*ia* ‹‹aš›› *ú-it na-an* [d]UTU-*ŠI* MÈ-*ia-nu-un nu-mu* [d]UTU [URU]*A- ri-in-na*
39. [GAŠAN-*IA*] ⌜[d]⌝U ⌜NIR⌝.GÁL EN-*IA* [d]*Me-ez-zu-ul-la-aš* DINGIR.MEŠ *ḫu-u-ma-an-te-eš pé-ra-an* ⌜*ḫu*⌝-*i-e-er*
40. [*nu-za* ŠA K]UR [URU]*Kaš-ga* ÉRIN.MEŠ *NA-RA-RÙ tar-uḫ-ḫu-*⌜*un*⌝ *na-an-kán* *ku-e-nu-un*
41. [*nu-za* ŠA KUR [UR]][U]*Dur-mi-it-ta* [URU]*Ga-aš-ga-aš da-a!-an* EGIR-*pa* ÌR-*aḫ-ta-at*
42. [*nu-mu* ÉRIN.MEŠ] *pé-eš-ke-u-an da-a-er*

---

43. [*nam-ma* [d]UTU-*ŠI* EGI]R-*pa ú-wa-nu-un nu-mu ŠA* KUR [URU]*Iš-ḫu-pí-it-ta ku-it* [URU]*Ga-aš-ga-aš*
44. [*ku-u-ru-ri-ia-aḫ-ḫa-an ḫar-t*]*a nu-mu* ÉRIN.MEŠ *Ú-UL pé-eš-ke-et nu* [d]UTU-*ŠI I-NA* KUR [URU]*Iš-ḫu-*⌜*pí-it*⌝-*ta*
45. [*pa-a-un nu* [URU]X-*ḫ*]*u-mi-eš-še-na-an* GUL-*un na-an IŠ-*⌜*TU* NAM⌝.RA $GU_4$ ⌜UDU⌝
46. [*ša-ra-a da-aḫ-ḫu-un*] *na-an* [URU]KÙ.BABBAR-*ši ar-ḫa ú-da-aḫ-ḫu-un* URU-*an-ma ar-ḫa*
47. [*wa-ar-nu-nu-un nu-za ŠA*] KUR [URU]*Iš-ḫu-pí-it-ta* [URU]*Ga-aš-ga da-a-an* EGIR-⌜*pa* ÌR-*aḫ-ḫu*⌝-*un*
48. [*nu-mu* ÉRIN.MEŠ *pé-eš-ke-u-an da-a-e*]*r nu ki-i* erasure *I-NA* MU.1.KAM *i-ia-nu-*⌜*un*⌝

---

49. [MU-*an-ni-ma* I-NA KUR UGU-*TI*] ⌜*pa*⌝-*a-un nu-mu* KUR [URU]*Ti-pí-ia ku-it ku*![1]-*u-ru-ri-ia-aḫ-ḫa*‹-*an*› *ḫar-ta*
50. [*nu-mu* ÉRIN.MEŠ *Ú-UL pé-eš-ke-et n*]*u* [d]UTU-*ŠI* [URU]*Kat-ḫa-id*![2]-*du-wa-an* GUL-⌜*un*⌝
51. [*na-an IŠ-TU* NAM.RA $GU_4$ UDU [URU]K]Ù.BABBAR-*ši ar-ḫa ú-da-aḫ-ḫu-*⌜*un*⌝
52. [URU-*an-ma ar-ḫa wa-ar-nu-nu-u*]*n*

---

(Traces of eight more lines before column breaks off)

---

1 Tablet has GIŠ.
2 Tablet has DA.

ii

1. *nam-ma* [*pa-r*]*a-* ⌜*a* I⌝ [-N]A URU*Iš-ḫu-pí-it-ta pa-a-un nu* URU ⌜*Pal-ḫu*⌝ [*-iš*]*-š*[*a-an*]
2. GUL*-un* <u>*nu-mu-uš-ša-an*</u> I-NA URU*Pal-ḫu-iš-ša* EGIR*-an* x LÚ.KÚR [*Pí-*]*eš*!*-hu-ru-* ⌜*uš*⌝
3. MÈ*-ia ti*[3]*-ia-* ⌜*at*⌝ *na-an*![4] ⌜*za*⌝ *-aḫ-ḫi-ia-nu-un nu-mu* dUTU URU*A-ri-in-na* GAŠAN*-IA*
4. dU NIR.GÁL BE-LÍ-IA d*Me-ez-zu-ul-la-aš* DINGIR.MEŠ*-ia ḫu-u-ma-an-te-es pé-ra-an ḫu-i-e-er*
5. *nu-kán* LÚ.KÚR *Pí-iš-ḫu-ru-un* I-NA URU*Pal-ḫu-iš-ša* EGIR*-an ku-e-nu-un*
6. *nam-ma* URU*-an ar-ḫa wa-ar-nu-nu-un*

---

i 36–42. … (36–37 *maḫḫanma … warreššešta*) and came to me for battle. I, My Majesty, fought them (lit. him/her) and the Sun goddess of Arinna, [My Lady,] the mighty Storm god, My Lord, Mezzulla, (and) all the gods ran before me … (40–41 *nuza …* ÌR*-aḫtat*) and they began to give [me troops].

43–48. [Then I, My Majesty, r]eturned, and since the Gašgaean town of the area of Išhupitta [ha]d [turned hostile] towards me and was not giving me troops, I, My Majesty, [went] to the land of Išḫupitta … (45–47 *nu …* ÌR*-aḫḫun*) [and they bega]n [to give me troops.] This I did in one year.

49–52. [In the following year] I went [to the Upper Land.] Since the area of Tipiya had been hostile [and had not been giving me troops] … (50–52 [*n*]*u … warnunun*).

ii 1–6 Next I went [o]n to the town of Išḫupitta and I attacked the town of Palḫu[iš]š[a]. In Palḫuišša the Pešḫuruwean enemy engaged me in battle and I fought him. The Sun goddess of Arinna, My Lady, the mighty Storm god, My Lord, Mezzulla, and all the gods ran before me … (5–6 *nukan … warnunun*).

## Questions

1. Identify in the handcopy the cuneiform signs given in this and the previous Lessons.
2. Parse the underlined forms.
3. Translate the sentences that are left untranslated (marked by …, the first and last word and line number[s]).

---

[3] Written over erasure.

[4] Tablet has ŠI.

## Words

| | |
|---|---|
| 36. *ḫarninkuwar* | destruction |
| 37. KUR $^{URU}$*Gašga ḫūman* | "all Gašga-Land" |
| *anda warreššešš-* (Ia) | to help |
| 40. *kuenun* | "I destroyed" |
| ÉRIN.MEŠ | "troops, army" (usually referred back to with a sing. com.) |
| 41. *dān* (adv.) | for a second time |
| ÌR-*aḫḫ-* (IIa) | to subject, enslave |
| 46. *šarā daḫḫun* | "I captured" |
| *arḫa udaḫḫun* | "I carried off" |
| 47. ÌR-*aḫḫ-* | see i 41 |
| 51. *arḫa udaḫḫun* | see i 46 |

ii

| | |
|---|---|
| 5. *kuenun* | see i 40. |

# Lesson 5

## 5.1 *-nt-* and *-t-* noun stems

### 5.1.1

The first group of consonant stems to be introduced here is that of the **dental stems**: those in *-nt-* (Lesson 5.1.1) and -V*tt*- (Lesson 5.1.2). The stems in *-nt-* [GrHL 4.96–98] contain both nouns and adjectives; the nouns are of common gender only. A special group within the adjectives are the participles: see Lesson 5.3.3.

Again, the case endings are the same as those of the vowel stems of the preceding Lessons, but in two cases the combination of an ending with the final dental results in a slightly different form (see immediately below).

Examples for the *-nt*-stems: *išpant-* (GE$_6$, GE$_6$.KAM) "evening, night" for the nouns, *ḫumant-* "every, all" for the adjectives, and *walḫant-* "beaten, struck" (from *walḫ-* "to beat") for the participles.

| | Noun | Adjective | Participle |
|---|---|---|---|
| **Sing.** | | | |
| nom. com. | *išpanza* | *ḫumanza* | *walḫanza* |
| acc. com. | *išpantan* | *ḫumantan* | *walḫantan* |
| nom.-acc. neut. | | *ḫuman* | *walḫan* |
| gen. | *išpantaš* | *ḫumantaš* | *walḫantaš* |
| dat.-loc. | *išpanti* | *ḫumanti* | *walḫanti* |
| abl. | *išpantaz* (GE$_6$-*az*) | *ḫumantaz* | *walḫantaz* |
| instr. | | | *walḫantit* |
| **Plur.** | | | |
| nom. com. | | *ḫumanteš* | *walḫanteš* |
| acc. com. | *išpantiuš* | *ḫumantuš* | *walḫantuš* |
| nom.-acc. neut. | | *ḫumanta* | *walḫanta* |
| gen., dat.-loc. | | *ḫumantaš* | *walḫantaš* |

- The final dental of the stem is frequently written with the signs DA and DU (e.g., *ḫu-u-ma-an-du-uš*).
- The nom. sing. com. in *-an-za* is the orthographic result of the stem plus the nom. sing. com. ending *-š*: /-nt-s/. The final *-a* is therefore nothing but a graphic vowel; it has no linguistic reality.

- A special development is responsible for the nom.-acc. sing. neut.: With a zero ending for this case, one would expect *-*nt* (‹ -*nt*-Ø). However, this combination is not acceptable word-finally in Hittite, and the final -*t* is dropped: *-*nt* › -*n* (*ḫūman, walḫan*).
- The acc. plur. com. *išpantiuš* of *išpant-* is secondary and must have been influenced by the *i*-stems.

## 5.1.2

The *tt*-stems [GrHL 4.94–95] contain nouns only, of both common and neuter gender. Neuter presence is not very strong, however: it is restricted to words in –*itt*- like *militt*- "honey".

Examples: *naḫšaratt*- com. "fear, respect, awe," *šiwatt*- com. (UD, UD.KAM) "day."

| | | | |
|---|---|---|---|
| **Sing.** | | | |
| nom. com. | *naḫšaraz* | UD-*az* | (= *šiwat-š*) |
| acc. com. | *naḫšarattan* | UD-*an*, UD.KAM-*an* | (= *šiwattan*) |
| gen. | *naḫšarattaš* | UD-*aš* | (= *šiwattaš*) |
| dat.-loc. | *naḫšaratti* | *šiwatti*, UD-*ti*, | (= *šiwatti*) |
| | | *šiwat*, UD-*at* | (= *šiwat-Ø*) |
| abl. | *naḫšarataza* | UD.KAM-*az* | (= *šiwattaz*) |
| **Plur.** | | | |
| nom. com. | *naḫšaratteš* | UD.KAM.ḪI.A-*uš* | (= *šiwattuš*) |
| acc. com. | *naḫšaradduš* | UD.KAM.ḪI.A-*uš* | |
| nom.-acc. neut. | | | |
| gen., dat.-loc. | *naḫšarattaš* | UD.KAM.ḪI.A-*aš* | (= *šiwattaš*) |

- The nom. sing. com. *naḫšaraz* is the graphic way to represent /nahsarat-s/ (compare above *išpanza*).
- The declension of neuter nouns in -*itt*- is the same as those in -*att*- with a nom.-acc. sing. in -*it* (e.g., *milit* "honey").
- The form *šiwat* "on the day, by day" listed under the dat.-loc. is an example of the very archaic so-called endingless locative (see Lesson 1.1.1 in the "older" set of endings). It is also present in the frozen expression *anišiwat* "today."

## 5.2 Demonstrative pronoun *apā-*

### 5.2.1

To refer to something in the addressee's environment or to someone or something mentioned previously in a text we find the **demonstrative pronoun *apā-*** "that; he, she, it, they" [GrHL 7.3–9 (forms), 18.2–32 (use)]. The inflection runs almost completely parallel to that of *kā-* "this" (Lesson 4.2.1):

| | Sing. | Plur. |
|---|---|---|
| nom. com. | *apāš* | *apē, apūš* |
| acc. com. | *apūn* | *apūš, apē* |
| nom.-acc. neut. | *apāt* | *apē* |
| gen. | *apēl* | *apenzan, apēl* |
| dat.-loc. | *apēdani* | *apēdaš* |
| abl. | *apēz, apezza* | |
| instr. | *apedanda* | |

- Note that as opposed to the nom.-acc. sing. neut. *kī* "this," the corresponding form *apāt* shows the characteristic pronominal neuter ending *-t* (Lesson 1.2.1).
- The nom. sing. com. *apāš* can be further stressed to *apašila* "he himself/she herself, it was (s)he who …"
- For the interchange between the nom. and acc. plur. com. *apē* and *apūš*, as well as the gen. plur. *apēl*, see the remarks in Lesson 4.2.1.
- An original **apit* is preserved only in the frozen expression *apit(-)pantalaz* "from that moment on, since then."
- An allative *apēda* is attested in the adverbial sense "thither."
- Other adverbs derived from the stem *apā-* are:
  - *apiya* "there, then"
  - *apeniššan* "thus, in that way"
  - *apadda(n)* "therefore."

## 5.3 Thematic verb stems Ic, including *-ške*-imperfectives

### 5.3.1

The most extensive class of Hittite *mi*-verbs is the **thematic** one (Ic) [GrHL 12.21–40], so called after the *thematic* vowel, which comes between the verbal stem and the ending. In Hittite this vowel is either *-e-* (although mostly written *-i-*) or *-a-*, depending on the person: *-e/i-* in the 2. and 3. sing. pres. and pret., and *-a-* in the rest.

From an historical (Proto-Indo-European) point of view, one would expect the 2. plur. to also have the *-e-*, but no such form has been attested thus far. During the history of the Hittite language the -*a*- gradually replaced the -*e*-, resulting in paradigms with -*a*- throughout. Some forms, in which -*e*- is not expected to occur (e.g., 3. plur. pres. *ienzi* "they do/make" instead of *iyanzi*; see below), may have to be explained as the result of analogy or as "hypercorrection." In Older Hittite one still finds the -*e*-forms very frequently.

Four types (A–D) of thematic verbs can be distinguished:

**A.** basic thematic verbs = stem + thematic vowel -*e*-/-*a*-; example *zinne*/*zinna*- "to stop, end" (*zinn+a+mi, zinn+e+ši* etc.)
**B.** verbs with the thematic suffix -*ye*-/-*ya*-; example *iye*-/*iya*- "to do, make"
**C.** verbs ending in -*ae*-/*-*aa*- —› -*ā*-; example *ḫatrae*-/*ḫatrā*- "to write, send"
**D.** imperfective verbs in -*ške*-/-*ška*-; example *memiške*-/**memiška*- "to (be) speak(ing)"

In the first three types (A–C) the thematic vowel -*e*- is gradually replaced by -*a*-; in D the -*e*- rapidly spread and almost completely ousted -*a*-. The latter type is separately discussed in Lesson 5.3.2.

| | A | B | C |
|---|---|---|---|
| **Active** | | | |
| **Present** | | | |
| **Sing.** 1 | *zinnami, zinnaḫḫi* | *iyami, iyemi* | *ḫatrāmi* |
| 2 | *zinniši* | *iaši* | *ḫatrāši* |
| 3 | *zinnizi, zinnai* | *iezzi, iyazzi* | *ḫatrāezzi* |
| **Plur.** 1 | *zinnaweni* | *iyaweni* | *ḫatrāweni* |
| 2 | *zinnatteni* | | *ḫatrātteni* |
| 3 | *zinnanzi* | *iyanzi, ienzi* | *ḫatrānzi* |
| **Preterite** | | | |
| **Sing.** 1 | *zinnaḫḫun* | *iyanun* | *ḫatrānun* |
| 2 | *zinnit* | *iyeš, iyaš* | *ḫatrāeš* |
| 3 | *zinnit, zinnešta* | *iēt, iyat* | *ḫatrāet, ḫatraeš* |
| **Plur.** 1 | | *iyawen* | |
| 2 | | *iyatten* | |
| 3 | *zinner* | *iēr* | |
| **Medio-passive** | | | |
| **Present** | | | |
| **Sing.** 3 | *zinnattari* | | |
| **Plur.** 3 | *zinnantari* | | |
| **Participle** | *zinnant-* | *iyant-* | *ḫatrānt-* |

- Since ultimately almost all *-e-* thematic vowels disappeared, the stems of types A–B are usually presented in dictionaries and other secondary literature as *a*-stems: *zinna-*, *iya-*.
- The type-A verbs (*zinne-/zinna-*) have sometimes been reinterpreted as *ḫi*-verbs (of the semi-consonantal class IIc, see Lesson 8.3.1 *ešša-*) resulting in 1. and 3. sing. forms like *zinnaḫḫi*, *zinnaḫḫun*, and *zinnai*.
- For forms like the 3. plur. pres. *ienzi* (besides *iyanzi*), see already above.

5.3.2

In the paradigm of the so-called **imperfectives** in *-ške-/-ška-* [GrHL 12.31–40], i.e., type **D** of the thematic verbs Ic, the *-a-* vowel has rarely been preserved; it appears in forms like *pašgami* "I stick (something into something)" or *pišgaweni* "we give (repeatedly)." The only consistent *-a*-form is the 3. plur. pres. *-škanzi*, but a theoretical **-škenzi* would have become *-škanzi* regularly anyway. Often the 2. plur. *-škitteni* and *-škitten* are written with the KAT-sign (°*š*-KAT-*te*-) and are interpreted as such (*-škatteni, -škatten*). However, since the only other spellings for the 2. plur. display the *-e/i*-value (°*š-ki-te-*) and the KAT-sign can also be read $kit_9$, this form will be given here as *-škitten(i)*.

The *-ške*-suffix is immediately attached to the stem; for the phonology of this, see Lesson 5.5. For the semantics of this suffix, see Lesson 5.4. The paradigm given here is *memiške-*, derived from *mema-* "to speak, say," for which see Lesson 9.3.2.

| Ic D | | Present | Preterite |
|---|---|---|---|
| **Sing.** | 1 | *memiškemi* | *memiškenun* |
| | 2 | *memiškeši* | *memiškeš* |
| | 3 | *memiškezzi* | *memišket* |
| **Plur.** | 1 | *memiškeuwani* | |
| | 2 | *memišketteni* | *memišketten* |
| | 3 | *memiškanzi* | *memišker* |
| **Participle** | | *memiškant-* | |

- The medio-passive forms of the *-ške*-verbs conform to the distribution of the thematic vowel in the active conjugation: *i* throughout (with the reservation on the KAT sign just outlined) and *a* only in the 3. plur. pres.
- The medio-passive forms most frequently attested are the 3. sing. pres. (*-škittari*) and the 3. plur. pres. (*-škantari*).

### 5.3.3

In Lesson 5.1.1 mention was made of a **participle**, i.e., an adjective derived from a verb [GrHL 11.18–24]: "to eat" › "eaten" (= passive) or "eating" (= active). In Hittite, participles are derived from the verbal stems by adding the suffix *-ant-*: *walḫ-* —› *walḫant-*, *šipand-* —› *šipandant-*. The declension follows that of the other *nt*-stems (Lesson 5.1.1).

The participle normally indicates the state which lasts after the verb's action has been performed: *walḫ-* "to beat, strike" › *walḫant-* "beaten, struck", *akk-* "to die" › *akkant-* "dead." Sometimes, however, the participle also indicates an action, as in the case of *adant-* "eaten," but also "eating" from *ed-/ad-* (Ib, see Lesson 4.3), *akuwant-* "drunk," but also "drinking" from *eku-/aku-* (Ib), *ḫalziyant-* "calling."

For the forms of the participle for the verb classes presented in the preceding lessons, see Appendix 1.

## 5.4 Semantics

### 5.4.1

The **imperfective suffix *-ške-*** can be attached to most verbal stems [GrHL 24.4–26]. It can add a whole range of so-called **aspects** to the meaning of the verb, that is, it can present the action of the verb as being stretched out over a longer period of time (**durative** aspect), as being done regularly or repeatedly (**iterative** aspect), as involving several individual persons or things (**distributive**), as beginning (**inchoative**), or as being in progress (**progressive**).

Compare the following examples:

- durative: *n=at* INA UD.3.KAM *azzikkitten akkuškitten* "You ate (and) drank it for three days"
- iterative: LUGAL-*uš=ma=kan maḫḫan* UD-*tili šipanzakezzi* "when the king brings offerings daily (UD-*tili*)"
- distributive: *nu kāša apēdani memini* LIM DINGIR.MEŠ *tuliya ḫalziyanteš nu uškandu ištamaškandu=ya* "Behold, the thousand (LIM) gods have been called to meet for this matter, now let them watch and listen, each of them!"
- inchoative: *n=aš uiškezzi* "he starts crying"
- progressive: *nu anniškemi kuin* UN-*an* "the person I am treating …."

Two other less frequently attested suffixes cover the same range of aspects: *-anna/i-* and *-šša-* (see Lesson 8.3.1).

## 5.5 Phonology

### 5.5.1

The **imperfective suffix** *-ške-* is attached directly to the stem of the verb [GrHL 12.31.33]. If the verbal stem ends in a vowel, the cluster *-šk-* can easily be spread over two signs: e.g., *me-mi-iš-k°* from *mema-/memi-/memiya-* "to speak," *ti-it-ta-nu-uš-k°* from *tittanu-* "to put, install," *pé-eš-ši-iš-k°* from *peššiya-* "to throw, cast" etc. As is clear from the last example, verbal stems ending in °*a-* have °*eške-* instead of *°*aške-*.

If a verbal stem ends in °*š-* the two *šš* merge: e.g., *pu-nu-uš-k°* ‹ *punuš-ške-* from *punušš-* "to ask, question." With verbs ending in °*n-* the *-n-* assimilates to the *-š-*: from *kuen-* "to kill" we have *ku-wa-aš-k°* (‹ **kuen-šk°*).

In most cases where a consonant cluster appears, it is solved either by inserting a so-called anaptyctic vowel *-e/i-* in between the stem and the suffix (e.g., *akkiške-* from *akk-ške-* "to die") or between the *š* and the *k* of the suffix itself (e.g., *anšikke-* from **anš-ške-* "to wash"). The latter type is usually typical of older language: e.g., from the verb *ḫanna-* (IIc) "to judge" we find an older form *ḫaššikke-* (from **ḫan-ške-*) that was later changed to *ḫanneške-*.

## 5.6 Akkadian

### 5.6.1

In Lesson 4.4.3–4 we saw some possibilities for expressing possessive relations. Probably the most frequent way to do so used in written Hittite is the Akkadian possessive pronoun (already briefly mentioned in Lesson 4.6). The noun to which it is attached stands in the *status constructus* (see Lesson 4.6) whenever it is a nom. or acc.; if it is a gen. the **possessive suffix** comes behind the gen. ending in *-i*. The following forms can be encountered:

| | | | |
|---|---|---|---|
| -C-*IA*/-V-*I* | "mine" | -*NI* | "our" |
| -*KA* | "your" | -*KUNU* | "your" (plural) |
| -*ŠU*/-*ZU* | "his" | -*ŠUNU* | "their" (masc.) |
| -*ŠA* | "her" | -*ŠINA* | "their" (fem.) |

Examples: *ŠARR=I* "my king" (nom., acc.) but *ANA ŠARRI=YA* "to my king", *BĒL=KA* "your lord," *MĀR=ŠU* "his son" (*MĀRU* = DUMU), *MĀR=ŠA* "her son," *MĀR=NI* "our son," *ALAP=KUNU* "your (plur.) ox" (*ALPU* = GU$_4$), *ŠAR=ŠUNU/ŠINA* "their king." For *ABU* "father" with its *status constructus* *ABI=* we get: *AB=I* "my father" (but mostly we find incorrect *ABU=IA*), *ABI=KA* "your father" etc. Here too (see already Lesson 2.6) forms are often used incorrectly by the Hittite scribes.

## 5.7 Cuneiform signs

| | | | |
|---|---|---|---|
| GAM  | tén  | ḫi  | im  |
| eš  | še  | pu  | |
| zi  | uz  | | |
| aḫ/eḫ/ iḫ/uḫ  | ḫar/ḫur/mur  | | |

### Determinatives

The following determinatives are postponed, i.e., they are put at the end of the word (comparable to the Sumerian plural morphemes MEŠ and ḪI.A) instead of before it:

| | |
|---|---|
| □$^{\text{SAR}}$  | for plants |
| □$^{\text{KAM}}$  | for numbers and numbered items |
| □$^{\text{MUŠEN}}$  | for birds |
| □$^{\text{KI}}$  | for geographical names |

## 5.8 Exercises; KBo 3.4 ii 7–32

### 5.8.1 Translate:

1. (from a ritual for the renewal of kingship) MU.ḪI.A-*aš-ši* (i.e., the king) EGIR *ne-wa-aḫ-ḫe-er na-aḫ-ša-ra-at-ta-an ne-wa-aḫ-ḫe-er* (subject: the gods)
2. A-BU-IA-*an-na-aš-za* $^{\text{m}}$*Mur-ši-li-iš* 4 DUMU.ḪI.A $^{\text{m}}$*Ḫal-pa-šu-lu-pí-in* $^{\text{m}}$NIR.GÁL-*in* $^{\text{m}}$*Ḫa-at-tu-ši-li-in* $^{\text{f}}$DINGIR.MEŠ.IR-*in-na* DUMU.MUNUS-*an ḫa-aš-ta nu-za ḫu-u-ma-an-da-aš-pát* EGIR-*iz-zi-iš* DUMU-*aš e-šu-un*
3. *nu* KUR $^{\text{URU}}$*Pár-ḫa-an-na* IŠ-TU $^{\text{GIŠ}}$TUKUL *e-ep-zi nu-kán a-pa-a-aš-ša* A-NA LUGAL KUR $^{\text{URUd}}$U-*ta-aš-ša a-aš-ša-an-za*
4. *ki-nu-un-ma-aš-kán* (=*aš* refers to a deity's statue) $^{\text{GIŠ}}$*iš-ta-na-ni* GUB-*ri*
5. (from the colophon of a tablet) *ki-i* ṬUP-PU *ar-ḫa ḫar-ra-an e-eš-ta na-at* A-NA PA-NI $^{\text{m}}$*Ma-aḫ-ḫu-zi* Ù A-NA $^{\text{m}}$*Ḫal-wa*-LÚ *ú-uk* $^{\text{m}}$*Du-da-aš* EGIR-*pa ne-wa-aḫ-ḫu-un*
6. *a-pa-a-at-ma-kán ḫu-u-ma-an ar-ḫa ḫa-aš-pé-er-pát*
7. (said of a woman) *pár-ku-i-ša-aš a-pa-a-aš mi-iš-ri-wa-an-za a-pa-a-aš ḫar-ki-ša-aš a-pa-a-aš na-aš-kán ḫu-u-ma-an-da-az a-ša-nu-wa-an-za*
8. *di-iš-šu-um-mi-na* A-NA SAG.DU-ŠU *tu-wa-ar-ne-er*
9. GAL-*iš-za* $^{\text{d}}$UTU-*uš* EZEN$_4$ *i-e-et*
10. (from the laws) *ták-ku* LÚ-*aš* EL-LUM É-*er* ("house," nom.-acc. neut.) *lu-uk-ke-ez-zi* É-*er* EGIR-*pa ú-e-te-ez-zi*

11. DINGIR.MEŠ-*aš* ZI-*an-za da-aš-šu-uš*
12. *Ù* ŠA UDU *ka-ra-a-du-uš* IŠ-TU *ḫa-ap-pí-ni-it za-nu-uš-kán-zi*
13. *nu-mu* KUR.KUR.MEŠ *ḫu-u-ma-an-da me-na-aḫ-ḫa-an-da ku-ru-ri-aḫ-ḫe-er*
14. *nu-ut-ta* KUR $^{\text{URU}}$*Ḫa-at-ti ḫu-u-ma-an-za* KUR $^{\text{URU}}$*Ḫa-ia-ša* KUR.KUR.MEŠ-*ia ḫu-u-ma-an-te-eš a-ra-aḫ-zé-né-eš an-tu-ri-e-eš ar-ḫa iš-ta-ma-aš-šer*
15. *na-at ma-aḫ-ḫa-an* IŠ-TU DINGIR-LIM *ḫa-an-da-a-it-ta-ri na-at* QA-TAM-MA *i-ia-mi*

## 5.8.2

Read and transliterate the following sign combinations:

## Words for Lesson 5

| | | | |
|---|---|---|---|
| *anturiya-* | inner-, inside, interior | DUMU.MUNUS | daughter |
| | | É.DINGIR-(LIM) | temple |
| *appa(n)* | again, back, later | EGIR(-*an/pa*) | = *appa(n)* |
| *appezzi-* | last, youngest, low (in rank) | EGIR-*izzi-* | = *appezzi-* |
| | | GAL | = *šalli-* |
| *arḫa ištamaš-* (Ia) | to hear of/about | GUB | = *ar-*, dep. |
| *ašš-* (Ia) | to belong to, remain | SAG.DU | head |
| *aššanuwant-* | provided with | $^{\text{GIŠ}}$TUKUL | weapon |
| *duwarne-* (Ic) | to break | | |
| *ḫandae-* (Ic) | to ascertain | ZI(-*ant-*) | = *ištanzan(ant)-* |
| *ḫappina-*, com. | flame, fire | | |
| *ḫarki-* | fair, white | ANA (PANI) | to, for, in front of |
| *ḫarrant-* | damaged | ELLU(M) | free |
| *ḫaš-* (IIa) | to give birth to, sire | QADU | (together) with |
| *ḫašp-* (Ia) | to destroy | QATAMMA | likewise, just so |
| *ḫumant-* | all, every | TUPPU(M) | (clay) tablet |
| $^{\text{(GIŠ)}}$*ištanana-*, com. | table, altar | Ù | and |
| *ištanzan(ant)-*, com. | soul | | |
| | | **GN** | |
| *iya-* (Ic) | to do, make | (KUR) $^{\text{URU}}$*Parḫa* | (= classical Perge) |

| | | | |
|---|---|---|---|
| *karat-*, com. | innards | (KUR) URU dU-(*ta*)*šša* | Tarḫuntašša |
| *kururiyaḫḫ-* (IIa) | to be(come) hostile | | |
| *lukke-* (Ic) | to set fire to (+ acc.) | KUR URU*Ḫayaša* | (= mod. Armenia) |
| *menaḫḫanda* (adv.) | across, facing, opposite | | |
| | | **PN** | |
| *mišriwant-* | beautiful, shining | fDINGIR.MEŠ.IR-*i* | Maššanauzzi |
| *naḫšaratt-*, com. | fear, awe, respect | m*Duda* | |
| *newaḫḫ-* (Ia) | to renew, make new | m*Ḫalpašulupi* | |
| *parkui-* | clean, pure | m*Ḫalwa*-LÚ | Ḫalwaziti |
| | | m*Ḫattušili* | Hittite Great King (*c.* 1267–1240 BC) |
| *šu* (conj., cf. Lesson 1.4.2) | and | m*Kupanta*-dLAMMA | |
| | | m*Maḫḫuzzi* | |
| *wete-* (Ia) | to build | | |
| *zanu-* (Ia) | to cook, boil | 1-*an* | only |

## 5.8.3 *The Ten-Year Annals* of the Hittite King Muršili II

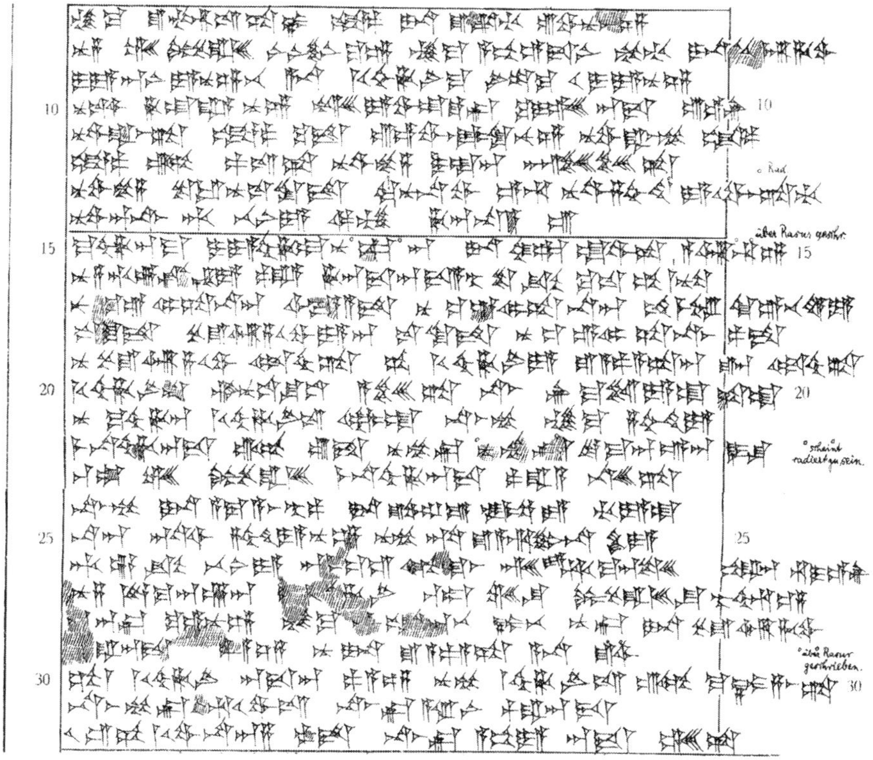

Figure 6

ii

7. *nam-ma* $^{\text{URU}}$*Pal-ḫu-iš-ša-az* EGIR-*pa I-NA* $^{\text{URU}}$⸢KÙ⸣.BABBAR-*ti ú-wa-nu*«-x»-*un*
8. *nu-za* ÉRIN.MEŠ ANŠE.KUR.RA.MEŠ *ni-ni-in-ku-un nam-ma a-pé-e-da-ni* MU-*ti I-NA* ⸢KUR⸣ [*A*]*r-za-u-wa*
9. *i-ia-an-ni-ya-nu-un-pát A-NA* $^{\text{m}}$*U-uḫ-ḫa*-LÚ-*ma* $^{\text{LÚ}}$*ṬE-MA u-i-ia-nu-un*
10. *nu-uš-ši ḫa-at-ra-a-nu-un* ÌR.MEŠ-*IA-wa-at-ták-kán ku-i-e-eš an-da ú-e-er*
11. *nu-wa-ra-aš-ta* EGIR-*pa ku-it ú-e-wa-ak-ki-nu-un nu-wa-ra-aš-mu* «EGIR-pa»
12. EGIR-*pa Ú-UL pa-iš-ta nu-wa-mu-za* DUMU-*la-an ḫal-zi-eš-še-eš-ta*
13. *nu-wa-mu-za te-ep-nu-uš-ke-et ki-nu-na-wa e-ḫu nu-wa za-aḫ-ḫi!-ia-u-wa-aš-ta-ti*
14. *nu-wa-an-na-aš* $^{\text{d}}$U *BE-LÍ-IA DI-NAM ḫa-an-na-a-ú*

---

15. *ma-aḫ-ḫa-an-ma i-ia-aḫ-ḫa-at nu* GIM-*an I-NA* $^{\text{ḪUR.SAG}}$*La-wa-ša a-ar-ḫu-un*
16. *nu-za* $^{\text{d}}$U NIR.GÁL EN-*IA pa-ra-a ḫa-an-da-an-da-a-tar te-ek-ku-ša-nu-ut*
17. *nu* $^{\text{GIŠ}}$*kal-mi-ša-na-an ši-ia-a-it nu* $^{\text{GIŠ}}$⸢*kal*⸣-*mi-ša-na-an am-me-el* KARAŠ.ḪI.A-*ia*
18. *uš-*⸢*ke*⸣-*et* KUR $^{\text{URU}}$*Ar-za-u-wa-ia-an uš-ke-et nu* $^{\text{GIŠ}}$*kal-mi-ša-na-aš pa-it*
19. *nu* KUR $^{\text{URU}}$*Ar-za-u-wa* GUL-*aḫ-ta ŠA* $^{\text{m}}$*U-uḫ-ḫa*-LÚ-*ia* $^{\text{URU}}$*A-pa-a-ša-an* URU-*an* GUL-*aḫ-ta*
20. $^{\text{m}}$*U-uḫ-ḫa*-LÚ-*na gi-nu-uš-šu-uš a-še-eš-ta na-aš ir-ma-li-ia-at-ta-at*
21. *nu ma-aḫ-ḫa-an* $^{\text{m}}$*U-uḫ-ḫa*-LÚ-*iš* GIG-*at na-aš-mu nam-ma za-aḫ-ḫi-ia*
22. *me-na-aḫ-ḫa-an-da Ú-UL ú-it nu-mu-kán* erased: nu-mu-kán $^{\text{m}}$SUM-*ma*-$^{\text{d}}$LAMMA-*an* DUMU-*ŠU*
23. *QA-DU* ÉRIN.MEŠ ANŠE.KUR.RA.MEŠ *me-na-aḫ-ḫa-an-da pa-ra-a na-eš-ta*
24. *na-aš-mu I-NA* $^{\text{ÍD}}$*A-aš-tar-pa I-NA* $^{\text{URU}}$*Wa-al-ma-a* MÈ-*ia ti-ia-at*
25. *na-an* $^{\text{d}}$UTU-*ŠI za-aḫ-ḫi-ia-nu-un nu-mu* $^{\text{d}}$UTU $^{\text{URU}}$*A-ri-in-na* GAŠAN-*IA*
26. $^{\text{d}}$U NIR.GÁL *BE-LÍ-IA* $^{\text{d}}$⸢*Me*⸣-*ez-zu-ul-*⸢*la*⸣-*aš* DINGIR.MEŠ-*ia*[1] *ḫu-u-ma-an-te-eš pé-ra-an ḫu-i-e-er*
27. *nu-za* $^{\text{m}}$SUM-*ma*-$^{\text{d}}$LAMMA-*an* ⸢DUMU $^{\text{m}}$*U-uḫ-ḫa*⸣-LÚ *QA-DU* ÉRIN.MEŠ-*ŠU* ANŠE.KUR.RA.MEŠ-*ŠU tar-uḫ-ḫu-un*
28. ⸢*na*⸣-*an-kán ku-e-nu-un* ⸢*nam*⸣-*ma-*⸢*an* EGIR-*an*⸣-*pát AṢ-BAT nu-kán I-NA* KUR $^{\text{URU}}$*Ar-za-u-wa*
29. [*pár*]-*ra-an-da* ⸢*pa*⸣-*a-un nu I-NA* $^{\text{URU}}$*A-pa-a-ša A-NA* URU-*LIM*
30. *ŠA* $^{\text{m}}$*U-uḫ-ḫa*-LÚ *an-da-an pa-a-un nu-mu* $^{\text{m}}$*Uḫ-ḫa*-LÚ-*iš Ú-UL ma-az-za-aš-ta*

---

[1] IA added above line.

31. *na-aš-mu-kán* ^d^*ḫu-u-wa-iš na-aš-kán a-ru-ni pár-ra-an-da*
32. ^d^*gur-ša-u-wa-na-an-za pa-it na-aš-kán a-pí-ia an-da e-eš-ta*

---

ii 7–14 … (7–10 *namma* … *ḫatrānun*): "Concerning the fact that I demanded back my subjects that had come to you, you have not given them back to me … (12–13 *nuwamuza* … *zaḫḫiyauwaštati*) and may the Storm god, My Lord, decide our lawsuit!"

15–32 When I marched and had reached Mount Lawaša … (16–19 *nuza* … GUL-*aḫta*), Uḫḫazidi sank to his knees … (20–27 *naš* … *taruḫḫun*) and I defeated him. Next, I arrested him. I crossed over into Arzawa-Land and entered Apaša, the city of Uḫḫazidi. Uḫḫazidi did not resist, but he escaped me. He went across the sea to the islands and there he stayed.

## Questions

1. Identify in the handcopy the cuneiform signs given in this and the previous Lessons.
2. Translate the sentences that are left untranslated (marked by …, the first and last word and line number[s]).

## Words

| | | |
|---|---|---|
| 7. | ^URU^*Palḫuišša* | (a town) |
| | ^URU^KÙ.BABBAR-*ti*/-*ša*- | Ḫatti/Ḫattuša |
| | *uwanun* | "I came" |
| 8. | ÉRIN.MEŠ ANŠE.KUR.RA.MEŠ | troops (and) chariots |
| | *nininkun* | "I mobilized" |
| | MU | year |
| | KUR *Arzauwa* | Arzawa-Land (in western Anatolia, partly overlapping with classical Lydia) |
| 9. | *iyanniya*- | to march, go, walk |
| | ^LÚ^*ṬEMU* | envoy, messenger |
| | *uiya*- | to send |
| 12. | *ḫalzieššešta* | "you called" |
| 13. | *tepnuške*- | to humiliate, belittle (here 2. sing.!) |
| | *kinun* | now |
| | *eḫu* | "come!" |
| | *zaḫḫiyauwaštati* | (pret. med.-pass with pres. [see Lesson 3.3.1], probably adhortative value: "let's …") |
| 16. | NIR.GÁL | mighty |
| | *parā ḫandandatar* neut. | guidance, providence |
| | *tekkušanu*- | to show |

| | |
|---|---|
| 17. $^{\text{GIŠ}}$*kalmišana-* com. | meteorite |
| *šae-*, *šiya-* | to hurl, shoot, press |
| KARAŠ.ḪI.A | army, troops |
| 18. *uške-* | to see, watch |
| *pait* | "it went" |
| 20. *irmaliya-* (Sum. GIG; dep.) | to fall ill |
| 21. *zaḫḫai-* (Sum. MÈ) com. | battle, fight |
| 22. *menaḫḫanda* | to(wards), against (+ dat.-loc.) |
| *uit* | "he came" |
| $^{\text{m}}$SUM-*ma*-$^{\text{d}}$LAMMA (partly Sum. writing for Luwian) | Piyamatarḫunta |
| 23. *parā naešta* | "he sent" |
| 24. $^{\text{ÍD}}$*Aštarpa* | (a river) |
| $^{\text{URU}}$*Walma* | (a town) |
| 25. *zaḫḫiya-* | to fight |
| 26. *peran ḫuiya-* | to run in front of (with dat.-loc., as a sign of leadership and support) |
| 28. *kuenun* | "I killed" |
| EGIR-*an* AṢBAT | "I pursued" |

# Lesson 6

## 6.1 *n*-stem nouns

6.1.1

The Hittite **nominal stems in -*n*-** [GrHL 4.68–72] distinguish two types: one with an Ablaut -*a*-/-Ø-, all neuters, and one without Ablaut, of common gender, with a nom. in -*aš* and all other cases in -*an*-. In the latter type, the nom. sing. cannot be distinguished from a regular *a*-stem noun since the final -*n*- of the stem has been assimilated to the nom. -*š* (see Lesson 6.5): **ḫaran-š* › *ḫaraš*. Sometimes the acc. plur. in this group also has an *a*-stem form: e.g., *arkammuš* from *arkamman*- "tribute."

Examples: *tekan/takn*- "earth" and *laman/lamn*- (‹ **naman*, Sum. ŠUM) neut. "name" for the first type, and *ḫaran*- "eagle" and *išḫiman*- "rope" for the second.

| | with Ablaut | | without Ablaut | |
|---|---|---|---|---|
| **Sing.** | | | | |
| nom. | | | *ḫaraš* | *išḫimaš* |
| acc. | | | *ḫaranan* | *išḫimanan* |
| nom.-acc. neut. | *tekan* | *laman* | | |
| gen. | *taknaš* | *lamnaš* | *ḫaranaš* | |
| dat.-loc. | *takni* | *lamni* | | |
| all. | *takna* | | | |
| abl. | *taknaz* | ŠUM-*za*/-*az* | | *išḫimanaz* |
| instr. | | *lamnit* | | *išḫimanta*, *išḫimanit* |
| **Plur.** | | | | |
| nom. | | | *ḫaraneš* | *išḫimaneš* |
| acc. | | | | *išḫimanuš* |
| gen., dat.-loc. | | *lamnaš*, ŠUM.ḪI.A-*aš* | | |

- Note the double change in the paradigm of *tekan/takn*- with the -*e*-/-*a*- Ablaut in the first syllable and the -*a*-/-Ø- Ablaut in the second syllable.
- Sometimes Ablaut changes are visible in the paradigm of *išḫiman*-, too, when we see such forms as the acc. sing. *išḫimenan* next to *išḫimanan*. These accusatives gave rise to new nom. sing. like *išḫimanaš* and *išḫiminaš*.

- The instr. *išḫimanta* contains the archaic ending *-t* (see Lesson 1.1.1) supported by a prop vowel to avoid its being dropped in word-final position (see Lesson 5.1.1, 6.5 for word-final **-nt › -n*).

### 6.1.2

An important but irregular *n*-stem is *memiyan-/memin-/memiya-* (Sum. INIM, Akkad. *AWĀTU*) "word, deed, thing" [GrHL 4.76]. It stands isolated not only because of the different stems throughout its paradigm, but also because its gender varies:

| | **Sing.** | **Plur.** |
|---|---|---|
| nom. com. | *memiaš* (INIM-*aš*) | *AWĀTE*^MEŠ |
| acc. com. | *memian* (INIM-*an*) | *memiyanuš* |
| nom.-acc. neut. | *memian* | |
| gen. | *memiyanaš* | *memiyanaš* (INIM.MEŠ-*aš*) |
| dat.-loc. | *memiyani, memini* (INIM-*ni*) | *memiyanaš* |
| abl. | *memiyanaz, meminaz, memiaz* (INIM-*za*) | |
| instr. | *memiyanit, meminit* | |

- The Sumerogram INIM can also stand for Hitt. *uttar* of the same meaning (see Lesson 7.1.3).

## 6.2 Relative and interrogative pronoun *kui-*

### 6.2.1

For both the **relative** ("who, whom, which, that") and the **interrogative** pronoun ("who?, which?, what?") Hittite has a single stem ***kui-*** [GrHL 8.2]. The interrogative pronoun can be used substantivally ("whom did you see?") or adjectivally ("what/which man did you see?"). The inflection shows all the pronominal characteristics (see Lesson 1.2.1):

| | **Sing.** | **Plur.** |
|---|---|---|
| nom. com. | *kuiš* | *kuieš, kueuš* |
| acc. com. | *kuin* | *kueuš, kuiuš, kuieš* |
| nom.-acc. neut. | *kuit* | *kue* |
| gen. | *kuel* | |
| dat.-loc. | *kuedani* | *kuedaš* |
| abl. | *kuez* | |

- For the use of the relative pronoun see Lesson 6.4.1.

### 6.2.2

From the relative stem *ku*(*i*)- several adverbs are derived [GrHL 8.9]:

- *kuwat* "why?"
- *kuwatka* "perhaps"
- *kuwapi* 1. "when, where," 2. "sometime, somewhere"
- *kuwapikki* "somewhere, ever"
- *kuitman* "when, as long as, until."

The nom.-acc. sing. neut. *kuit* can also be used as a subordinating conjunction "since, because, concerning the fact that."

## 6.3 Ablauting verbs Id, Ie, and If

### 6.3.1

Besides the verbs with an Ablaut -*e*-/-*a*- (Ib) discussed in Lesson 4.3, there are two other groups of *mi*-verbs with a change in the stem: those with an **Ablaut** -*e*-/-Ø- (Id) [GrHL 12.5–7] and those with an interchange -*n*-/-Ø- (Ie) [GrHL 12.8–9].

In the **conjugation Id** (-*e*-/-Ø-) the forms without -*e*- are the 3. plur. pres. (*kunanzi* "they kill" from *kuen*-) and the participle in -*ant*- (*kunant*- "(having been) killed," see Lesson 5.3.3). Originally, the entire plural was -*e*-less, but there was a strong tendency to restore the -*e*- in the rest of the paradigm.

In the **conjugation Ie** (-*n*-/-Ø-) we have verbs ending in -*nk*- or -*nḫ*-; the nasal in the stem is regularly dropped when the ending starts with a consonant: compare 3. plur. pres. *link-anzi* as opposed to 3. sing. pres. *lik-zi*. By analogy, however, the nasal may be restored: e.g., *linkzi*.

Examples: *ḫuek-*/*ḫuk-* "to slaughter; to cast a spell," *kuen-*/*kun-* "to kill, destroy" for Id, *link-*/*lik-* "to swear an oath," supplemented by *ḫarnink-*/*ḫarnik-* "to destroy," and *šanḫ-*/*šaḫ-* "to search, look for" for Ie.

| | | Id | Id | Ie | Ie |
|---|---|---|---|---|---|
| **Pres.** | | | | | |
| **Sing.** | 1 | *ḫuekmi* | *kuemi* | | *šanḫmi* |
| | 2 | | *kueši, kuenti* | | *šanḫti* |
| | 3 | *ḫuekzi* | *kuenzi* | *likzi, linkzi* | *šaḫzi, šanḫzi* |
| **Plur.** | 1 | *ḫuekkueni* | | *linkueni* | *šanḫueni* |
| | 2 | | | | *šaḫteni* |
| | 3 | *ḫukanzi* | *kunanzi* | *linkanzi* | *šanḫanzi* |

| | Id | Id | Ie | Ie |
|---|---|---|---|---|
| **Pret.** | | | | |
| **Sing.** 1 | | *kuenun* | *linkun* | *šanḫun* |
| 2 | | | *(ḫarnikta)* | |
| 3 | *ḫuekta* | *kuenta* | *likta, linkta* | *šanḫta* |
| **Plur.** 1 | | *kuewen* | *linkuen, lingawen* | |
| 2 | | | *likten* | |
| 3 | | *kuenner* | *linker* | *šanḫer* |
| **Participle** | *ḫukant-* | *kunant-* | *linkant-* | *šanḫant-* |

- In the 2. sing. pres. the *ḫi*-ending *-ti* occurs frequently (*kuenti, šanḫti*).
- For the loss of the nasal in *kuemi, kueši* and *kuewen*, see Lesson 6.5 below.
- The form *šanḫti* shows the irregular restoration of the *-n-* which we also find elsewhere: e.g., *linkzi, linkta.* The resulting clusters *-nkt-* and *-nḫt-* are spelled differently: for *link-* one finds mostly *li-in-ik-t*V-, for *šanḫ-* either *ša-an-aḫ-t*V- or *ša-na-aḫ-t*V-.
- The medio-passive of the conjugation Ie (*-n-*/-Ø-) follows the same rule; compare 3. sing. and plur. pres. of *tamenk-/tamek-* "to stick to": *tamektari* and *tamenkantari.*
- Medio-passive forms for Id (*-e-*/-Ø-) are not attested.
- As a passive for *kuen-/kun-* "to kill" the verb *akk-* "to die" (IIa) is used.

### 6.3.2

An isolated verb is ***ḫark-/ḫar-*** "to hold, have" (**If**) [GrHL 12.10]. Whenever the verbal ending starts with a consonant, the final *-k-* of the stem is dropped: e.g., *ḫar-mi* "I hold" vs. *ḫark-anzi* "they hold." Except for the intrusion, again, of the 2. sing. pres. ending *-ti* from the *ḫi*-conjugation (compare Lesson 6.3.1), the inflection is otherwise regular:

| | Pres. Sing. | Plur. | Pret. Sing. | Plur. |
|---|---|---|---|---|
| 1 | *ḫarmi* | *ḫarweni* | *ḫarkun* | *ḫarwen* |
| 2 | *ḫarši, ḫarti* | *ḫarteni* | | *ḫarten* |
| 3 | *ḫarzi* | *ḫarkanzi* | *ḫarta* | *ḫarker* |

This verb is important because of its frequent combination with the participle, for which see Lesson 6.4.2. Watch out for the verb ***ḫark-*** (Ia) "to perish" that never loses its *-k-*!

| Present | | Preterite | |
|---|---|---|---|
| **Sing.** 1 *ḫarkmi* | **Plur.** 1 *ḫarkueni* | **Sing.** 1 *ḫarkun* | **Plur.** 1 *ḫarkuen* |
| 2 *harkši* | 2 *ḫarkteni* | 2 *ḫarkta* | 2 *ḫarkten* |
| 3 *ḫarkzi* | 3 *ḫarkanzi* | 3 *ḫarkta* | 3 *ḫarker* |

- The cluster /-rkC-/ is usually spelled *ḫar-ak-CV*.

## 6.4 Syntax and semantics

### 6.4.1

Hittite **relative clauses** [GrHL 30.58–64] usually precede the main clause they depend on, as in the following example:

| | | | | | |
|---|---|---|---|---|---|
| | *nu* | DUMU-*an kuin* | *ḫuekmi* | *n=an=kan* | *tēmi* |
| lit. | | "what child | I treat magically, | that (child) | I will call." |

In normal English this would be: "I will call the child that/whom I treat magically." The part "that/whom I treat magically" is the relative clause, introduced by the relative pronoun "that." The latter refers back to "the child" in the main clause, which we call the antecedent. From the Hittite example and the literal translation it can be seen that in Hittite the antecedent (the child = DUMU-*an*) stands within the relative clause (*nu* DUMU-*an kuin ḫuekmi*) and is taken up in the following main clause (*n=<u>an</u>=kan tēmi*) by the enclitic personal pronoun *-an* (*n=<u>an</u>=kan*) "it/that (one)." So we get:

| | |
|---|---|
| *nu* DUMU-*an kuin ḫuekmi* | *n=an=kan tēmi* |
| RELATIVE CLAUSE | MAIN CLAUSE |
| antecedent | |
| relative | pron. (referring back to antecedent) |

- Instead of the enclitic personal pronoun *-a-* (Lesson 2.2) we also frequently find the pronoun *apā-* (Lesson 5.2) used in the main clause to refer to the relative and the antecedent (see an example immediately below).
- Sometimes there is nothing in the main clause referring back, and we have to supply it ourselves from the context.

Depending on the position of the relative pronoun in the relative clause, Hittite is able to distinguish between *determinate and indeterminate relative clauses.* A determinate relative clause speaks about an antecedent which was introduced earlier in the text and is therefore familiar to the reader. In the above example the priest is referring not to just any child, but to a specific child under his care.

But in the following sequence a king gives a *general* rule for succession whenever a king dies:

| | |
|---|---|
| *nu kuiš tān pēdaš* DUMU-RU | *nu* LUGAL-*uš apāš kišari* |
| "who<u>ever</u> (is) a son of second rank, | that one will become king." |

Here, it should be noted, the relative pronoun comes in so-called *first position*, preceded only by the connective *nu*. Whether or not the connective is followed by any clitics is of no importance. The relative pronoun might also have stood in *initial position*, that is, it could have been the very first word of the clause without even a connective in front (*kuiš tān pēdaš* etc.). The indeterminate nature of such clauses can be stressed in the translation by using words like "who*ever*." In our first example above, however, the relative pronoun was preceded by yet another constituent (DUMU-*an*) and, as a consequence, marks a determinate relative clause. As a rule it can be stated that *whenever the relative pronoun stands in initial or first position, the relative clause is indeterminate; if it comes in any later position, it is determinate.*

6.4.2

The combination of the verb *ḫark-/ḫar-* "to have, hold" and the nom.-acc. sing. neuter of a participle can be used as a **periphrastic perfect** ("I have done") [GrHL 22.19–25]: *nu=za=kan* $\text{GU}_4$ *kunan ḫarzi* "he has killed the ox." Originally it literally meant "to hold someone/something in a certain state," a meaning sometimes still noticeable: *nu=za* LUGAL KUR.KUR.MEŠ LÚ.KÚR *taruḫḫan ḫarta* "the king held (*ḫarta*) the enemy countries subjected/in subjection (*taruḫḫan*)." That *ḫark-/ḫar-* eventually lost this meaning and developed into a real auxiliary verb is shown by combinations with an intransitive verb like, for instance, *paršnae-* "to kneel (down)" (where there is no object to hold): e.g., $^{\text{LÚ}}$*ḫeštā ... paršnān ḫarta* "the *ḫeštā*-man had knelt down (by the hearth)."

## 6.5 Phonology

6.5.1

When a **nasal** is followed by a dorsal (*k*, *g*) or a laryngeal (*ḫ*) + stop (C), it is regularly dropped, as we saw in Lesson 6.3.1 [GrHL 1.135]. Likewise, a nasal before *š*, another nasal (*m*), or a glide (*w*) is lost: compare above *kueši*, *kuemi*, and *kuewen* from **kuenši*, **kuenmi*, and **kuenwen* respectively. Nasals in general were apparently rather weakly pronounced; in places where they are expected, such as in the *nt*-stems, they are often not written: *ḫu-u-ma-da-az* for *ḫūma<u>n</u>daz*. These spellings may point at a frequent nasalization of vowels in the spoken language ([ḫūmãdats]).

Hittite cannot have a word ending in a resonant + a stop – thus the loss of the final dental in the nom.-acc. sing. com. of the *nt*-stems: compare Lesson 5.1.1 on *ḫūman, walḫan* etc.

## 6.6 Akkadian

### 6.6.1

Besides Sumerian and Akkadian nominal forms and grammatical elements, Hittite scribes also regularly used some Akkadian **verb forms**. The most common ones are listed here:

| | |
|---|---|
| *ADDIN* | "I gave" |
| *AQBI* | "I said" |
| *AṢBAT* | "I took, seized" |
| *AŠPUR* | "I wrote, sent" |
| *IDDIN* | "he gave" |
| *IMUR* | "he saw" |
| *IQBI* | "he said" |
| *IṢBAT* | "he took, seized" |
| *IŠME* | "he heard" |
| *IŠPUR* | "he wrote, sent" |
| *IŠṬUR* | "he wrote" |
| *QIBI* | "speak!" |

## 6.7 Cuneiform signs

tu  te 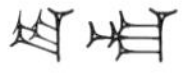 li 

in  šar 

me  MEŠ 

a  za  ḫa 

## 6.8 Exercises; KBo 3.4 ii 33–56

### 6.8.1 Translate:

1. *ku-e* GAL.ḪI.A *ak-ku-uš-ke-ez-zi ta a-pé-e-pát e-ku-zi*
2. (from a prayer) *nu ke-e-ta-aš A-NA* KUR.KUR.ḪI.A *šu-me-en-za-an ŠA* É.ḪI.A DINGIR.MEŠ-*KU-NU ku-e e-eš-ta na-at* LÚ.MEŠ URU*Ga-aš-ga ar-ḫa pí-ip-pé-er* ("have destroyed")
3. *nu-kán* NAM.RA.ḪI.A *ku-iš* $GU_4$ UDU *an-da e-eš-ta na-an ḫu-u-ma-an-da-an e-ep-ta* (note: take NAM.RA.ḪI.A and $GU_4$ UDU as subject)

4. *na-aš-ta* DINGIR.MEŠ *ḫu-u-ma-an-du-us lam-ni-it ḫal-za-a-i*
5. (from a ritual) *na-aš-ta* $^{\text{DUG}}$*iš-nu-u-re-eš ku-e-ez* *IŠ-TU* GADA DINGIR-*LIM* *ka-ri-ia-an-te-eš na-at* *PA-NI* $^{\text{LÚ}}$EN É-*TIM* *ša-ra-a ap-pa-an-zi*
6. *nu nam-ma* $^{d}$*Ḫé-pa-du-uš* DINGIR.MEŠ-*aš ḫa-lu-ga-an Ú-UL iš-ta-ma-aš-zi*
7. (from prayer to the Sun deity) *nu mi-e-ú-uš* (add: animals) *ku-i-uš* $^{d}$UTU-*uš* *tu-u-ri-ia-an ḫar-ši nu-uš-ma-aš ka-a-ša* DUMU.NAM.LÚ.U$_{19}$.LU-*aš ḫal-ki-in šu-uḫ-ḫa-aš* ("[he/she] has poured")
8. (from prayer to the Sun goddess of Arinna) *nu-un-na-aš* $^{d}$UTU $^{\text{URU}}$PÚ-*na* GAŠAN-*IA* *ku-e-da-ni pí-di ti-it-ta-nu-ut na-at tu-el a-aš-ši-ia-an-ta-aš* DUMU-*aš* *ŠA* $^{d}$IM $^{\text{URU}}$*Ne-ri-ik* *AŠ-RU* (supply a form of *eš-/aš-* "to be")
9. *nu-un-na-aš* *A-BU-IA* *an-da ar-nu-ut nu-un-na-aš le-en-qa-nu-ut*
10. *ša-an-kán e-ep-per* *QA-DU* DUMU.MEŠ-*ŠU-ia ku-en-ner*
11. *nu-mu* $^{d}$IŠTAR GAŠAN-*IA* *ku-it ka-ni-iš-ša-an ḫar-ta* ŠEŠ-*IA*-*ia-mu* $^{\text{m}}$NIR.GÁL *a-aš-šu ḫar-ta*
12. *nu-uš-kán ma-a-an ku-e-mi ma-a-nu-uš ar-nu-mi*
13. (omen: "if so-and-so happens, then ...") *nu* É.DINGIR-*LIM* *im-ma* 1-*an ḫar-ak-zi* $^{\text{URU}}$*Ḫa-at-tu-ša-aš-ma* LUGAL-*aš a-aš-šu* UL *ḫar-ak-zi*
14. EGIR-*an*("from behind")-*ma-an-kán* LÚ.KÚR *ku-en-ta*
15. É.MEŠ.DINGIR.MEŠ-*kán pa-ra-a ša-an-ḫa-an-zi*
16. *nam-ma ku-e-da-ni pí-di* *ŠA* $^{\text{GIŠ}}$KIRI$_{6}$.GEŠTIN $^{d}$*Ma-li-ia-an-ni-uš a-ša-an-zi nu* $^{d}$*Ma-li-ia-an-na-aš pé-ra-an te-kán pád-da-aḫ-ḫi*
17. *nu-za-kán* *A-NA* $^{\text{GIŠ}}$GU.ZA *A-BI-IA* *ku-wa-pí e-eš-ḫa-at nu-za ke-e a-ra-aḫ-zé-na-aš* KUR.KUR.MEŠ $^{\text{LÚ}}$KÚR *I-NA* MU.10.KAM *tar-uḫ-ḫu-un na-at-kán ku-e-nu-un*
18. *nu-wa-za zi-ik* LUGAL.GAL *am-mu-uk-ma-wa-kán* 1-*EN* *ḪAL-ZI* *ku-in da-li-ia-at nu-wa-za* *ŠA* 1-*EN* *ḪAL-ZI* LUGAL-*uš*

### 6.8.2

Read and transliterate the following sign combinations:

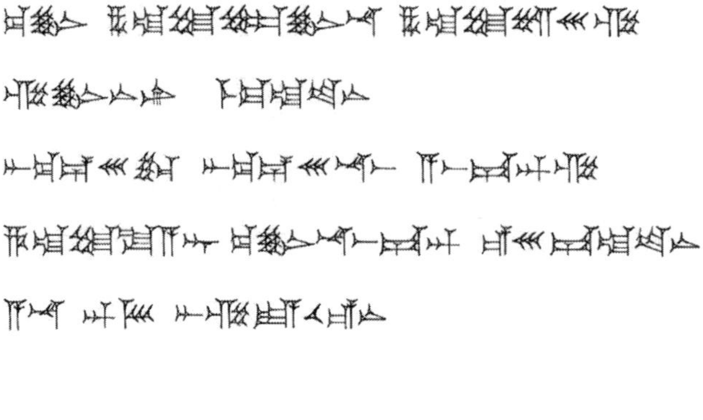

## Words for Lesson 6

| | |
|---|---|
| *anda*(*n*) | in(to), inside |
| *araḫzena-* | foreign, hostile |
| *arnu-* (Ia) | to bring |
| *anda arnu-* | to bring together |
| *aššiyant-* | beloved |
| *aššu* | (neut. plur.) goods |
| *dalae-*/*daliya-* (Ic) | to abandon, leave |
| *ḫaluga-*, com./ | message |
| *ḫark-* (Ia) | to perish |
| *imma* (adv.) | (emphasizing adv.) |
| *kappuwauwar*, neut. | count(ing) |
| *kariya-* (Ic) | to cover |
| *kuwapi* (conj., adv.) | 1. where(to)<br>2. somewhere<br>3. when |
| *laman*, neut. | name |
| *mān* … *mān* … | either … or … |
| *memiya*(*n*)-, com. neut. | word, matter, deed |
| *miu-* | four |
| *padda-* (IIc) | to dig |
| *peda-*, neut. | place, position |
| *šnaḫ-* | to search, to sweep |
| *šumenzan* | see Lesson 3.2.1 |
| *tekan*, neut. | earth, ground |
| *tittanu-* (Ia) | to place, install |
| *turiya-* (Ic) | to harness |
| *uwate-* (Ia) | to bring, lead |
| 1-*an*/1-*EN* | one, only, single |

| | |
|---|---|
| DUMU.NAM.LÚ.$U_{19}$.LU | mortal, human being |
| É.DINGIR | temple |
| GADA | cloth, textile |
| $GU_4$ | ox, bovine |
| $^{GIŠ}KIRI_6$.GEŠTIN | vineyard |
| KUR.KUR | lands |
| NAM.RA | inhabitant, deportee |
| NU.GÁL | there is no(t) |
| UDU | sheep |
| *AŠRU* | = *peda-* |
| *ḪALZU* | fortress |
| *IŠTU* | out of, by, with |
| (*ANA*) *PANI* | = *ANA* |

**DN**

| | |
|---|---|
| $^{d}$UTU-*u-* | Ištanu, the Sun deity |
| $^{d}$UTU $^{URU}$PÚ-*na* | the Sun goddess of (the town) Arinna |
| $^{d}$*Ḫepadu-* | Ḫepat |
| $^{d}$*Maliyanneš*/*-nniuš* | (plur.) |

**GN**

| | |
|---|---|
| $^{URU}$*Nerik* | Nerik (an important Hittite cult center in the north) |
| $^{URU}$KÙ.BABBAR | = Ḫattuša, Ḫatti |

### 6.8.3 *The Ten-Year Annals* of the Hittite King Muršili II

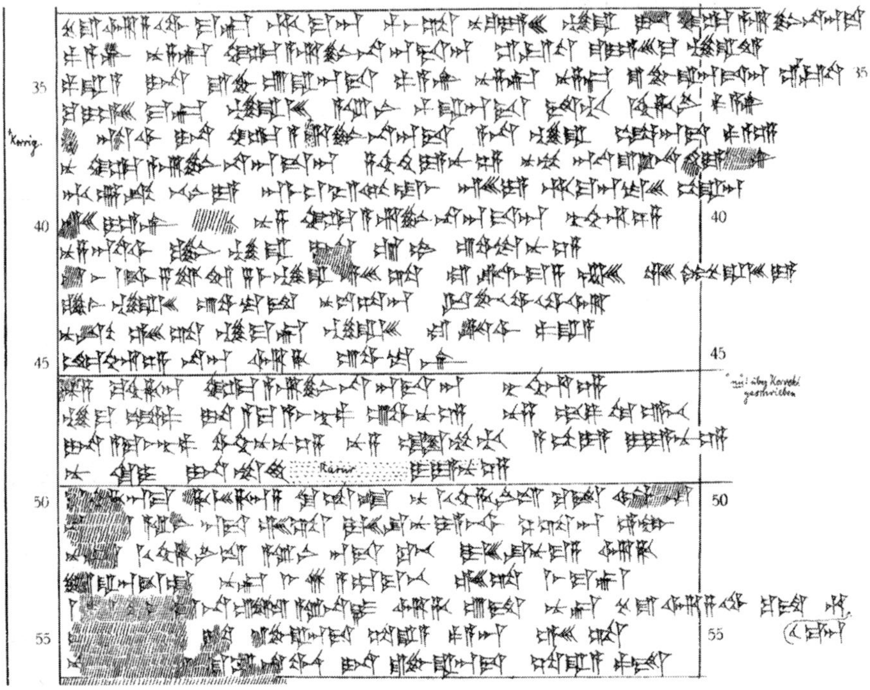

Figure 7

ii

33. KUR $^{URU}$*Ar-za-u-wa-ma-kán ḫu-u-ma-an pár-aš-ta nu ku-i-e-eš* NAM.RA *I-* ⌈*NA*⌉ $^{ḪUR.SAG}$*A-ri-in-na-an-da*
34. *pa-a-er nu-za-kán* $^{ḪUR.SAG}$*A-ri-in-na-an-da-an e-ep-per ku-i-e-eš-ma* NAM.RA.ḪI.A
35. *pa-ra-a I-NA* $^{URU}$*Pu-ú-ra-an-da pa-a-er nu-za-kán* ‹‹nu-za-kán›› $^{URU}$*Pu-ra-an-da-an e-ep-per*
36. *ku-i-e-eš-ma-kán* NAM.RA.MEŠ *a-ru-ni pár-ra-an-da IT-TI* $^{m}$*Uḫ-ḫa-*LÚ *pa-a-er*
37. ⌈*nu*⌉ $^{d}$⌈UTU⌉ *-ŠI I-NA* $^{ḪUR.SAG}$*A-ri-in-na-an-da A-NA* NAM.RA EGIR-*an-da pa-a-un*
38. *nu* $^{ḪUR.SAG}$*A-ri-in-na-an-da-an za-aḫ-ḫi-ia-nu-un nu-mu* $^{d}$UTU $^{URU}$ ⌈PÚ⌉ *-na* ⌈GAŠAN⌉ *-IA* ‹‹[o?] er››
39. $^{d}$U NIR.GÁL *BE-LÍ-IA* $^{d}$*Me-ez-zu-ul-la-aš* DINGIR.MEŠ-*ia ḫu-u-ma-an-te-eš pé-ra-an*
40. *ḫu!-u!*[1]*-i-e-er* erasure *nu-za* $^{ḪUR.SAG}$*A-ri-in-na-an-da-an tar-uḫ-ḫu-un*

[1] Tablet has DINGIR.MEŠ.

41. *nu-za* ᵈUTU-*ŠI* *ku-in* NAM.RA ⸢*I-NA*⸣ É.LUGAL *ú-wa-te-nu-un*
42. ⸢*na*⸣ *-aš* 1 $SIG_7$ 5 *LI-IM* 5 ME NAM.RA ⸢*e*⸣ *-eš-ta* ᵁᴿᵁKÙ.BABBAR-*aš-ma-za* EN.MEŠ ÉRIN.MEŠ ANŠE.KUR.RA.MEŠ-*ia*
43. *ku-in* NAM.RA.MEŠ *ú-wa-te-et nu-uš-ša-an kap-pu-u-wa-u-wa-ar*
44. NU. ⸢GÁL⸣ *e-eš-ta nam-ma-kán* NAM.RA.MEŠ ᵁᴿᵁ ⸢KÙ⸣ .BABBAR-*ši pa-ra-a*
45. *ne-eḫ-ḫu-un na-an ar-ḫa ú-wa-te-er*

---

46. *nu-za*[2] *ma-aḫ-ḫa-an* ᴴᵁᴿ.ˢᴬᴳ*A-ri-in-na-an-da-an tar-uḫ-ḫu-un*
47. *nam-ma* EGIR-*pa* *I-NA* ᴵᴰ*A-aš-tar-pa ú-wa-nu-un nu-za* BÀD.KARAŠ
48. *I-NA* ᴵᴰ*Aš-tar-pa wa-aḫ-nu-nu-un nu-za* $EZEN_4$ *MU-TI a-pí-ya i-ia-nu-un*
49. *nu ki-i* *I-NA* MU.1.KAM erasure *i-ia-nu-un*

---

50. ⸢*ma-aḫ-ḫa*⸣ *-an-ma* <u>*ḫa-me-eš-ḫa-an-za*</u> *ki-ša-at nu* ᵐ*U-uḫ-ḫa*-LÚ-*iš ku-it* ⸢GIG-*at*⸣
51. ⸢*na*⸣ [*-aš-ká*]*n a-ru-* ⸢*ni*⸣ *an-da e-eš-ta* DUMU.MEŠ-*ŠU-NU-ia-aš-ši kat-ta-an* <u>*e-šer*</u>
52. *nu-* ⸢*kán*⸣ ᵐ*U-uḫ-ḫa*-LÚ-*iš a-ru-ni an-da* BA.ÚŠ DUMU.MEŠ-*ŠU-NU-ma-za ar-ḫa*
53. <u>⸢*šar*⸣ *-ra-an-da-at*</u> *nu-kán* 1-*aš* ŠÀ A.AB.BA-*pát e-eš-ta* 1-*aš-ma-kán*
54. ᵐ ⸢*Ta-pa-la-zu*⸣ *-na-ú-li-iš a-ru-na-az ar-ḫa ú-it nu-kán* KUR ᵁᴿᵁ*Ar-za-u-wa ku-it ḫu-u-ma-an*
55. x [ o o o o ] ⸢*I-NA* ᵁᴿᵁ⸣ *Pu-ra-an-da ša-ra-a pa-a-an e-eš-ta*
56. *nu*[*-kán* ᵐ*Ta-p*]*a*[*-l*]*a-* ⸢*zu-na*⸣ *-wa-liš* *I-NA* ᵁᴿᵁ*Pu-ra-an-da ša-ra-a pait*

---

## Questions

1. Identify in the handcopy the cuneiform signs given in this and the previous Lessons.
2. Parse the underlined forms.
3. Translate the text with the notes below.

## Words

| | |
|---|---|
| 33. *pāer* | "(they) went/had gone" |
| 33, 34, 36 *kuiēš* | "some …, others …, others" (cf. Lesson 7.4.2) |
| 36. *parranda* | across, over |

---

[2] *nu-za* written over erasure.

| | |
|---|---|
| *ITTI* | together with |
| 37. EGIR-*anda* (*appanda*) | after, behind |
| *pāun* | "I went" |
| 41. *uwate-* (Ia) | to bring, lead |
| 42. SIG$_7$ | 10,000 |
| *LIM* | 1000 |
| ME | 100 |
| 43. *kappūwauwar*, neut. | counting |
| 44. NU.GÁL (*ēš-*) | there is no(t) |
| 44-45 *parā neḫḫun* | "I sent" |
| 47. *uwanun* | "I came" |
| BÀD.KARAŠ | army camp |
| 48. *waḫnu-* (Ia) | to turn, move |
| EZEN$_4$ | cultic celebration, (religious) festival |
| *apiya* | there, then |
| 50. *ḫamešḫant-*, com. | spring |
| 51. DUMU.MEŠ-*ŠU-NU* | (here and in line 52) translate as DUMU.MEŠ-*ŠU*(-) |
| *kattan* | with, next to (with dat.-loc.) |
| 52. BA.ÚŠ | "he died" |
| 52-53. *arḫa šarrandat* | "(they) split up" |
| 53. A.AB.BA | sea |
| 54. *uit* | "(he) came" |
| 55. *pān ēšta* | "had gone" |
| 56. *pait* | "(he) went" |

# Lesson 7

## 7.1 *-r-/-n-* or heteroclitic noun stems

### 7.1.1

There is a large class of neuter nouns with a nom.-acc. sing. ending in *-r*, Ablauting with an oblique stem in *-n-*, that are called *-r-/-n-* or **heteroclitic noun stems**: e.g., nom.-acc. sing. neut. *meḫur* with an oblique stem *meḫun-* (gen. *meḫun-aš*, dat.-loc. *meḫun-i* etc.).

This *-r-/-n-* declension can be roughly divided into two groups: one with a nom.-acc. sing. neut. in -C*ar*, changing with an obl. stem in -C*n*- (Lesson 7.1.2) [GrHL 4.104–113], and a second with a nom.-acc. sing. neut. in -C*ar*/-C*ur*, changing with an obl. stem in -CV*n*- (Lesson 7.1.3) [GrHL 4.101–103]. So, whereas the vowel preceding the *-r* of the nom.-acc. sing. is dropped in the oblique stem of the first group, the second group retains a vowel in the oblique stem.

### 7.1.2

The first group with the Ablaut -C*ar*/-C*n*- contains four types of noun:

**A** nom.-acc. sing. *-tar* – gen. (*-tnaš* ›) *-nnaš* (e.g., *paprātar, paprannaš* "defilement, uncleanness"; for the assimilation *-tnaš* › *-nnaš* see Lesson 7.5.2)
**B** nom.-acc. sing. *-šar* – gen. *-šnaš* (e.g., *ḫanneššar, ḫannešnaš* "trial, lawsuit," *uppeššar, uppešnaš* (lit. sending -›) "gift")
**C** nom.-acc. sing. *-war* – gen. *-unaš* (e.g., *partawar, partaunaš* "wing")
**D** nom.-acc. sing. *-mar* – gen. *-mnaš* (e.g., *ḫilammar, ḫilamnaš* "portico").

- The nouns in *-tar* (A) are predominantly abstract nouns co-occurring with causatives in *-aḫḫ-* (see Lesson 2.4.2), often derived from adjectives: e.g., *idalu-/idalaw-* "bad, evil" › *idalawaḫḫ-* "treat badly" › *idalawatar* "evil, evil treatment."
- Similarly, the nouns in *-šar* (B) can be connected to fientives and statives in *-ešš-* (see Lesson 2.4.2): *parkui-* "clean" › *parkuešš-* "to be(come) clean" › *parkueššar* "purity."
- The declension for all four types A–D is identical, but note the assimilation of the dental in *-tar* (A) into *-n-* in the oblique stem **-tnaš* › *-nnaš*.
- It should also be noted that the intervocalic sonant *-w-* in *-war* (C) changes into the vowel *-u-* before the *-n-* of the oblique stem: *-awar/-awn-* -› *-aun-*.
- For a special function of the allative of nouns in *-tar* (A), see Lesson 7.3.3.

- The plural is only poorly attested; originally, the final syllable of the nom.-acc. plur. was lengthened, as opposed to the short singular: sing. *-ar* vs. plur. *-ār*. Sometimes this can be recognized by a plene spelling: *-a-ar*.
- Possibly, this lengthening explains the loss of the final *-r* (*paprata*) which can be observed in a number of instances in the older language. If so, this *-r* was restored again afterwards.
- Occasionally, we also find a plural ending *-i* of unknown origin (e.g., *zanki-latarri*ḪI.A; for the ending, see already Lesson 1.1.1). Very often, however, the nom.-acc. plur. is identical to the sing. and is distinguishable only by the Sumerian plural morpheme ḪI.A added to the Hittite word (e.g., *uppeššar*ḪI.A "gifts").

The declension is as follows (the paradigm of *papratar* is supplemented by the allative of *appatar* "(the act of) capturing, capture," for which see Lesson 7.3.3; similarly, *zankilatar* in the nom.-acc. pl. neut., and *ḫaršauwar* "harvest" in the *partauwar* paradigm):

| | A | B | C | D |
|---|---|---|---|---|
| **Sing.** | | | | |
| nom.-acc. | *papratar* | *ḫanneššar* | *partawar* | *ḫilammar* |
| gen. | *paprannaš* | *ḫannešnaš* | *partaunaš* | *ḫilamnaš* |
| dat.-loc. | *papranni* | *ḫannešni* | *partauni* | *ḫilamni* |
| all. | (*appanna*) | | | *ḫilamna* |
| abl. | *paprannaz* | *ḫannešnaz* | *partaunaz* | *ḫilamnaz* |
| instr. | | *ḫannešnit* | *partaunit* | |
| **Plur.** | | | | |
| nom.-acc. | *paprata* (*zankilatarri*ḪI.A) | *uppeššar*ḪI.A | | |
| dat.-loc. | | | (*ḫaršaunaš*) | |

## 7.1.3

Whereas in the above group the final *-a-* of the nom.-acc. sing. is lost in the oblique stem (cf. *-šar* vs. *-šn-*), in the second group discussed here a vowel remains. If the nom.-acc. sing. had *-a-*, that vowel can be either *-a-* (*uddar/uddan-*) or *-e-* (*watar/weten-*); it remains *-u-* (*meḫur/meḫun-*) or turns into *-ue-* (*paḫḫur/paḫḫuen-*), if the nom.-acc. sing. had a *-u-*. The latter two variants can exist side by side (*paḫḫun-* and *paḫḫuen-*).

Examples: *uddar* "word, deed, thing" (INIM; but see Lesson 6.1.2), *watar* "water" (A), and *meḫur* "time, moment, period."

| | | | |
|---|---|---|---|
| **Sing.** | | | |
| nom.-acc. | *uddar* | *watar* | *meḫur* |
| gen. | *uddanaš* | *wetenaš* | *meḫunaš* |
| dat.-loc. | *uddani* | *weteni* | *meḫuni, meḫueni* |
| all. | | *wetena* | |
| abl. | *uddanaz* | *wetenaz* | |
| instr. | *uddanit, uddanta* | *wedanda, wetenit* | |
| **Plur.** | | | |
| nom.-acc. | *uddār* | *widār* | *meḫurri*ḪI.A |
| gen., dat.-loc. | *uddanaš* | A.ḪI.A-*aš* | *meḫunaš* |

- The form *wedanda* is an archaic instr., for which see Lessons 1.1.1, 6.1.1 (*išḫimanta*).
- Note the double Ablaut in *watar* vs. *weten-* (the latter is also spelled *witen-*).
- Besides this *-r-/-n-*stem there is also a short stem *wit-*: e.g., dat.-loc. sing. *witi* "in the water."
- The Hittite word for "blood" *ešḫar/ešḫan-* occasionally has an oblique stem *ešn-* (gen. *ešnaš*).

## 7.2 Indefinite pronoun *kuiški*

### 7.2.1

The **indefinite pronoun** ("any-/someone, any-/something, some,") [GrHL 8.3–8] is derived from the relative stem *kui-* (see Lesson 6.2.1) by adding an indeclinable suffix *-ki/-ka* to the inflected form: *kuiš-ki, kuel-ka.* The inflection is that of the relative pronoun. It can be used both substantively ("someone, something") and adjectivally ("some …, a certain …"). For syntax involving indefinite pronouns, see Lesson 7.4.1.

| | **Sing.** | **Plur.** |
|---|---|---|
| nom. com. | *kuiški* | *kuieška* |
| acc. com. | *kuinki* | *kuiuška* |
| nom.-acc. neut. | *kuitki* | *kueka, kuekki* |
| gen. | *kuelka* | |
| dat.-loc. | *kuedanikki* | *kuedaška* |
| abl. | *kuezka* | |

- The *-ka* seems to be written mostly with the sign $KA_4$/QA, and is found in the gen. sing., the abl., and in the plural.

## 7.3 Ablauting verbs IIb, Ig, and infinitive II

### 7.3.1

After some classes of Ablauting *mi*-verbs in the previous two lessons, we now turn to *ḫi*-verbs with similar patterns. The first of these is a class with an Ablaut *-a-/-e-* **(IIb)**, that is, with *-a-* originally in the singular and *-e-* in the plural [GrHL 13.1–2]. This system is frequently abandoned, however, with *-a-* intruding in the plural and *-e-* in the singular.

Examples: *šakk-/šekk-* "to know," *ḫaš-/ḫeš-* "to open," and *ašaš-/ašeš-* "to settle, make sit down."

| | | | |
|---|---|---|---|
| **Present** | | | |
| **Sing.** 1 | *šākḫi* | | *ašašḫi* |
| 2 | *šākti* | | *ašašti* |
| 3 | *šākki* | *ḫāši, ḫašzi, ḫešzi* | *ašaši* |
| **Plur.** 1 | | | |
| 2 | *šekteni, šakteni* | | |
| 3 | | *ḫešanzi, ḫaššanzi* | *ašešanzi* |
| **Preterite** | | | |
| **Sing.** 1 | | *ḫašḫun* | *ašašḫun* |
| 3 | *šakkiš* | *ḫašta* | *ašašta, ašešta* |
| **Plur.** 1 | | *ḫešuwen* | |
| 3 | *šekker* | *ḫešer, ḫašer* | *ašešer, ašašer* |
| **Medio-pass. pret.** 3. sing. | | *ḫeštat* | |
| **Participle** | *šakkant-* | *ḫaššant-, ḫešant-* | *ašešant-* |

- Note the intrusion of the 3. sing. pres. *-mi*-conjugation ending *-zi* in *ḫa/ešzi.*
- The verb *ar/er-* "to arrive" can be easily confused with *ar-* (Ia) "to stand," even though no forms are the same, because *ar-* "to stand" is a deponent (see Lesson 3.3.2); for the two verbs in the same sentence, see Lesson 7.7.1 sentence 6 below.

### 7.3.2

There is only one verb of the *mi*-conjugation showing the same Ablaut with *-a-* in the singular and *-e-* in the plural: *damašš-/damešš-* **(Ig)** "to oppress." Here too we see analogy at work, with *-a-* and *-e-* turning up where they were not at home originally.

| | Sing. | Plur. |
|---|---|---|
| **Active** | | |
| **Present** 1 | *tamašmi* | |
| 2 | *tamašti* | |
| 3 | *tamašzi, dammešzi* | *dameššanzi, tamaššanzi* |
| **Preterite** 1 | *damaššun* | *tameššuwen* |
| 3 | *damašta, dammešta* | *tameššer, tamaššer* |
| **Medio-pass.** | | |
| **Present** 3 | *damašta(ri)* | |
| **Preterite** 3 | *tamaštat* | |
| **Participle** | *tameššant-, damaššant-* | |

### 7.3.3

The original allative case -*(a)nna* of the nouns in -*(a)tar* (see Lesson 7.1.2 A) developed into an infinitive, the so-called **infinitive II** (for the infinitive I, see Lesson 10.3.2) [GrHL 11.18–24]. This infinitive is mostly formed from Ablauting *mi*-verbs of classes Ib (*ed-/ad-* "to eat") and Id (*kuen-/kun-* "to kill"). In these cases the infinitive is formed on the "downgraded" stem: *adanna, kunanna.*

The meaning is mainly final: *epp-/app-* "to take, capture" -› *appatar* "(the act of) capturing" -› all. *appanna* "to(wards) capturing -› to capture." E.g., URU*Nerikkan* URU-*an appanna* UL *kuiški šanḫta* "nobody strived towards capturing -›nobody sought to capture the town of Nerik," ANA d*Kumarbi* GIŠ*ḫašalli ašanna tianzi* "they put down a chair (GIŠ*ḫašalli*) for Kumarbi towards sitting on -› to sit on."

## 7.4 Syntax and semantics

### 7.4.1

If a clause is introduced by the **conditional** conjunction *mān* "if" or by a relative pronoun (*kui-* Lesson 6.2.1), and if that clause contains a form of the **indefinite pronoun** (*kuiški, kuitki* etc., Lesson 7.2), the latter may shed its suffix -*ki/-ka* [GrHL 8.1]. Compare e.g.:

- with -*ki/-ka*: *kinun=a mān* DUMU.LUGAL *kuiški waštai* "but if now some (*kuiški*) prince commits a sin"
- vs. without: *nu=kan mān* INA É.LUGAL *kuit ḫurtiyaš uttar nūwa* EGIR-*an* "if in the palace there still (is left) behind some (*kuit*) word of cursing."

The following example illustrates the leaving-out of *-ki/-ka* in a relative sentence: *kuiš=ma=za* ŠA *MAMETI* *kuedani kišari* "but whoever becomes (a man) of the oath (i.e., a sworn comrade) to somebody, …" with *kuedani* instead of *kuedanikki*.

### 7.4.2

The **relative pronoun** sometimes occurs in a pair or in a series (*kui-* … *kui-*), meaning "one … the other/another … (yet another … )" or "some … others … (again others … )"; compare already Lesson 6.8.3 lines 33–36 or the following passage:

> *nu* KUR.KUR.ḪI.A LÚ.KÚR *kue šullanta*
> *kuēš=kan tuk* ANA $^{d}$*Telipinu* Ù ANA DINGIR.MEŠ $^{URU}$*Ḫatti* UL *naḫḫanteš*
> *kuēš=ma* BIBRI$^{ḪI.A}$ GAL.ḪI.A *danna šanḫanzi*
> *kuēš=ma=šmaš=za* $^{A.ŠÀ}$A.GÀR=*KUNU* $^{GIŠ}$KIRI$_6$.GEŠTIN *dannattaḫḫuwanzi šanḫanzi*
>
> "And as to the enemy countries that are fighting, some do not show respect to you, Telipinu, nor to the Gods of Ḫatti, others seek to seize (your) rhyta (and) cups, again others seek to lay waste your field(s and) vineyard(s)."

Note, by the way, the change of gender from the neuter KUR.KUR.ḪI.A *kue* "the countries that" to the common gender relative pronoun forms *kuēš* which each time refer back to those countries. This phenomenon will be explained in Lesson 9.4.2.

The form *šullanta* is the nom.-acc. plur. neut. of the participle *šullant-* from the verb *šulla-* "to fight, quarrel," serving as the nominal predicate; for the agreement, see Lesson 3.4.5.

### 7.4.3

To express a modality of the verb, i.e., either a wish (*optative*), a possibility (*potentialis*), or an impossibility (*irrealis*), there exists the so-called **modal particle *man*** [GrHL 23.10–16]. It is distinguished from the conditional conjunction *mān* (*ma-a-an*) "if" by the usual absence of plene spelling (*ma-an*). This modal particle can stand on its own in initial position (for the term "initial position," see Lesson 6.4.1) or can be used enclitically (*-man*) attached to the first word of the sentence. If attached to the conjunction *mān* we can get *māmman* with double *-mm-* ‹ **mān=man*.

Each of the three modes, the optative, the potentialis, and the irrealis, can be used with the indicative of the present or preterite tense, resulting in:

- an **optative**
  - of the present ("may such-and-such happen" or the subject "wishes to ...")
  - and the past (the subject "wished to ...")
- an **irrealis**
  - of the present ("if such-and-such were the case, I would ...")
  - and the past ("if such-and-such had been the case, I would have ...").
- a **potentialis**
  - of the present ("could/might")
  - and the past ("could have/might have")

For each of these we will give an example:

**Optative**

- with a pres.: *apāš=man* URU-*aš ammel kišari* "May that city become mine" (a speaker's wish)
- with a pret.: *man=an=kan* $^{\mathrm{m}}$*Aškaliyaš kuenta* "Aškaliya wanted/wished to kill him"

**Irrealis**

- with a pret.: *man* INA $^{\mathrm{URU}}$*Ḫaiaša pāun=pat nu=za* MU.KAM-*za tepaweššanza ēšta*

"I would indeed (*-pat*) have gone to Ḫayaša but the year was too short"

**Potentialis**

- with a pres.: *mān=mu* 1-*an* DUMU-*KA paišti man=aš=mu* $^{\mathrm{LÚ}}$MUTI=IA *kišari* "If you give (*paišti*) me one son of yours, he may/can become my husband"
- with a pret.: *ammel=man=mu* DUMU-*RU*=IA *arḫa uppešta* "you could have sent (*uppešta*) my son home to me!"

  - To negate any of the above modes, *nūman* or *nūwan* is used: *n=e nūman pānzi* "they do not wish to/would not go."
  - *Nūman/nūwan* is never used in first position, probably to avoid confusion with the connector *nu*.
  - Which of the three modalities (optative etc.) is meant in a given clause depends on the context only and should be decided in each individual case.
  - An urgent wish of the 1. sing. ("I want to ...") can also be expressed by using the 1. sing. of the imperative, also called *voluntative*, for which see Lesson 8.3.4.

## 7.5 Phonology

### 7.5.1

In the paradigms of the heteroclitic declension above (Lesson 7.1.2) we noticed the occasional loss of word-final *-r* in forms like *paprata* = *papratar* [GrHL 1.133]. Whether these forms are interpreted as regular after a long vowel or not, they do illustrate the apparently weak pronunciation of this sound in Hittite. In the middle of the word especially, *-r-* can be left out in writing, as exemplified by the frequent spelling of the adverb *peran* (*pé-ra-an*) as *pé-an*.

### 7.5.2

Apart from a few exceptions, the cluster *-tn-* assimilates to *-nn-* [GrHL 1.112], as seen in the oblique stem of the heteroclitic nouns in **-tar/-tn-* › *-tar/-nn-* (Lesson 7.1.2 A). Sometimes the cluster is preserved, as in *ḫuitar* "animals, fauna" with its gen. *ḫuitnaš*.

## 7.6 Numerals

### 7.6.1 Numerals [GrHL 9]

Usually numerals are written with the numeral signs (see Lesson 7.7), occasionally with phonetic complements. Only rarely are they written out fully syllabically.

Of the Hittite **cardinals 1, 2, and 3**, only the reading of the first (*šia-*) and last (*teri(ya)-*) are known. "Two" is only attested written with the number sign plus or minus phonetic complements. The inflection is mostly pronominal; the most important forms are given here.

| | 1 | 1 | 2 | 3 |
|---|---|---|---|---|
| nom. com. | 1-*aš* | 1-*iš* | 2-*e*, 2-*uš* | 3-*ieš* |
| acc. com. | 1-*an* | 1-*in* | | |
| nom.-acc. neut. | 1-*an* | | 2-*e* | 3-*e* |
| gen. | *šīēl* | | | *teriyaš*, 3-*aš* |
| dat.-loc. | *šiedani*, 1-*edani* | | | |
| abl. | *šīēz*, 1-*ez*, 1-*edaz*, | | | 3-*az* |
| instr. | 1-*etanda* | | | |

- The numeral "one" is also used in the sequence 1-*aš* … 1-*aš* … "one … the other …"
- There are some **adjectives** derived from the numbers, built on the pronominal gen. in -*el*: 1-*ela*- "of one (mind)," 2-*ela*- "of two, in a pair."
- **Adverbs** are *dān*/2-*an* "secondly, again," 3-*an*/3-*in* "thirdly."
- Besides these, there are compounds like *duyanalli*- "of second rank," *teriyalla* (a drink with three ingredients or the like).
- **Distributives** (once, twice, thrice/three times) are often found in rituals indicating, for instance, the number of times a deity is libated to. They end in -*šu*, which is usually taken as an Akkadian phonetic complement (1-ŠU, 2-ŠU, 3-ŠU), but inner-Anatolian (Luwian and Lycian) evidence actually justifies a Hittite reading 1-*šu*, 2-*šu*, 3-*šu*.
- Other distributives seem to be some forms in -*anki* (1-*anki*, 2-*anki*, 3-*anki*) and perhaps also in -*iš* (2-*iš*, 3-*iš*).

## 7.7 Cuneiform signs

iš  uš  du 

da  it 

ḫu  ri  ar 

kán 

1  2  3 

## 7.8 Exercises; KBo 3.4 ii 57–78

### 7.8.1 Translate:

1. (from the Hittite laws) *ták-ku* $\text{GU}_4$-*aš* A.ŠÀ.ḪI.A-*ni* *ku-el-ka*$_4$ *a-ki* BE-EL A.ŠÀ 2 $\text{GU}_4$ *pa-a-i* ("he will give")
2. ÌR-IA-*ma nu-u-ma-an da-aḫ-ḫi* ("I take/will take")
3. *zi-ik-ma-wa-za* DUMU-*aš nu-wa* Ú-UL *ku-it-ki ša-ak-ti na-aḫ-šar-nu-ši-ma-mu* Ú-UL
4. *šu-uš ta-me-eš-šer še a-ker*
5. *nu* KÁ.GÁL.ḪI.A EGIR-*pa ḫe-še-er*
6. *ma-aḫ-ḫa-an-ma* LUGAL-*uš* I-NA É-TIM GAL *a-ri ḫa-an-te-ez-zi-az* ("in front")-*ma* LÚ.MEŠALAN.$\text{ZU}_9$ (a kind of cult personnel, leave untranslated "the ALAN.ZU-men") *ka-ru-ú a-ra-an-ta-ri*
7. *nu-wa-za-kán* URU*Ḫa-pa-ra-an i-ni-iš-ša-an ta-ma-aš-ta*

8. *na-aš-ta* DINGIR-*LUM* (i.e., his/her statue) *IŠ-TU* É.DINGIR-*LIM* *pa-ra-a ú-da-an-zi* ("they bring") *na-an-kán* $^{\mathrm{GIŠ}}$*ḫu-lu-ga-an-ni a-še-ša-an-zi*
9. (omen) *ma-a-an* I-*NA* UD.15.KAM $^{\mathrm{d}}$SÎN-*aš a-ki a-ru-na-aš a-aš-šu har-ak-zi na-aš-ma šu-up-pa-la-an te-pa-u-e-eš-zi*
10. *na-at du-li-ya-aš pí-di an-da e-re-er*
11. *nu* SILA$_4$ *ú-e-te-ni-it kat-ta a-an-ša-an-zi*
12. *na-pa* $^{\mathrm{m}}$*Mur-ši-i-li-ia-aš e-eš-ḫar* DINGIR.MEŠ-*iš ša-an-ḫe-er* (i.e., for revenge)
13. *nu* $^{\mathrm{LÚ}}$KÚR $^{\mathrm{URU}}$*A-ra-u-wa-an-na-aš ku-iš* KUR $^{\mathrm{URU}}$*Ki-iš-ši-ia-a* GUL-*an-ni-eš-ke-et na-at me-ek-ki ta-ma-aš-ša-an ḫar-ta*
14. (from the parable with talking deer, cf. Lesson 2.8.1:14) *ú-e-ši-ia-aḫ-ḫa-ri ku-e-da-ni* ḪUR.SAG-*i ma-a-na-an pa-aḫ-ḫu-e-na-an-za ar-ḫa wa-ar-nu-zi*

## Words for Lesson 7

| | | | |
|---|---|---|---|
| *anš-* (Ia) | to wash, wipe | A.ŠÀ | field |
| *ar-/er-* (IIb) | to reach, arrive | É.GAL | palace |
| *aruna-*, com. | sea | GUL | = *walḫ-* |
| *ašaš-/ašeš-* (IIb) | to make sit, seat | ÌR(*-i-*, com.) | servant, subject |
| *ešḫar*, neut. | blood | KÁ.GAL | gate |
| *ḫaš-/ḫeš-* (IIb) | to open | SILA$_4$ | lamb |
| *iniššan/eniššan* | in that way, thus | | |
| *naḫšarnu-* (Ia) | to cause to fear, instill respect | *BĒLU* | lord, officer, owner |
| *numan* | (modal negation) | | |
| *šakk-/šekk-* (IIb) | to know | **GN** | |
| *šuppala-*, neut. | cattle | $^{\mathrm{URU}}$*Arauwanna* | |
| *takku* (conj.) | if | $^{\mathrm{URU}}$*Ḫapara* | |
| *tamašš-/tamešš-* (Ig) | to oppress | $^{\mathrm{URU}}$*Kiššiya* | |
| | | | |
| *tuliya-*, com. | assembly, meeting | **PN** | |
| *watar*, neut. | water | $^{\mathrm{m}}$Muršili | Hittite Great King |
| *wešiya-* (Ic) | to graze, pasture | | (*c.* 1318–1295 BC) |

## 7.8.2 *The Ten-Year Annals* of the Hittite King Muršili II

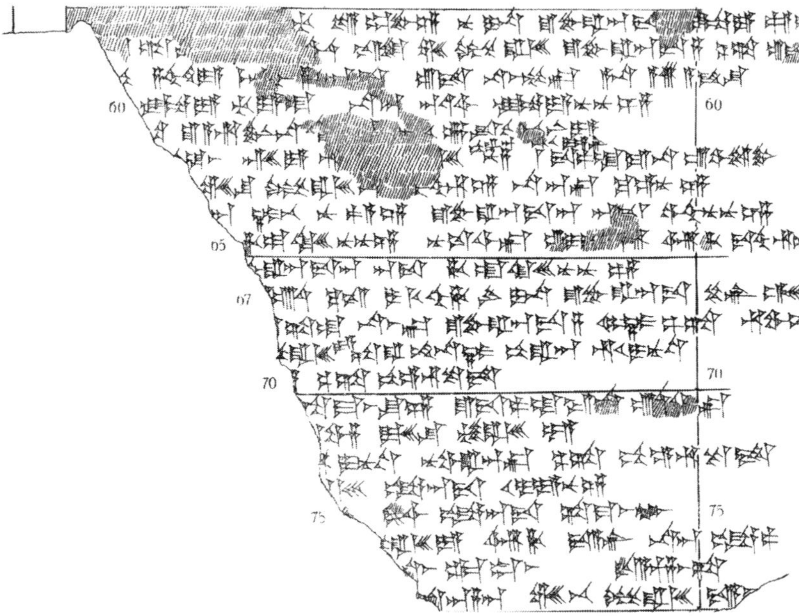

Figure 8

ii

57. [*ma-aḫ-ḫa-an-ma-za-kán* EZEN$_4$ MU-]*TI kar-ap-pu-un nu I-NA* $^{URU}$*Pu-ra-an-da* [M]È-*ia pa-a-un*
58. [*nu-kán*] $^{m}$*Ta-p*[*a-la-zu-na-*] ⌈*wa*⌉ *-liš IŠ-TU* ÉRIN.MEŠ ANŠE.KUR.RA.MEŠ $^{URU}$*Pu-ra-an-da-za kat-ta ú-* ⌈*it*⌉
59. [*na-aš-m*]*u za-aḫ-ḫi-ia me-* ⌈*na-aḫ-ḫa-an-da*⌉ *ú-it na-aš-mu-kán A-NA* $^{A.ŠÀ}$A.GAR-*ŠU*
60. [*an-da*] MÈ-*ia ti-ia-at na-an* $^{d}$UTU-*ŠI* MÈ-*ia-nu-nu-un*
61. [*nu-mu* $^{d}$]UTU $^{URU}$*A-ri-in-na* GA[ŠAN-*I*]*A* ⌈$^{d}$⌉ U NIR.GÁL *BE-LÍ-IA*
62. [$^{d}$*Me-ez-zu-u*]*l-la-aš* DINGIR.MEŠ-*ia* ⌈*ḫu*⌉ [*-u-ma-an-t*]*e-eš pé-ra-an ḫu-u-i-e-er*[1] *nu-za* $^{m}$*Da-pa-la-zu-na-ú-wa-li-in*
63. [ … QA-DU] ÉRIN.MEŠ-*ŠU* ANŠE.KUR.RA.MEŠ- ⌈*ŠU tar*⌉ *-uḫ-ḫu-un na-an-kán ku-e-nu-un*
64. [*nam-ma-an* EGIR-]*an AṢ-BAT nu pa-a-un* $^{URU}$*Pu-ra-an-da-an an-* ⌈*da*⌉ *wa-aḫ-nu-nu-un*

---

[1] *pé-ra-an ḫu-u-i-e-er* added above the line.

65. [*na-an-kán an-da*] *ḫa-at-ke-eš-nu-nu-un nu-uš-ši-kán ú-i-d*[*a-a-a*]*r ar-ḫa da-aḫ-ḫu-un*

---

66. [*nu-kán ma-aḫ-ḫa-an* $^{uru}$*P*]*u-ra-an-da-an an-da ḫa-at-ke-eš-nu-nu-un*
67. [*nu-kán* $^{m}$*Ta-pa-la-zu-n*]*a-ú-liš ku-iš* DUMU $^{m}$*U-uḫ-ḫa*-LÚ I-*NA* $^{URU}$*Pu-ra-an-da še-er e-eš-ta*
68. [*na-aš na-aḫ-ša-ri-ia-a*]*t-ta-at na-aš-kán* $^{URU}$*Pu-ra-an-da-za* GE$_6$*-az kat-ta ḫu-wa-iš*
69. [*nam-ma-za* DUMU.MEŠ-*ŠU* NA]M.RA.MEŠ-*ia*[2] *ša-ra-am-na-az pé-ra-an ḫu-u-i-nu-ut*
70. [*na-an-kán* $^{URU}$*Pu-ra-an-da-z*]*a kat-ta pé-e-ḫu-te-et*

---

71. [*ma-aḫ-ḫa-an-ma* $^{d}$UTU-*ŠI iš-t*]*a-ma-aš-šu-un* $^{m!}$[3]*Da-pa-la-zu-na-ú-*⌈*liš-wa*⌉*-kán*
72. [GE$_6$*-az kat-ta ḫu-u-wa-a-iš* DAM-*ZU-i*]*a-wa-za* DUMU.MEŠ-*ŠU* NAM.RA.MEŠ-*ia*
73. [*sa-ra-am-na-za pé-ra-an ḫ*]*u-i-nu-ut nu-wa-*⌈*ra*⌉*-an-kán kat-ta pé-e-ḫu-te-et*
74. [*nu-uš-ši* $^{d}$UTU-*ŠI* ÉRIN.MEŠ ANŠE.KUR.R]A.MEŠ EGIR-*an-da u-i-ia-nu-un*
75. [*nu* $^{m}$*Ta-pa-la-zu-na-ú-li-i*]*n* KASKAL-*ši* EGIR-*an-da ta-ma-aš-*⌈*šer*⌉
76. [*nu-uš-ši-kán* DAM-*ZU* DUMU.MEŠ-*ŠU* NA]M.RA.MEŠ-*ia ar-ḫa da-a-er na-an* EGIR-*pa*
77. [*ú-wa-te-er* $^{m}$*Ta-pa-la-zu-na-ú-li-is-ma-ká*]*n* 1-*aš* SAG.DU-*aš iš!*[4]*-pár-za-aš-ta*
78. [NAM.RA-*ma-kán ku-in* KASKAL-*ši ta-ma-aš-šer*] ⌈*na*⌉*-an-za-an* ÉRIN.MEŠ-*pát* ANŠE.KUR.RA.MEŠ *da-a-aš*

---

(traces of seven more lines before column breaks off)

## Questions

1. Identify in the handcopy the cuneiform signs given in this and the previous Lessons.
2. Parse the underlined forms.
3. Translate the text with the notes below.

---

2 *ia* added above the line.
3 Tablet has URU.
4 Tablet has DA-A.

## Words

| | |
|---|---|
| 57. *karp-* (Ia) | to lift; take care of |
| *pāun* | "I went" |
| 58. *uit* | "(he) came" |
| 59. $^{\text{A.ŠÀ}}$A.GAR | field, territory |
| 64. *pāun* | "I went (and)" |
| *anda waḫnu-* | to surround, encircle |
| 65. *ḫatkešnu-* | to close, isolate |
| 68. *naḫšariya-* (dep.) | to be(come) afraid |
| 68. *ḫuwaiš* | 3. sing. pret. indic. of *ḫuiya-* to run, flee |
| 69. *šaramnaz* | "from above" |
| *peran ḫuinu-* | to make run in front of |
| 70. *peḫute-* | to bring, carry |
| (*n*)=*an* | i.e., DUMU.MEŠ-*ŠU* NAM.RA.MEŠ-*ia* |
| 75. EGIR-*anda tamašš-* | to oppress from behind, to be on someone's heels |

# Lesson 8

## 8.1 *r*- and *l*-stem nouns

### 8.1.1

There is a small class of ***r*-stems** containing both nouns and adjectives [GrHL 4.80–86]. The gender of the nouns is often difficult to establish, since common gender and neuter gender forms coexist even in Old Hittite.

Examples: (DUG)*ḫuppar* com./neut. (a container), *kurur* neut. "hostility" (but evolving into an adjective "hostile") for the nouns, and *šakuwaššar*- "entire, complete" for the adjectives.

| | | | |
|---|---|---|---|
| **Sing.** | | | |
| nom. com. | *ḫupparaš* | | *šakuwaššaraš* |
| acc. com. | *ḫupparan* | | *šakuwaššaran* |
| nom.-acc. neut. | *ḫuppar* | *kurur* | *šakuwaššar* |
| gen. | *ḫupparaš* | *kururaš* | *šakuwaššaraš* |
| dat.-loc. | *ḫuppari* | *kururi* | *šakuwaššari* |
| abl. | *ḫupparaz* | | *šakuwaššaraz* |
| instr. | *ḫupparit* | | *šakuwaššarit* |
| **Plur.** | | | |
| nom. com. | | | *šakuwaššaruš* |
| acc. com. | | | *šakuwaššaruš* |
| nom.-acc. neut. | *ḫuppari*ḪI.A | *kururi*ḪI.A | |

- Note again the -*i* ending in the nom.-acc. plur. neut. combined with Sum. ḪI.A (see Lesson 7.1.2).
- The regular nom.-acc. plur. neut -*a* is attested in *šittara* "sun disks" from *šittar*-.
- The declension of *šakuwaššar*- might be mistaken for an *a*-stem (Lesson 1.1.2) were it not for the nom.-acc. sing. neut. *šakuwaššar* with its zero ending (-Ø).

### 8.1.2

A rare *r*-stem showing Ablaut is *keššar/keššer-/kešr*- (ŠU, *QĀTU*) "hand" [GrHL 4.82]. Originally it was a common gender word, with an asigmatic (i.e., *s*-less) nominative (*keššar*-Ø) next to an acc. sing. *keššeran*. Since such a common gender nom. sing. stood isolated within the Hittite nominal system, it was prone to be reinterpreted in two ways: as an *r*-stem neuter with a new acc. sing.

*keššar* (ŠU-*šar*) identical to the nom., or as an *a*-stem with a new nom. *kešširaš* by analogy to the acc. *kešširan*. The first syllable is written both *ki-iš-* and *ke-eš-*.

| | Sing. | Plur. |
|---|---|---|
| nom. | *keššar, kiššeraš,* ŠU*(-aš)* | |
| acc. | *kiššeran,* ŠU*-an,* ŠU*-šar* | *kiššeruš,* ŠU.MEŠ*-uš* |
| gen. | *kišraš* | *kišraš,* ŠU.ḪI.A*-aš* |
| dat.-loc. | *kiššari,* ŠU*-i* | |
| all. | *kišra* | |
| abl. | *kišraz, kiššaraz,* ŠU*-az* | |
| instr. | *kiššarta, kišše/arit,* ŠU*-ta/it* | |

- For the old instrumental *kiššarta*, compare above *išḫimanta* (Lesson 6.1.1) and *wedanda* (Lesson 7.1.3).

8.1.3

The ***l*-stems** comprise mostly neuter nouns, most notable among them deverbatives in *-ul*: e.g., *waštul* "sin, crime" from *wašta-* (IIc) "to sin, err" [GrHL 4.63–64].

Examples: *waštul* "sin, crime," *išḫiul* "treaty, bond" (from *išḫiya-* "to bind"), and *tawal* (a drink).

| | | | |
|---|---|---|---|
| **Sing.** | | | |
| nom.-acc. | *waštul* | *išḫiul* | *tawal* |
| gen. | *wašdulaš* | *išḫiulaš* | *tawalaš* |
| dat.-loc. | *wašduli* | *išḫiuli* | *tawali* |
| abl. | | *išḫiullaza* | |
| instr. | *wašdulit* | | *tawalit* |
| **Plur.** | | | |
| nom.-acc. | *wašdul*ḪI.A | *išḫiuli*ḪI.A | |

- For both the zero-ending and the *-i* of the nom.-acc. plur. neut., compare the *-r-/-n-*stems in Lesson 7.1.1–3.

## 8.2 Distributive pronoun *kuišša*

8.2.1

For the **distributive pronoun** ("each, every") the relative stem *kui-* is used again [GrHL 8.2–4]. This time it is combined with the conjunction *-a/-ya* "and, too" which comes after the case ending. It should be remembered (see Lesson 1.4.3) that the *-y-* of this enclitic conjunction assimilates to a preceding consonant, which is then doubled.

| | Sing. | Plur. |
|---|---|---|
| nom. com. | *kuišša* | *kuešša* |
| acc. com. | *kuinna* | *kuiušša* |
| nom.-acc. neut. | *kuitta* | |
| gen. | *kuella* | |
| dat.-loc. | *kuedaniya* | |
| abl. | *kuezziya* | |

- For the abl. *kuezziya*, see Lesson 8.5.

## 8.3 Half-consonantal verb stems IIc, Ih, and Ii

### 8.3.1

In the group of *ḫi*-verbs presented here (**IIc**) the singular of the verbal stem ends in a vowel (e.g., *išša-/ešša-* in *ešša-ḫḫi* "I do") but the plural shows a consonant stem (e.g., *i/ešš-* in *eš-weni* "we do") [GrHL 13.15–16]. The verbs extended with the aspectual suffix *-išša-* (e.g., *ḫalziššа-* to *ḫalzai-* "to call," cf. Lesson 5.4) belong to this class.

Examples: *ešša-* (older often *išša-*) "to do, make," and *tarna-* "to let go, release."

| | Present | Preterite |
|---|---|---|
| **Active** | | |
| **Sing.** 1 | *eššaḫḫi* | *iššaḫḫun* |
| 2 | *eššatti* | |
| 3 | *iššai* | *iššišta, tarnaš* |
| **Plur.** 1 | *iššuweni* | *iššuwen* |
| 2 | *išteni, iššatteni* | |
| 3 | *iššanzi* | *iššer* |
| **Medio-passive** | | |
| **Sing.** 3 | *tarnattari* | *tarnattat* |
| **Plur.** 3 | *tarnantari* | |
| **Participle** | *tarnant-* | |

- The forms of the 1. plur. pres. and pret. *iššuwen(i)* of course represent /iswen(i)/.
- Already in the older language the *-a-* of the singular starts invading the plural in forms like *iššatteni* (next to *išteni*). This tendency may originate from the 3. plur. pres. *iššanzi*, which can be analyzed in two ways: *išš-anzi* and *išša-(a)nzi*.

### 8.3.2

Two isolated but very frequently used *mi*-verbs of motion are ***pai***- "to go" (**Ih**) and ***uwa***- "to come" (**Ii**) [GrHL 12.41–43].

| | Present | Preterite |
|---|---|---|
| **Sing.** 1 | *paimi* | *pāun* |
| 2 | *paiši* | *paitta* |
| 3 | *paizzi* | *pait* |
| **Plur.** 1 | *pa(i)weni, paiwani* | *pa(i)wen* |
| 2 | *paitteni* | |
| 3 | *pānzi* | *pāer* |
| **Participle** | *pānt-* | |

| | Present | Preterite |
|---|---|---|
| **Sing.** 1 | *uwami* | *uwanun* |
| 2 | *uwaši* | *ueš, uwaš* |
| 3 | *uezzi* | *uet* |
| **Plur.** 1 | *uwaweni* | *uwawen* |
| 2 | *uwatteni* | *uwatten* |
| 3 | *uwanzi* | *uēr* |
| **Participle** | *uwant-* | |

For the semantics of these motion verbs, see Lessons 8.4.1, 8.4.4.

### 8.3.3

The only verbally inflected mode other than the indicative and the infinitive is the **imperative** [GrHL 11.1–9]. There are separate endings for all persons except the 1. plur. The 1. sing. form is quite rare and is less an imperative than a so-called voluntative, expressing a fervent wish of the subject ("I want to …").

Here too a distinction between the *mi*- and *ḫi*-conjugation, as well as between **active and medio-passive**, is made:

| | -mi- | | -ḫi- |
|---|---|---|---|
| **Active** | | | |
| **Sing.** 1 | | *-allu, -allut, -lu, -lut, -lit* | |
| 2 | | *-Ø, -t, -i* | |
| 3 | *-tu* | | *-u* |
| **Plur.** 2 | | *-ten* | *-šten* |
| 3 | | *-antu* | |

| | -mi- | | -ḫi- |
|---|---|---|---|
| **Medio-passive** | | | |
| **Sing.** 1 | | *-ḫaru, -ḫaḫaru* | |
| 2 | | *-ḫut, -ḫuti* | |
| 3 | *-taru* | | *-aru* |
| **Plur.** 2 | | *-dumat* | |
| 3 | | *-antaru* | |

- Examples for the voluntative are:
  - *akallu* "I want to die!"
  - *ašallu/ešlut/ešlit* "I want to be ..."
  - *memallu* "I want to speak of ...."
- The ending *-t* for the 2. sing. is found with the causatives in *-nu-* (e.g., *tittanut* "you must put") and with some isolated verbs like *tet* "speak!" from *te-/tar-* (see Lesson 9.3.3) and *it* "go!"
- The 2. sing. ending *-i* is mainly attested with verbs in °*š*-: *paḫši* "protect, take care!" But compare also from *kuen-* "to kill, destroy" the form *kuenni* "you must destroy!" in KBo 3.4 i 26 (the Sun goddess speaking to Muršili II; see Lesson 3.8.5).
- Only the 3. sing. (*-tu* and *-taru* vs. *-u* and *-aru*) distinguishes between the *mi-* and *ḫi*-conjugation.
- Note that the 2. plur. act. *-ten* and the 2. plur. medio-pass. *-dumat* can also be preterite indicatives (*walḫten* "you struck" and "you must strike!", *ardumat* "you stood" and "you must stand!")!

The imperative forms of all verb classes including those presented in the preceding lessons can be found in Appendix 1. For a negated imperative or prohibitive, see Lesson 8.4.3.

## 8.4 Syntax and semantics

### 8.4.1

The verbs ***uwa***- and ***pai***- are both compounds of the ancient Indo-European root $^{*}h_1ei$- "to go, walk" (compare Latin *i-re*, Greek *ei-mi*) with two different **prefixes, *u*- and *pe*-**, indicating a motion towards and a motion away from a certain point respectively [GrHL 18.32]. Contractions of the root and the vocalic ending of the prefixes have largely obscured this origin, however. The prefixes *pe*- and *u*- can be seen in a series of other pairs:

| | | | |
|---|---|---|---|
| *uda-* | "to bring (towards)" | *peda-* | "to bring (away)" |
| *uwate-* | "to lead (towards)" | *peḫute-* | "to lead (away)" |
| *unna-* | "to drive (towards)" | *penna-* | "to drive (away)" |

The choice for *u*- or *pe*- depends on the communicative situation.

- In a situation with a speaker and an addressee, *u*- is used for motion towards both of them ("I come to you and you come to me"), *pe*- for any motion towards a third goal ("I tell you: I will go to Paris/Mary").
- In a narrative with a first person narrator, all motion towards the narrator have *u*- ("Mary comes to me") and all other motion has *pe*- ("I went to Paris").
- In a non-personal narrative *u*- and *pe*- seem to shift.

In the verbs just mentioned, including *uwa*- and *pai*-, the prefixes still mostly retain their original value; sometimes, however, they have become fossilized as, e.g., in *uššiya*- "to pull up (a curtain)" which probably once formed a pair with *peššiya*- "to throw, cast away."

### 8.4.2

Frequently the motion verbs ***uwa***- "to come" and ***pai***- "to go" (see Lesson 8.3.2) appear in clause-initial or first position (for these terms, see Lesson 6.4.1), or in second position if preceded by the conjunctions *mān*, *maḫḫan* or *kuitman*. A second verb in the same person, number, tense, and mood follows in the common position at the end of that same clause, i.e., without any intervening connective. This is known as the **phraseological construction** or phraseological use of the verbs *uwa*- and *pai*- [GrHL 24.31–42].

A characteristic example is: *n=at uwami* INA É.GAL-LIM *memaḫḫi* "I will come (and) tell it to the palace." That we are not dealing with two short asyndetic clauses here is shown by the enclitic anaphoric pronoun *-at* "it" (nom.-acc. sing. neut.), which cannot belong to the 1. sing. of the intransitive verb *uwami* ("I come/will come") but can function only as the object to the second verb *memaḫḫi* "I will tell." Initial position is especially frequent in questions and commands: e.g., *paimi=kan* $^{d}$UTU-*ŠI anduḫšan* INA $^{URU}$*Šamuḫa parā neḫḫi* "Should I, My Majesty, go (and) send forth a man to the city of Šamuḫa?"

The translation given here, using an inserted "(and)," is the most literal and the one commonly used. Often the phraseological verb seems to indicate an action which follows logically or expectedly from a preceding action. In this sense, the phraseological construction can be said to mark a relation which is causal in a general way. Compare the following passage: "I, the Great King, marched concealed with my troops and chariots. The mighty Storm god, My Lord, had called for me Ḫašammili, My Lord, and he kept me concealed, so that no one saw me. *nu=ššan pāun* KUR *Piggainarešša šašti walaḫḫun* Thereupon I attacked (the country) Piggainarešša in its sleep." In most cases a translation with "thereupon" seems to bring out the required relation most appropriately.

A special use of the phraseological construction involves *uwa-* only and might be termed "impersonal." The construction is the same, but the form of *uwa-* is translated "it will happen (that), it happened (that)": the second verb in the same clause becomes the main verb of the English "that"-clause. E.g., EGIR-*pa=ma uit* $^{m}$*Ammunaš* DUMU.LUGAL BA.ÚŠ "later, however, it happened that Ammuna, the prince, died." From the context it is obvious that the writer does not mean that Ammuna first came and subsequently died.

8.4.3

A **prohibitive**, or order for someone *not* to do something, can be expressed by the prohibitive particle *lē* (invariably spelled *le-e*) [GrHL 26.16–22] followed by the indicative: e.g., *lē paiši* "don't go!", *lē paizzi* "he/she must/shall not go!" Only rarely is the particle *lē* combined with an imperative: *lē paiddu* "he must/shall not go!"

8.4.4

The generalizing **indefinite** notion "whoever, whatever" (see Lesson 7.2) can also be expressed in other ways, for instance, by doubling the relative pronoun [GrHL 8.7]: *kuit=ši=ššan kuit anda ēšta* "whatever (clothing) was on him" or $^{m}$*Ibri*-LUGAL-*maš=mu kue kue* UNUTE$^{MEŠ}$ EGIR-*pa maniaḫda* "Whatever weapons Ibrišarruma assigned me again."

There is also the possibility of combining *kui-* with the emphasizing adverb *imma* and the enclitic personal pronoun *-a-* "he, she, it" (see Lesson 2.2). This can take various forms: *kuiš imma, kuiš imma kuiš, kuiš=aš imma kuiš.* E.g., *kuit=kan imma kuit kēdani* ANA ṬUPPI GAR-*ri* "whatever is laid down (in writing) on this tablet" or *kuiš=aš imma kuiš* ŠA É.GAL-*LIM* MUNUS "whatever palace woman she (might be)."

## 8.5 Phonology

### 8.5.1

If the enclitic **conjunction *-a/-ya*** is attached to an abl. we do not get an expected doubled **-zza*, but *-zziya* instead [GrHL 1.116]: e.g., Lesson 8.2 *kuez+-ya* › *kuezziya*. This is due to the origin of the abl. ending *-z*: it was assibilated from **-ti*, the ending which is preserved as the regular abl. in Luwian. The final *-i* was dropped after the assibilation of **-t-* › *-z* but surfaces again when *-ya* is attached.

## 8.6 Numerals

### 8.6.1

The cardinal number best known in its reading and inflection is the number 4. From 5 onwards the evidence becomes very scanty and it is not certain how and to what extent these **cardinals** were inflected.

| | 4 | 7 | 8 | 9 | 10 |
|---|---|---|---|---|---|
| nom. com. | *miewaš* | | | | |
| acc. | *mieuš*, 4-*uš*, 4-*aš* | 7-*an* (= *šiptan*?) | | | |
| gen. | *miuwaš* | | | | |
| dat.-loc. | *miuwaš*, 4-*taš* | | 8-*taš* | 9-*anti* | |
| abl. | | | | | |
| instr. | 4-*it* | | | | 10-*antit* |

- If the phonetic complement *-taš* in 4-*taš* (and 8-*taš*?) represents the pronominal *-edaš*, then the inflection is partly pronominal at least. But it could also stand for an *-ant*-extension, in which case the pronominal declension for the numerals would be restricted to numbers 1–3.
  - Besides the forms given above, there is also evidence for ordinals like 4-*in* "fourth."
  - For a distributive we find 4-*šu* (for the reading of *-šu*, see Lesson 7.6).
- For numbers 5 and 6 we have certain evidence only for ordinals (5-*in*, 6-*an*) and distributives (5-*šu*, 6-*šu*).
  - It is possible that the Hittite word for "all, totality" *panku-* is the corresponding form to Proto-Indo-European **penk*$^w$e, which became the word for "five" in, e.g., Greek (*pente*) and Latin (*quinque* assimilated from

**pinque*). There is, however, no evidence *panku* was ever used as a cardinal in Hittite or that it is the reading behind the number sign "5."

- The reading of 7-*an* as **šiptan* comes from the name of a drink called *šiptamiya* which is also written as 7-*miya.*
  - Here again there are ordinals and distributives (7-*an* "seventh," 7-*anki*, 7-*iš*, 7-*šu* "seven times").
- The material for 9 and 10 offers further -*nt*-derivations for the cardinals, 8-*taš* may stand for -*antaš.*
  - A special form is 8-*inzu*, possibly meaning "octad."
  - Besides these there are the usual distributives and occasional ordinals.

## 8.7 Cuneiform signs

| | | | |
|---|---|---|---|
| ra  | al  | ka  | |
| ši  | wa  | ul  | kum  |
| ru  | | | |
| ut  | di  | ki  | |
| 4  | 5  | 6  | 7  |
| 8  | 9  | 10  | |

## 8.8 Exercises; KBo 3.4 iii 10–38

### 8.8.1 Translate:

1. *ta* LUGAL-*uš* URU*Ta-ḫur-pa-za* URU*A-ri-in-na an-da-an* GIŠGIGIR-*it pa-iz-zi*
2. *nu* 1-*aš* 1-*e-da-ni le-e i-da-la-a-u-e-eš-zi* ( … ) *nu* 1-*aš* 1-*an ku-na-an-na le-e ša-an-ḫa-zi*
3. *ar-ḫa-wa-mu da-a-li* dGILGAMEŠ *nu-wa-mu-za zi-ik* EN-*aš e-eš am-mu-uk-ma-ad-du-za* ÌR-*iš e-eš-lu-ut*
4. *na-aš-ta an-da-ia* Ú-UL *ku-in-ki tar-na-i pa-ra-a-ia-kán* Ú-UL *ku-in-ki tar-na-i*
5. *nu* I-NA KUR URU*Tág-ga-aš-ta pa-a-un nu-mu iš-ta-ma-aš-ša-an ku-it ḫar-ke-er nu-uš-ma-aš-kán nam-ma* UD.KAM-*az* GÉŠPU-*it* EGIR-*pa-an-da* Ú-UL *pa-a-un nu* $GE_6$-*az i-ia-aḫ-ḫa-at*
6. (Ḫebat is waiting for her husband, standing on the roof. Upon hearing the bad news…) *ma-na-aš-kán šu-uḫ-ḫa-az kat-ta ma-uš-ta-at na-an* MUNUS.MEŠSUḪUR.LÀL *e-ep-per na-an* Ú-UL *tar-ne-er*
7. (rhetorical question) URU*Ni-ḫi-ir-ia-za-kán* Ú-UL 1-*aš arḫa u-un-na-aḫ-ḫu-un*

8. *na-at* 2-*e-la* *A-NA A-BU-IA* *kat-ta-an ú-e-er*
9. ("I want you to do so and so!") *ma-a-an* Ú-*UL-ma ú-wa-ši ḫar-ak-ši*
10. *zi-ik ku-e-da-ni* EGIR-*an ti-ia-ši nu a-pu-u-un-na ḫar-ni-in-kán-du*
11. *nu ku-e-ez-za ud-da-a-na-az ak-ki-iš-ki-it-ta-ri na-at ú-e-mi-ia-at-ta-ru*
12. DUB.ḪI.A-*ia ku-e u-da-an-zi nu ne-eš-um-ni-li ḫa-at-re-eš-ki*
13. *na-at-kán ša-aḫ-ḫa-na-za lu-zi-ia-za a-ra-u-e-eš a-ša-an-du*
14. (from the Hittite laws) *ták-ku* GU$_4$-*un* ANŠE.KUR.RA ANŠE.GÌR.NUN.NA *ku-iš-ki ú-e-mi-ia-zi na-an* LUGAL-*an a-aš-ka u-un-na-i*
15. (from a prayer) $^{d}$U EN-*IA ud-da-a-ar-mu iš-ta-ma-aš ud-da-a-ar-ta ku-e me-mi-iš-ki-mi*
16. *nu-za* KUR.KUR.MEŠ *ku-e ke-e* EGIR-*pa a-še-ša-nu-un nu* KARAŠ ANŠE.KUR.RA.MEŠ *ke-e-el ŠA* KUR-*TI* (translate as plural) *A-NA* ŠEŠ-*IA la-aḫ-ḫi I-NA* KUR *Mi-iz-ri-i* GAM-*an pé-e-ḫu-te-nu-un*
17. *nu* $^{d}$UTU-*ŠI ú-ki-la pa-i-mi*

## Words for Lesson 8

| | | | |
|---|---|---|---|
| *appan tiya-* (Ic) | to step behind, support | A.ŠÀ(.ḪI.A) | field(s) |
| | | ANŠE.GÌR.NUN.NA | mule, donkey |
| *appanda* | after(wards), behind | ANŠE.KUR.RA | horse, equid |
| | | DUB | (clay) tablet |
| *arawa-* | free | EGIR-*az* | later |
| *dalai-/daliya-* (Ic) | to abandon, leave | GAM-*an* | = *kattan* |
| *gimmant-*, com. | winter | GE$_6$ | = *išpant-* |
| *ḫarnink-* (Ie) | to destroy | GÉŠPU | force, violence |
| *idalawešš-* (Ia) | to become evil | GEŠTIN | wine |
| *išpant-*, com. | night | $^{GIŠ}$GIGIR | wheeled vehicle, chariot, wagon |
| *iya-*, (Ic dep.) | to walk, march, go | | |
| *keššar*, com. | hand | GÙB(-*la-*) | left (side) |
| *kuit* (conj.) | since, because | KARAŠ | army, troops |
| *laḫḫa-*, com. | military campaign | $^{MUNUS}$SUḪUR.LÀL | (female) servant |
| *luzzi-*, com. | corvée, labor | | |
| *nešumnili* (adv.) | in Hittite | *MAḪAR* | before, in front of |
| *nink-* (Ie) | to make move, mobilize | | |
| | | **GN** | |
| *pai-* (Ih) | to go | $^{URU}$*Arinna* | |
| *peḫute-* (Ia) | to bring, lead (away) | $^{URU}$*Gašga* | |
| | | $^{URU}$*Katḫaidduwa* | |
| *šaḫḫan*, neut. | tax(es) | KUR $^{URU}$*Mizri* | Egypt |
| *šuḫḫa-*, com. | roof | $^{URU}$*Niḫiriya* | |
| *tarna-* (IIc) | to let go | $^{URU}$*Taggašta* | |

| | | |
|---|---|---|
| *uda-* (IIc) | to bring, carry | $^{\text{URU}}$*Taḫurpa* |
| *ukila* | see Lesson 1.2.2 | |
| *unna-* (IIc) | to drive | **PN** |
| *uppa-* (IIc) | to send | $^{\text{m}}$Gilgameš |

## 8.8.2 *The Ten-Year Annals* of the Hittite King Muršili II

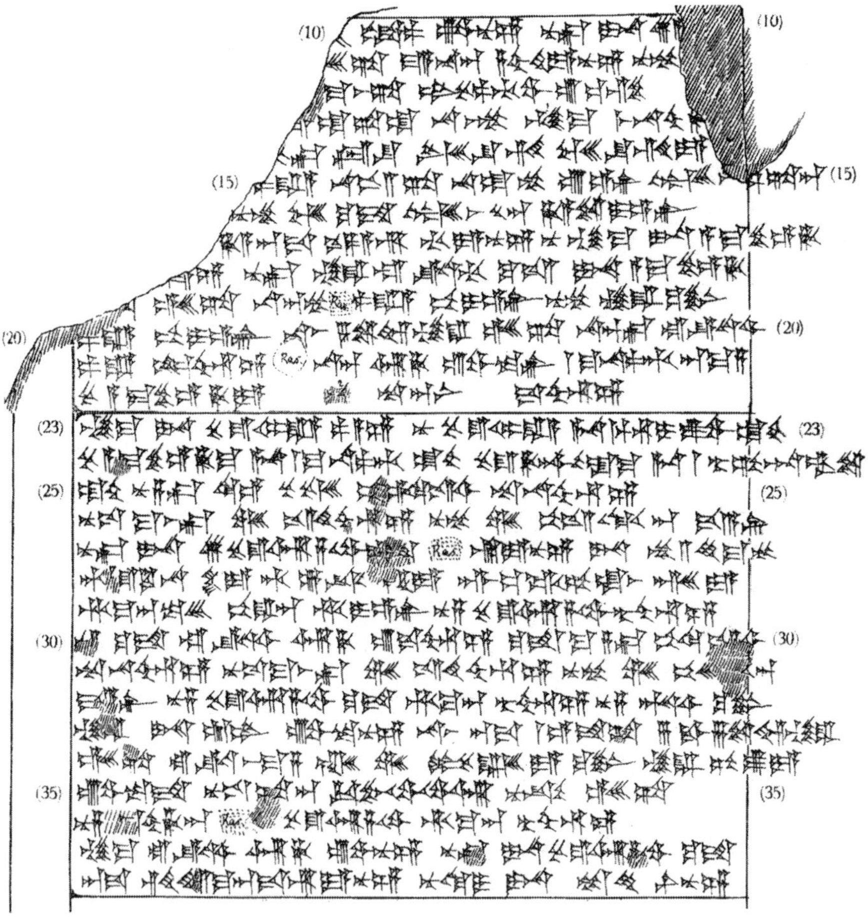

Figure 9

The ends of lines of iii 10–15 are preserved in the small fragment Bo 8245, given below (Figure 10) and published as KUB 23.125, which joins KBo 3.4 physically in the top right-hand corner of the fragment in Figure 9. Note that in the drawing in Figure 10 part of KBo 3.4 is copied again to make the join clear; the line numbers of KBo 3.4 are given in parentheses on the right. Of course, only lines KUB 23.125 iii 13–16 (= KBo 3.4 iii 10–13) are relevant here.

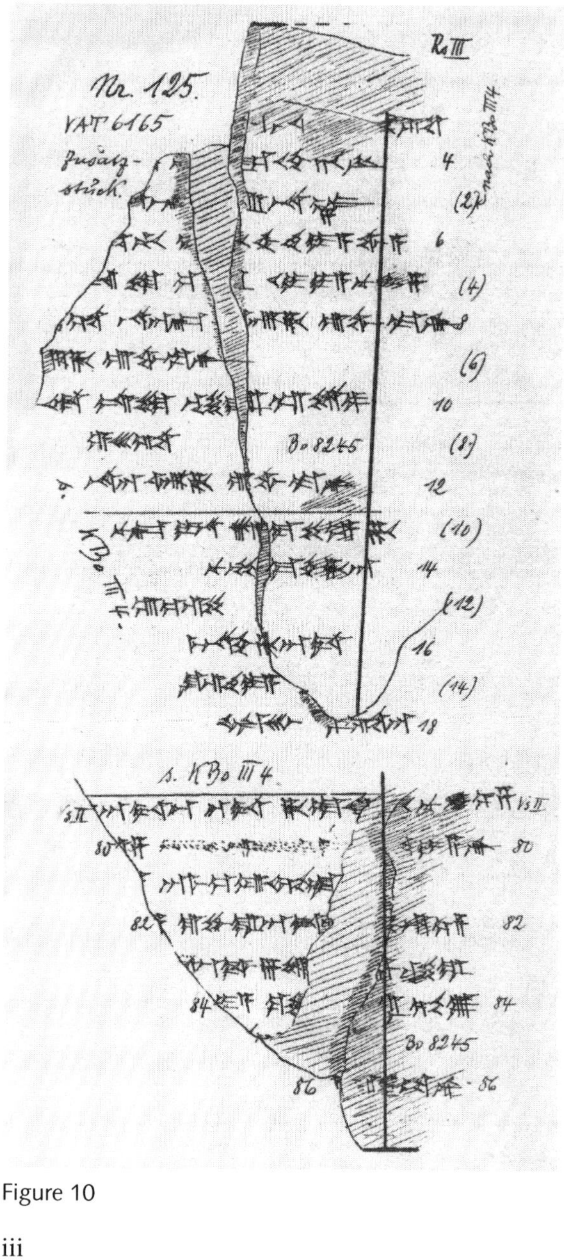


Figure 10

iii

(lines 1–9 too fragmentarily preserved)

10. [GIM-*an-ma-kán* I-NA KUR $^{\text{ÍD}}$*Še-e-ḫ*]*a* EGIR-*pa ú-wa-nu-un nu-kán* I-NA ŠÀ $^{\text{ÍD}}$*Še-e-ḫa*

11. [$^{\text{m}}$*Ma-na-pa-*$^{\text{d}}$U-*aš ku-iš* EN-*aš e*]-*eš-ta ma-a-na-an za-aḫ-ḫi-ia-nu-un nu-mu ma-aḫ-ḫa-an*

12. [$^{\text{m}}$*Ma-na-pa-*$^{\text{d}}$U-*aš iš-ta*]-*ma-aš-ta* LUGAL KUR *Ḫat-ti-wa ú-iz-zi*

13. [*na-aš na-aḫ-ša-ri-i*]*a-at-ta-at na-aš-mu nam-ma me-na-aḫ-* ⌈*ḫa*⌉ *-an-da*
14. [*Ú-UL ú-it nu-m*]*u-kán* AMA-*ŠU* LÚ.MEŠ ŠU.GI MUNUS.MEŠ ŠU.GI-*ia*
15. [*me-na-aḫ-ḫa-an-da*] ⌈*pa*⌉ *-ra-a na-iš-ta na-at-mu ú-e-er* GÌR.MEŠ-*aš* ⌈*kat*⌉ *-ta-an*
16. [*ḫa-a-li-i-e-er*] *nu-mu* MUNUS.MEŠ *ku-it* GÌR.MEŠ-*aš* GAM-*an ḫa-a-li-i-e-er*
17. [*nu A-NA* MUNUS.MEŠ] *ḫa-a-an-da ka-a-ri ti-ia-nu-un nu nam-ma I-NA* $^{\mathrm{ÍD}}$*Še-e-ḫa*
18. [*Ú-UL p*]*a-* ⌈*a*⌉ *-un nu-kán* NAM.RA $^{\mathrm{URU}}$KÙ.BABBAR-*ti ku-iš I-NA* $^{\mathrm{ÍD}}$*Še-e-ḫa*
19. [*an-d*]*a e-eš-ta na-an-mu* erasure *pa-ra-a pí-i-e-er nu-mu* NAM.RA *ku-in*
20. ⌈*pa*⌉ *-ra-a pí-i-e-er na-aš* 4 *LI-IM* NAM.RA *e-eš-ta na-an-kán* $^{\mathrm{URU}}$KÙ.BABBAR-*ši*
21. *pa-ra-a ne-eḫ-ḫu-un* erasure *na-an ar-ḫa ú-wa-te-er* $^{\mathrm{m}}$*Ma-na-pa-*$^{\mathrm{d}}$U*-an-ma-za*
22. KUR $^{\mathrm{ÍD}}$*Še-e-ḫa-ia* erasure ÌR-*an-ni da-aḫ-ḫu-un*

---

23. *nam-ma I-NA* KUR $^{\mathrm{URU}}$*Mi-ra-a pa-a-un nu* KUR $^{\mathrm{URU}}$*Mi-ra-a A-NA* $^{\mathrm{m}}$*Maš-ḫu-i-lu-wa AD-DIN*
24. KUR $^{\mathrm{ÍD}}$*Še-e-ḫa-ma A-NA* $^{\mathrm{m}}$*Ma-na-pa-*$^{\mathrm{d}}$U *AD-DIN* KUR $^{\mathrm{URU}}$*Ḫa-pal-la-ma A-NA* $^{\mathrm{m}}$*Tar-ga-aš-na-al-li*
25. *AD-DIN nu-za-kán ke-e* KUR.KUR.MEŠ *pé-e-di-iš-ši* ÌR-*na-aḫ-ḫu-un*
26. *nu-uš-ma-aš-kán* ÉRIN.MEŠ *iš-ḫi-iḫ-ḫu-un nu-mu* ÉRIN.MEŠ *pí-iš-ke-u-an da-a-er*
27. *nu-kán I-NA* ŠÀ KUR $^{\mathrm{URU}}$*Ar-za-u-wa* ⌈*ku-it*⌉ erasure ŠE$_{12}$*-ia-nu-un I-NA* MU.2.KAM-*ma-mu*
28. $^{\mathrm{d}}$UTU $^{\mathrm{URU}}$PÚ-*na* GAŠAN-IA $^{\mathrm{d}}$U NIR.GÁL EN-*IA* $^{\mathrm{d}}$*Me-ez-zu-ul-la-aš* DINGIR.MEŠ-*ia*
29. *ḫu-u-ma-an-te-eš pé-ra-an ḫu-u-i-e-er nu-za* KUR $^{\mathrm{URU}}$*Ar-za-u-wa tar-uḫ-ḫu-un*
30. ⌈*nu-za*⌉ *ku-it* $^{\mathrm{URU}}$KÙ.BABBAR-*ši ar-ḫa ú-da-aḫ-ḫu-un ku-it-ma-za-kán pé-di-* ⌈*iš-ši*⌉
31. ÌR-*na-aḫ-ḫu-un nu-uš-ma-aš-kán* ÉRIN.MEŠ *iš-ḫi-iḫ-ḫu-un nu-mu* ÉRIN.MEŠ *pé-eš*[*-ke*]*-u-an*
32. ⌈*da-a*⌉ *-er nu-za* KUR $^{\mathrm{URU}}$*Ar-za-u-wa ku-it ḫu-u-ma-an tar-uḫ-ḫu-un nu-za* $^{\mathrm{d}}$UTU-*ŠI ku-in*
33. NAM.⌈RA⌉ *I-NA* É.LUGAL *ú-wa-te-nu-un na-aš an-da* 1*-e-et-ta* 6 SIG$_{7}$ 6 *LI-IM* NAM.RA
34. *e-eš-ta* $^{\mathrm{URU}}$KÙ.BABBAR-*aš-ma-za* EN.MEŠ ÉRIN.MEŠ ANŠE.KUR.RA.MEŠ-*ia ku-in* NAM.RA GU$_{4}$ UDU-*ia*
35. *ú-wa-te-et nu-uš-ša-an kap-pu-u-wa-u-wa-ar* NU.GÁL *e-eš-ta*
36. *nu-za* ⌈*ma*⌉ *-aḫ-ḫa-an* erasure KUR $^{\mathrm{URU}}$*Ar-za-u-wa ḫu-u-ma-an tar-uḫ-ḫu-un*

37. *nam-ma* $^{\text{URU}}$KÙ.BABBAR-*ši ar-ḫa ú-wa-nu-un nu-kán* I-*NA* KUR $^{\text{URU}}$*Ar-*⌜*za*⌝*-u-wa ku-it*

38. *an-da gi-im-ma-an-da-ri-ia-nu-un nu ki-i* I-*NA* MU.1.KAM DÙ-*nu-un*

---

## Questions

1. Identify in the handcopy the cuneiform signs given in this and the previous Lessons.
2. Parse the underlined forms.
3. Translate the text using the notes below.

## Words

| | |
|---|---|
| 10. $^{\text{ÍD}}$*Šēḫa* | (a river) |
| 11. *ma-a-n(a-)* | translate as modal particle *man* (see Lesson 7.4.3) |
| 14. AMA | mother |
| ŠU.GI | old, elderly |
| 15. GÌR | foot |
| 16. *ḫaliya-* (Ic) | to kneel |
| 17. *ḫanda* (adv.) | because of (with preceding dat.-loc.) |
| *kāri tiya-* (Ic) | to comply, show clemency |
| 18. $^{\text{URU}}$KÙ.BABBAR-*ti* | = $^{\text{URU}}$*Ḫatti* |
| 20. *piyēr* | "(they) handed (over)" (formally, *piyēr* can also be derived from *piya-* to send) |
| 21. *parā neḫḫun* | "I sent" |
| *uwater* | subject is Muršili's troops |
| 22. ÌR-*atar*, neut. | subjection |
| *daḫḫun* | "I took" |
| 25. *pedišši* | "on the spot" |
| 26. *išḫiya-* (Ic) | to bind, impose |
| *piškeuan dāer* | "(they) began to give" |
| 27. ŠE$_{12}$-*yanu-* | = *gimmandariyanu-* to spend the winter |
| 30. *kuit … kuit* | cf. Lesson 7.4.2 |
| 33. 1-*ētta* | in one, all told |
| 37. *kuit* | since (temporal here) |
| 38. *gimmandariyanu-* (Ia) | to spend the winter |

# Lesson 9

## 9.1 *s*-stem nouns

### 9.1.1

The last real class of Hittite nouns is that of the **s-stems** [GrHL 4.87–90]. They all seem to be neuters. There is one type with Ablaut (*aiš/išš-*) and one without (*nepiš*). There is a rare third type *tunnakiš/tunnakišnaš*: the oblique cases inflect like the *r/n*-stems of the type *ḫanneššar/ḫannešnaš* (see Lesson 7.1.2 B), but the nom.-acc. sing. originally ended in *-iš*. Through analogy the nom.-acc. sing. was often changed into *-iššar*.

Examples: *aiš-/išš-* (Sum. KAxU, pronounced "ka-times-u", indicating a ligature of the signs KA and U) "mouth," *nepiš-* "heaven," *tunna*(*k*)*kiš* "inner chamber."

| | | | |
|---|---|---|---|
| **Sing.** | | | |
| nom.-acc. | *aiš* | *nepiš* | *tunnakiš*, *tunnakeššar* |
| gen. | *iššaš* | *nepišaš* | *tunnakkešnaš* |
| dat.-loc. | *išši* | *nepiši* | |
| all. | *išša* | *nepiša* | *tunnakišna* |
| abl. | *iššaz* | *nepišaz*, *nepišza* | *tunnakkešnaz* |
| instr. | *iššit* | | |
| **Plur.** | | | |
| nom.-acc. | KAxU.ḪI.A | | |
| gen., dat.-loc. | *iššaš* | | |

- For the Sumerogram KAxU there are also some common gender forms attested, for instance an acc. sing. KAxU-*an* and an acc. plur. KAxU-*uš*. This does not necessarily mean that the gender of *aiš-/išš-* was unstable: there may have been more Hittite words for "mouth" that could be hidden behind KAxU.

## 9.2 Suffixed possessive pronoun

### 9.2.1

Typical of the older language is the use of the Hittite **suffixed possessive pronoun** [GrHL 6]. From the fifteenth to fourteenth centuries BC onwards it seems to have been gradually replaced by the Akkadian enclitic possessive pronoun (see

Lesson 5.6). In the later language it is almost completely restricted to frozen expressions like *pediššì* (= *pedi=šši* lit. "in its place") "on the spot." Whether this means that it was also no longer used in the spoken language remains a matter of debate. If it was indeed no longer used, the question is what to read behind the numerous Akkadian possessive forms that we saw in Lesson 5.6.

The suffixed possessive pronoun is attached to the word it belongs to; it agrees in gender, case, and number. So both the "possessed" noun as well as the suffix are inflected, but they are written together as one single word:

- *atta-* "father" + *-mi-* "my" gives the nom. sing. *attaš=miš* "my father"
- *uttar* "word" + *-šmi-* "your" (plur.) gives nom.-acc. sing. *uttar=šmet* "your word"
- *kiššar* "hand" + *-ti-* "your" (sing.) gives a dat.-loc. *kiššari=ti* "in your hand."

The nom.-acc. sing. neut. ending *-t* is the only pronominal characteristic in the inflection, which is otherwise that of the nouns. Note that there is no ablative in *-(a)z*. The stem changes between °*a-* and °*i-* (cf. acc. sing. *-min/-man*):

| | | Singular | | Plural | |
|---|---|---|---|---|---|
| **Sing.** | **1: -mi/-ma** | **2: -ti/-ta** | **3: -ši/-ša** | **1: -šummi/a-** | **2–3: -šmi/a-** |
| nom. com. | *-miš* | *-tiš* | *-šiš* | *-šummiš* | *-šmiš* |
| acc. com. | *-min/-man* | *-tin* | *-šin/-šan* | *-šummi/an* | *-šman* |
| nom.-acc. neut. | *-mit* | *-tit* | *-šit* | *-šummit* | *-šmit* |
| voc. | *-mi* | | | | |
| gen. | *-maš* | *-taš* | *-šaš* | | |
| dat.-loc. | *-mi* | *-ti* | *-ši* | | *-šmi* |
| all. | *-ma* | *-ta* | *-ša* | | *-šma* |
| instr. | | *-tit* | *-šit* | | *-šmit* |
| **Plur.** | | | | | |
| nom. com. | *-miš* | *-tiš* | *-šiš* | | |
| acc. com. | *-muš/-miš* | *-tuš* | *-šuš* | *-šummuš* | *-šmuš* |
| nom.-acc. neut. | *-mit* | | *-šit* | | |
| gen. | *-man* | | | | |
| dat.-loc. | | *-taš* | | | *-šmaš* |

- Most forms with *-i-* (*-miš*, *-mit*, *-šit* etc.) are also frequently written with *-e-* (*-meš*, *-met*, *-šet* etc.).
- The final *-n* of a noun in the (nom.-)acc. sing. often assimilates to a following *-m-*, *-š-*, or *-t-* of an enclitic pronoun:

- *attamman* ‹ **attan=man* "my father"
- *ḫalugatallattin* ‹ **ḫalugatallan=tin* "your envoy"
- *peraššet* ‹ **peran=šet* lit. "(to) his front" › "in front of him" (for more on the last form, see Lesson 10.4.5).

• The cluster of consonants -*Cšm*-, resulting from the combination of a consonantal case ending and the beginning of the enclitic possessive -*šmi/a*-, can be spelled with -*ša-m°*, -*ši-m°*, or -*še-m°*: e.g., *pa-ap-ra-a-tar-ša-me-et* "your defilement," *e-eš-ḫar-ši-mi-it/-še-me-et* "your blood."

## 9.3 Verb class IId, IIe, Ij, IIIa, and supinum

### 9.3.1

The stem of the *ḫi*-verbs presented here (**IId**) [GrHL 13.20–29] is usually given in dictionaries as ending in °*ai*-: e.g., *pai*- "to give," *dai*- "to put, place," and *nai*- "to turn." We find, however, various different stems in the paradigm: stems in °*a*-, °*e*-/*i*-,°*iya*- and °*ai*-. For instance, from the verb *dai*- we have *te-ḫḫi* "I put," *dai-ti* "you put," *tiya-weni* "we put," and *da-er* "they put" (pret.).

Adding to this somewhat confusing picture is the fact that the distribution of these stems is not the same from verb to verb, especially in the plural, as can be observed below in, for instance, the 1. pret. plur. *pi-wen* "we gave" vs. *dai-wen* "we placed" and *neya-wen* "we turned." To this class also belong the verbs extended with the imperfective suffix -*anna*-/-*anni*- (e.g., *ḫuittiyanna/i*- from *ḫuittiya*- "to pull"):

Here are the paradigms of *pai*- "to give," *dai*- "to put, place," and *nai*- "to turn":

**Active**

| | | | |
|---|---|---|---|
| **Pres. sing.** 1 | *peḫḫi* | *teḫḫi* | *neḫḫi* |
| 2 | *paiti, paišti* | *daiti* | *naitti* |
| 3 | *pāi* | *dāi* | *nāi* |
| **plur.** 1 | *piweni* | *tiiaweni* | *naiwani* |
| 2 | *pišteni, paišteni* | *taitteni, taišteni* | *naišteni* |
| 3 | *pianzi* | *tianzi* | *neanzi* |
| **Pret. sing.** 1 | *peḫḫun* | *teḫḫun* | *neḫḫun, neyaḫun* |
| 2 | *paitta, paišta* | *daišta* | *naitta* |
| 3 | *pais, paišta* | *daiš* | *naiš, naišta* |
| **plur.** 1 | *piwen* | *daiwen* | *neyawen* |
| 2 | *pišten, paišten* | *daišten* | |

| | | | |
|---|---|---|---|
| 3 | *pier* | *daer, tier* | *naer, neier* |
| **Medio-passive** | | | |
| **Pres. sing.** 1 | | | *neyaḫḫari* |
| 2 | | | *neyattati, naištari* |
| 3 | | | *nea, neyari* |
| **plur.** 3 | | | *neanda, neantari* |
| **Pret. sing.** 1 | | | *neyaḫḫat* |
| 3 | | | *neat, neyattat* |
| **plur.** 3 | | | *neantati, neyantat* |
| **Imperative** | | | |
| **sing.** 2 | *pai* | *dāi* | *nāi, neya* |
| 3 | *pāu* | *dāu* | *nāu* |
| **plur.** 2 | *pešten, paišten* | *dāišten* | *naišten* |
| 3 | *piyandu* | *tiyandu* | *neyandu* |
| **Participle** | *piant-* | *tiant-* | *neant-* |

- The ending 2. plur. ending *-šten(i)* seems to be restricted to the *ḫi*-conjugation.
- Although there are actually no overlapping forms, the paradigm of *pai-* "to give" might easily be confused with *pai-* "to go" (see Lesson 8.3.2).

### 9.3.2

Comparable to the verbs of Lesson 9.3.1 is a class of verbs (**IIe**) whose stem is often presented as ending in °*a-*, although in fact we find within the paradigm stems in °*a-*, °*-i*, and °*iya-*.

Example: *mema-/memi-/memiya-* "to speak, say."

| | Present | Preterite |
|---|---|---|
| **Sing.** 1 | *memaḫḫi* | *memaḫḫun* |
| 2 | *mematti* | *memišta* |
| 3 | *memai* | *memišta, memaš* |
| **Plur.** 1 | *memiweni, memiaweni* | *memawen, memiawen* |
| 2 | *mematteni, memišteni* | *memišten* |
| 3 | *memianzi, memanzi* | *memer* |
| **Imperative** | | |
| **sing.** 1 | *memallu* | |
| 2 | *memi* | |
| 3 | *memau* | |

| | Present | Preterite |
|---|---|---|
| **plur.** 2 | *memišten* | |
| 3 | *memandu* | |
| **Participle** | *memant-*, *memiant-* | |

9.3.3

Another verb of speaking is *te-/tar-* (**Ij**) [GrHL 12.48–49]. Its *mi*-inflection stands isolated and is built on two different so-called suppletive stems, *te-* and *tar-*:

| | Sing. | Plur. |
|---|---|---|
| **Present** | | |
| 1 | *temi* | *tarweni* |
| 2 | *teši* | *tarteni* |
| 3 | *tezzi* | *taranzi* |
| **Preterite** | | |
| 1 | *tenun* | |
| 2 | *tēš* | |
| 3 | *tet* | *terer* |
| **Imperative** | | |
| **sing.** 2 | *tet* | |
| 3 | *teddu* | |
| **plur.** 2 | *teten* | |
| 3 | *tarandu* | |
| **Participle** | *tarant-* | |

9.3.4

The inflection of the verb ***auš-/au-/u-*** "to see" (**IIIa**) [GrHL 13.32–33] is highly irregular, not just because of its three stem forms but also because of its oscillation between *mi*- and *ḫi*-conjugation.

| | Present | Preterite |
|---|---|---|
| **Active** | | |
| **sing.** 1 | *ūḫḫi* | *uḫḫun* |
| 2 | *autti* | *aušta* |
| 3 | *aušzi* | *aušta* |
| **plur.** 1 | *umeni, aumeni* | *aumen* |
| 2 | *ušteni, autteni* | *aušten* |
| 3 | *uwanzi* | *auer* |

| | Present | Preterite |
|---|---|---|
| **Medio-passive** | | |
| **plur.** 3 | *uwanta* | |
| **Imperative** | | |
| **sing.** 1 | *uwallu* | |
| 2 | *au* | |
| 3 | *aušdu* | |
| **plur.** 2 | *aušten* | |
| 3 | *uwandu* | |
| **Participle** | *uwant-* | |
| **-ške-** | *uške-*, *uškiške-* | |

Note that the 3. plur. pres. and imperative *uwanzi* "they see" and *uwandu* "they must see, let them see" are identical to the same forms of the verb *uwa-* "to come" (Ii, see Lesson 8.3.2)!

### 9.3.5

A further infinite verbal form besides the infinitive II in *-anna* (see Lesson 7.3.3) is the so-called **supinum** [GrHL 11.18–24].

- It has an indeclinable ending -(*u*)*wan* to be attached directly to the verbal stem: e.g., *walḫuwan* "to beat" (from *walḫ-* Ia), *iššuwan* "to do, make" (from *ešša-/ešš-* IIc).
- The supinum is very frequently found with imperfectives in *-ške-*: e.g., *walḫiškewan* (from *walḫiške-*), *memiškeuwan* (from *memiške-*), *akkiškeuwan* (from *akkiške-*). For its use and meaning, see immediately below (Lesson 9.4.1).

## 9.4 Syntax and semantics

### 9.4.1

The **supinum** in *-wan* is almost completely restricted to a combination with the main verb *dai-/tiya-* (IId, see Lesson 9.3.1) [GrHL 25.37–38] "to put, place." In this combination the latter verb means "to begin, start," and the supinum marks the verb dependent on it: e.g., *n=an=za namma* $^{\mathrm{MU\check{S}}}$*Illuyankan taruḫḫuwan dāiš* "he then started defeating (*taruḫḫuwan*) him, Illuyanka" (for the particle *-za* here, see Lesson 3.4.1), or $^{\mathrm{d}}$*Tašmišuš* $^{\mathrm{d}}$U-*ni* EGIR-*pa memiškeuwan dāiš* "Tašmišu began to talk back (i.e., to answer) to the Storm god." The latter example is a frequent formula introducing direct speech in Hittite myths and epics.

Sometimes instead of the verb *dai-/tiya-* the *mi*-verb *tiya-* "to step" is used with the same meaning "to start, begin": e.g., *tešḫaniškeuwan tiyat* "it started to appear in (my) dreams."

9.4.2

In Hittite a word of neuter gender cannot function as the subject of a transitive verb with an expressed or overt object. If a word which is normally a neuter becomes the subject of a transitive verb, that neuter is transformed into common gender by adding the personifying or **ergative suffix** ***-ant-*** to the neuter stem [GrHL 3.8–10]. This *-ant*-stem is inflected (nom.sg.com.-anza) according to the normal *-nt*-stems of Lesson 5.1.1.

Compare the following passage, in which the word "water" in its normal neuter form *watar* (see Lesson 7.1.3) is first used as the object of *pešten* "you must give" and subsequently as the subject of the transitive verb *parkunu-* "to cleanse" in its personified or ergative form *wetenant-* (i.e., the obl. stem of *watar* = *weten-* + *-ant-*):

- *nu=wa=mu apāt wātar pešten parkunummaš=wa kuiš witenanza ēšḫar* *NIŠ* DINGIR-*LIM* *parkunuzi* "give me that water (*wātar*), the water of cleansing which (*parkunummaš witenanza kuiš*) cleanses bloodshed (and) perjury!"

For further examples, see Lesson 7.7.1 sentence 14 and Lesson 9.7.1 sentence 10 with *paḫḫuenant-* as the personified form of the neuter *paḫḫur* "fire," and the passage discussed in Lesson 7.4.2, where the neuter KUR.KUR.ḪI.A is the subject of the (intransitive) nominal predicate *šullanta* (showing it to be a neuter) and is then taken up three times by the common gender relative pronouns *kuēš*, each as the subject of transitive verbs, and two of which have direct objects in the accusative. A real *-ant*-derivation of the Hittite neuter word behind KUR is KUR-*eant-* "country, population" (see Lesson 10.1). See also Lesson 9.7.1 sentence 8 (*tuppiant-* vs. *tuppi-*).

## 9.5 Numerals: higher than 10

9.5.1

Except for an *-ant*-extension of the number 12 (12-*ta-a-ti* probably being 12-*ta*$^{n}$ti), there is no evidence for cardinals with phonetic complements higher than 10. Other complements mostly comprise the usual distributives (*-iš*, *-šu*, *-anki*).

Most higher numerals are expressed by way of cuneiform signs used as numbers:

20  40  60  80 
30  50  70  90 

For 100 (ME), 1000 (*LIM*), and 10,000 ($\text{SIG}_7$), we find Sumero- and Akkadograms.

## 9.6 Cuneiform signs

mu  mi  lum  lam 

dam  šu  ik/GÁL  ak 

šir  lu/UDU  kat  mar 

 az ḫé  zé 

az/uk 

 uk

## 9.7 Exercises; KBo 3.4 iii 39–72

9.7.1 Translate:

1. (from a letter to the king) *ma-an-kán* ᵈUTU-*ŠI BE-LÍ-IA BE-LU ku-in-ki pa-ra-a na-it-ti ma-na* KUR-*i* LÚ.KÚR *Ú-UL dam-mi-iš-ḫa-iz-zi*
2. *nu e-eš-ḫar-šum-mi-it e-eš-šu-wa-an ti-i-e-er*
3. *ma-a-aḫ-ḫa-an* ᴳᴵˢ*ḫu-lu-ga-an-ni-iš pár-na-aš-ša* (*parna-* = “house”) *pa-iz-zi* ᴸᵁ́*ša-la-aš-ḫa-aš-ma* ᴳᴵˢŠUKUR.ḪI.A *A-NA* ᴸᵁ́Ì.DUḪ *pa-a-i*
4. *ap-pí-iz-zi-ya-na* (“later however”) ᵐ*A-ni-it-ta-aš* LUGAL.GAL ᵈ*Ši-ú-šum-mi-in* ᵁᴿᵁ*Za-a-al-pu-wa-az a-ap-pa* ᵁᴿᵁ*Ne-e-ša pé-e-taḫ-ḫu-un*
5. (from a prayer) *na-at ši-i-ú-ni-mi tu-uk me-e-mi-iš-ki-mi*
6. (from a prayer) *nu-mu-za am-me-el* DINGIR-*IA* DUMU.NAM.$\text{U}_{19}$.LU *tu-ug-ga-aš-ta-aš iš-ta-an-za-na-aš-ta-aš* ÌR-*KA ḫal-za-it-ta*
7. (from a letter to a group of addressees) *nu-uš-ma-aš ma-aḫ-ḫa-an ka-a-aš tup-pí-an-za an-da ú-e-mi-iz-zi nu* I-NA ᵁᴿᵁ*Ka-še-pu-u-ra ḫu-it-ti-ya-at-tén* ( … ) *ka-a-aš-ma-aš-ma-aš tup-pí* ᵐ*Pi-še-ni-ya-aš up-pa-aḫ-ḫu-un-pát*
8. (proverb) *mar-ta-ri-wa-ra-at-kán nu-wa-ra-at-kán a-aš-zi*
9. ᵈIM-*aš-ma-na-an wa-la-aḫ-zi pa-aḫ-ḫu-e-na-an-za-ma-na-an ar-ḫa wa-ar-nu-zi*
10. *an-da-ma-kán* UDU-*un ku-wa-a-pí ku-e-u-e-en nu li-in-ki-ya kat-ta-an ki-iš-ša-an da-i-ú-en*
11. (from a letter to Mr. Ḫulla) *na-aš-ta tu-uk* ᵐ*Ḫu-ul-la-an ku-wa-pí gi-im-ma-an-ti pa-ra-a ne-eḫ-ḫu-un nu-ut-ta a-pí-ya Ú-UL iš-ta-ma-aš-še-er*

12. (from a prayer to the gods) *na-aš-ta* A-NA LUGAL MUNUS.LUGAL *an-da aš-šu-li na-iš-du-ma-at*
13. *na-aš* A-NA DUMU.É.GAL GÙB-*li-it* ŠU-*it pa-a-i* DUMU.É.GAL-*ma-aš* GÙB-*la-az ki-iš-ša-ra-az* LUGAL-*i pa-a-i*
14. ŠA $^{d}$IŠTAR *pa-ra-a ḫa-an-da-an-da-tar me-ma-aḫ-ḫi na-at* DUMU.NAM.LÚ.U$_{19}$.LU-*aš iš-ta-ma-aš-du*
15. *nu ka-a-aš ku-it me-ma-i na-at zi-ik ša-ak-ti zi-ga ku-it me-ma-at-ti na-at ka-a-aš ša-a-ak-ki*
16. *ka-ru-ú-i-li-ia-aš* MU.ḪI.A-*aš* $^{d}$*A-la-lu-uš* AN-*ši* LUGAL-*uš e-eš-ta*
17. *ki-i-wa* Ú-UL GEŠTIN *šu-me-en-za-an-wa e-eš-ḫar*
18. *nu-kán ka-ru-ú-i-li-ia* $^{URUDU}$*ar-da-a-la pa-ra-a ti-ia-an-du ne-pí-iš te-kán-na ku-e-ez ar-ḫa ku-e-re-er*

## Words for Lesson 9

| | | | |
|---|---|---|---|
| *anda=ma* | furthermore | *tu(e)kka-*, com. | body |
| *ardala-*, neut. | saw | | |
| *aššul*, neut. | benevolence | *wemiya-* (Ic) | to find, meet |
| *duwarne-* (Ic) | to break | | |
| *dai-/tiya*, (IId) | to put, place | AN | = *nepiš* |
| *parā dai-/tiya-* | to put forth, get | DUMU.É.GAL | palace attendant |
| *dammešḫae-* (Ic) | to bring damage to, punish | GÙB(-*la-*) | left |
| *ešḫar išša-* (IIc) | to shed blood | $^{LÚ}$Ì.DUḪ | guard, doorman |
| *gimmant-*, com. | winter | $^{GIŠ}$ŠUKUR | spear |
| *ḫalzae-* (Ic) | to call, invoke | | |
| *(parā) ḫandandatar* | (divine) guidance, providence | **DN** | |
| | | $^{d}$*Šiušummi-* | lit. "our god" |
| *ḫuittiya-* (Ic) | to (with)draw | | |
| *karuili-* | old, ancient | **PN** | |
| *kāša/kāšma* | (just) now, behold | $^{m}$*Anitta* | Great King, founder of the Hittite royal dynasty in Neša (*c.* 1750–1700 BC) |
| *kiššan* | thus, in this way | | |
| *kuer-* (Id) | to cut | | |
| *mar-/mer-* (IIb) | to disappear | | |
| *mema-* (IIe) | to speak, say | | |
| *nai-* (IId) | to turn | $^{m}$*Ḫulla-* | |
| *anda nai-* | to turn to(wards) | $^{m}$*Pišeni-* | |
| *parā nai-* | to send out, dispatch | **GN** | |
| *pai-* (IId) | to give | $^{URU}$*Kašepura* | |
| *peda-* (IIc) | to bring (away) | | |
| $^{LÚ}$*šalašḫa-*, com. | groom, stable boy | $^{URU}$*Zalpuwa* | |

## 9.7.2 *The Ten-Year Annals* of the Hittite King Muršili II

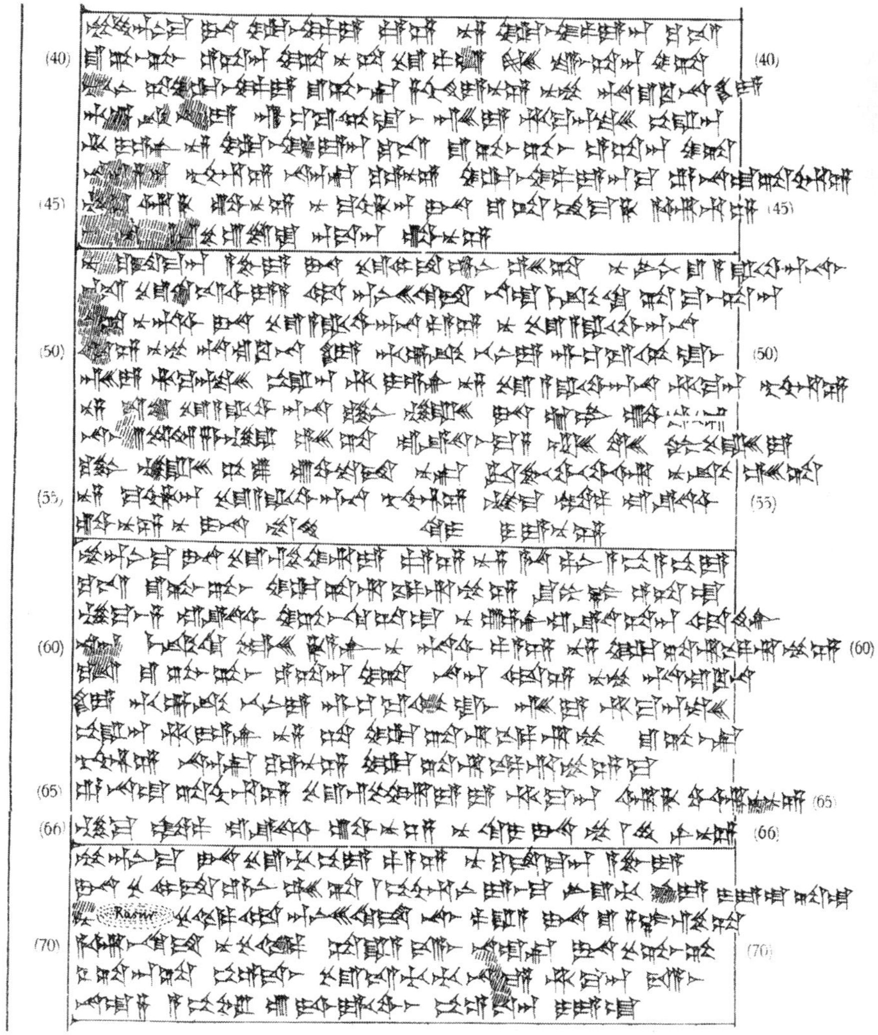

Figure 11

iii

39. MU.KAM-*an-ni-ma* I-NA $^{\text{ḪUR.SAG}}$*Aš-ḫar-pa-ia pa-a-un nu-za* $^{\text{ḪUR.SAG}}$*Aš-ḫar-pa-ia-an ku-iš*

40. $^{\text{URU}}$*Ga-aš-ga-aš e-ša-an ḫar-ta nu* ŠA KUR $^{\text{URU}}$*Pa-* ⌈*la*⌉ *-a* KASKAL.MEŠ *kar-aš-ša-an ḫar-ta*

41. ⌈*nu*⌉ *u-ni* ŠA $^{\text{ḪUR.SAG}}$*Aš-ḫar-pa-ia* $^{\text{URU}}$*Ga-aš-kán za-aḫ-ḫi-ia-nu-un nu-mu* $^{\text{d}}$UTU $^{\text{URU}}$PÚ-*na* GAŠAN-IA

42. $^{\text{d}}$U ⌈NIR.GÁL BE⌉ [-LÍ]-IA $^{\text{d}}$ ⌈*Me*⌉ *-ez-zu-ul-la-aš* DINGIR.MEŠ-*ia ḫu-u-ma-an-te-eš pé-ra-an*

43. *ḫu-u-i-e-er nu-za* $^{\text{ḪUR.SAG}}$*Aš-ḫar-*⌈*pa*⌉*-ia-an ku-iš* $^{\text{URU}}$*Ga-aš-ga-aš e-ša-an ḫar-ta*

44. ⌈*na-an*⌉*-za-an tar-uḫ-ḫu-un na-an-kán ku-e-nu-un* $^{\text{ḪUR.SAG}}$*Aš-ḫar-pa-ia-an-ma dan-na-at-ta-aḫ-ḫu-un*

45. ⌈*nam-ma*⌉ *ar-ḫa ú-wa-nu-un nu ma-aḫ-ḫa-an* I-NA $^{\text{URU}}$*Ša-am-ma-ḫa a-ar-ḫu-un*

46. *n*[*u* I-] ⌈NA⌉ $^{\text{URU}}$*Zi-ú-li-la an-da-an ú-wa-nu-un*

---

47. *nu ku-it-ma-an* A-BU-IA I-NA KUR $^{\text{URU}}$*Mi-it-*⌈*tan*⌉*-ni e-eš-ta nu* LÚ.KÚR $^{\text{URU}}$*A-ra-u-wa-an-na-aš*

48. ⌈*ku*⌉*-iš* KUR $^{\text{URU}}$ ⌈*Ki*⌉*-iš-ši-ia-a* GUL-*an-ni-eš-ke-et na-at me-ek-ki ta-ma-aš-ša-an*

49. [*ḫa*]*r-ta nu* $^{\text{d}}$UTU-*ŠI* I-NA KUR $^{\text{URU}}$*A-ra-u-wa-an-na pa-a-un nu* KUR $^{\text{URU}}$*A-ra-u-wa-an-na*

50. ⌈GUL⌉*-un nu-mu* $^{\text{d}}$UTU $^{\text{URU}}$PÚ-*na* GAŠAN-IA $^{\text{d}}$U NIR.GÁL BE-LÍ-IA $^{\text{d}}$*Me-ez-zu-ul-la-aš*

51. DINGIR.MEŠ-*ia ḫu-u-ma-an-te-eš pé-ra-an ḫu-u-i-e-er nu-za* KUR $^{\text{URU}}$*A-ra-u-wa-an-na ḫu-u-ma-an tar-uḫ-ḫu-un*

52. *nu-za* ⌈IŠ-TU⌉ KUR $^{\text{URU}}$*A-ra-u-wa-an-na ku-in* NAM.RA.MEŠ I-NA É.LUGAL *ú-wa-te-nu-un*

53. *na-aš* 3 LI-IM 5 ME NAM.RA *e-eš-ta* $^{\text{URU}}$KÙ.BABBAR-*aš-ma-za* EN.MEŠ ÉRIN.MEŠ ANŠE.KUR.RA.MEŠ-*ia*

54. *ku-in* NAM.RA.MEŠ GU$_4$ UDU *ú-wa-te-et nu-kán kap-pu-u-wa-u-wa-ar* NU.GÁL *e-eš-ta*

55. *nu-za ma-aḫ-ḫa-an* KUR $^{\text{URU}}$*A-ra-u-wa-an-na tar-uḫ-ḫu-un nam-ma* EGIR-*pa* $^{\text{URU}}$KÙ.BABBAR-*ši*

56. *ú-wa-nu-un nu* I-NA MU.1.KAM *ki-i i-ia-nu-un*

---

57. MU-*an-ni-ma* I-NA KUR $^{\text{URU}}$*Zi-ḫar-ri-ia pa-a-un nu-za* A-NA PA-NI A-BI A-BI-IA

58. *ku-iš* $^{\text{URU}}$*Ga-aš-ga-aš* $^{\text{ḪUR.SAG}}$*Ta-ri-ka-ri-mu-un* GÉŠPU-*az e-ša-at*

59. *nam-ma-aš-za* $^{\text{URU}}$KÙ.BABBAR-*ši ḫar-ga-aš ki-ša-at nu ú-e-er* $^{\text{URU}}$KÙ.BABBAR-*ša-an* GUL-*ḫe-er*

60. ⌈*na-an*⌉ *me-ek-ki dam-me-eš-ḫa-a-er nu* $^{\text{d}}$UTU-*ŠI pa-a-un nu-za* $^{\text{ḪUR.SAG}}$*Ta-ri-ka-ri-mu-un*

61. *ku-*⌈*iš*⌉ $^{\text{URU}}$*Ga-aš-ga-aš e-ša-an ḫar-ta na-an* GUL-*un nu-mu* $^{\text{d}}$UTU $^{\text{URU}}$PÚ-*na*

62. GAŠAN-IA $^{\text{d}}$U NIR.GÁL BE-LÍ-IA $^{\text{d}}$*Me-ez-zu-ul-la-aš* DINGIR.MEŠ-*ia ḫu-u-ma-an-te-eš*

63. *pé-ra-an ḫu-u-i-e-er nu-za* ŠA $^{\text{ḪUR.SAG}}$*Ta-ri-ka-ri-mu* $^{\text{URU}}$*Ga-aš-kán*

64. *tar-uḫ-ḫu-un na-an-kán ku-e-nu-un* $^{\mathrm{ḪUR.SAG}}$*Ta-ri-ka-ri-mu-un-ma*
65. *dan-na-at-ta-aḫ-ḫu-un* KUR $^{\mathrm{URU}}$*Zi-ḫar-ri-ia-ia ḫu-u-ma-an ar-ḫa wa-ar-nu-nu-un*
66. *nam-ma* EGIR-*pa* $^{\mathrm{URU}}$KÙ.BABBAR-*ši ú-wa-nu-un nu ki-i* I-NA MU.1.KAM DÙ-*nu-un*

---

67. MU-*an-ni-ma* I-NA KUR $^{\mathrm{URU}}$*Ti-pí-ia pa-a-un nu ku-it-ma-an* A-BU-IA
68. I-NA KUR *Mi-it-tan-ni e-eš-ta* $^{\mathrm{m}}$*Pí-iḫ-ḫu-ni-ia-aš-ma* LÚ $^{\mathrm{URU}}$*Ti-* ⌈*pí*⌉ *-ia i-ia-at-ta-at*
69. ⌈*nu*⌉ erasure KUR.UGU GUL-*an-ni-eš-ke-et na-aš pa-ra-a* I-NA $^{\mathrm{URU}}$*Za-az-zi-ša*
70. *a-ar-aš-ke-et nu* KUR.UGU *ša-ra-a da-a-aš na-at-kán* I-NA KUR $^{\mathrm{URU}}$*Ga-aš-ga*
71. *kat-ta-an-ta pé-e-da-aš* KUR $^{\mathrm{URU}}$*Iš-ti-ti-na-* ⌈*ma*⌉ *-za ḫu-u-ma-an da-a-aš*
72. *na-at-za a-pé-el ú-i-ši-ia-u-wa-aš pé-e-* ⌈*da*⌉ *-an i-ia-at*

---

## Questions

1. Identify in the handcopy the cuneiform signs given in this and the previous Lessons.
2. Translate the text using the notes below.

## Words

| | |
|---|---|
| 39. MU(.KAM)-*anni* | in the following year |
| 40. $^{\mathrm{URU}}$*Gašga-* | Gašgaean |
| 40. *ešan* | nom.-acc. neut. sing. of participle of *eš-/aš-* "to sit down, occupy" |
| *karš-* (Ia) | to cut |
| 41. *uni* | "that (Gašgaean)" |
| 44. *dannattaḫḫ-* (IIa) | to empty, lay waste |
| 48. GUL-*anniya-* | = *walḫanniya-* = *walḫ-* with imperfective *-anni(ya)-* suffix |
| 57. ANA PANI | in front of, in the time of |
| A-BI A-BI-IA | "my grandfather" (lit. my father's father) |
| 58. GÉŠPU | force, violence |
| 59. *ḫarga-*, com. | nuisance, pest, destruction, death |
| 60. *dammešḫae-* (Ic) | to damage, harass, punish |
| 68. LÚ $^{\mathrm{URU}}$*Tipiya* | apposition to Piḫḫuniyaš |
| 69. KUR UGU | the Upper Land (= area to the north-east of Ḫattuša) |
| 72. *wišiyauwaš* | "of/for grazing" |

# Lesson 10

## 10.1 Irregular nouns *ker, per, utne*

### 10.1.1

The overview of nouns concludes with three **irregular** and isolated paradigms: *ker/kard-/kardi-* neut. (ŠÀ) "heart," *per/parna-* neut. (É) "house, household, domain," and *utne-/utni-* neut. (KUR) "land" [GrHL 4.114–116, 4.58]. As already indicated, all three of them are neuters.

| | | | |
|---|---|---|---|
| **Sing.** | | | |
| nom.-acc. | *ker*, ŠÀ-*er* | *per*, É-*er* | *utne*, KUR-*e* |
| gen. | *kardiyaš*, ŠÀ-*aš* | *parnaš*, É-*aš* | *utniyaš, utneyaš*, KUR-*eaš* |
| dat.-loc. | *kardi*, ŠÀ-*i* | *parni*, É-*ni*, É-*ri* | *utni, utniya, utneya, utne*, KUR-*e* |
| all. | *karta*, ŠÀ-*ta* | *parna*, É-*na* | *utniya* |
| abl. | *kartaz*, ŠÀ-*az/za* | *parnaz*, É-*az/za*, É-*erza* | *utniyaz, utneaz*, KUR-*az* |
| instr. | *kardit*, ŠÀ-*it* | | |
| **Plur.** | | | |
| nom.-acc. | *ker* | É-*er* | *utne*, KUR.KUR(.ḪI.A) |
| gen., dat.-loc. | | *parnaš*, É-*naš* | |

- The declension of *ker* and *per* runs more or less parallel; the only real *i*-stem form of the former is the gen. sing. *kardiyaš*.
- Judging by forms like the dat.-loc. É-*ri* and the abl. É-*erza*, there was also an inflection using the stem *per-*.
- Note that *utne* can be nom.-acc. sing. and plur. as well as dat.-loc. sing.! For the derived stem *utneant-* "population," see Lesson 9.4.2.

## 10.2 Demonstrative and anaphoric pronoun *aši*

### 10.2.1

A less frequently attested **demonstrative and anaphoric pronoun** "that (one) over there (with a third person)" or simply "he, she, it" is ***aši*** [GrHL 7.10–16]. It is the third of the series to which *kā-* "this one with me" (see Lesson 4.2.1) and *apā-* "that one with you" (Lesson 5.2) belong. It can also have a depreciative or pejorative value ("that horrible/despicable …").

The pronoun *aši* consists of a single vowel pronoun *a-* (for the nom. sing. com.) Ablauting with *e-* (nom.-acc. sing. neut. and oblique stem) and *u-* (acc. sing. com., compare the *u* in the accusatives *kūn* and *apūn*). This vowel is followed by a case ending and an indeclinable *deictic* (i.e., demonstrative) particle *-i*: *a+š+i*, *u+n+i*, *e+n+i*.

Since it is a pronoun, the case ending can include the pronominal characteristic *-(e)d-*, *-(e)dan-*. Note that the neuter *ini* does not show the *-t* typical of the pronouns (cf. *apāt*).

| | Sing. | Plur. |
|---|---|---|
| nom. com. | *aši* | *uniuš* |
| acc. com. | *uni, unin, aši* | |
| nom.-acc. neut. | *ini, eni* | |
| gen. | *aši, el, uniaš* | |
| dat. | *edani* | *edaš* |
| loc. | *edi* | |
| abl. | *edez* | |

- It seems that the structure of this pronoun was no longer very clear to Hittite speakers; several new forms emerge over the course of the language. The acc. sing. com. *unin*, gen. sing. *uniaš*, and the nom. plur. com. *uniuš* are later secondary formations on a stem *uni-*.
- The abl. *edez* is mainly attested as an adverb meaning "on that side," especially in opposition to *kez* "on this side" (see Lesson 4.2.1).
- The loc. *edi* occurs adverbially only as "there" or "thither."
- An adverb derived from the same stem and comparable to *kiššan* "thus, in this way" and *apeniššan* "thus, in that way" is *iniššan*/*eniššan* "thus."

## 10.3 Verb class IIf, infinitive I and verbal noun, infinite verb

### 10.3.1

An important verb is *dā-* "to take, seize" (**IIf**). The only other verb to be inflected in the same way is *lā-* "to detach, release, set free." Apart from the 1. plur. pres. *tumeni*, the inflection is otherwise regular [GrHL 13.11–12]:

| | | Sing. | Plur. |
|---|---|---|---|
| **Active** | | | |
| **Present** | 1 | *dāḫḫi* | *tumeni, dāweni* |
| | 2 | *dātti* | *datteni* |
| | 3 | *dāi* | *dānzi* |
| **Preterite** | 1 | *dāḫḫun* | *dāuen* |
| | 2 | *dātta* | *datten* |
| | 3 | *dāš, datta* | *dāēr* |
| **Medio-passive** | | | |
| **Present** | 3 | *dattari* | |
| **Preterite** | 3 | *dattat* | |
| **Imperative** | | | |
| | 2 | *dā* | *dātten* |
| | 3 | *dāu* | *dandu* |
| **Infinitive II and I** | | *danna, dauwanzi* | |
| **Participle** | | *dānt-* | |

- For the infinitive I *dauwanzi*, see immediately below Lesson 10.3.2, 10.4.3.

### 10.3.2

Besides the infinite verb forms that we already saw (the inf. II in *-anna* Lesson 7.3.3, the supinum in *-wan* Lesson 9.3.5), there is [GrHL 11.18–24]:

- an **Infinitive I** in *-wanzi*
- and a **verbal noun** in nom.-acc. sing. neut. *-war* with a gen. sing. in *-waš* (or *-mar*/*-maš* after *-u-*: cf. Lesson 3.5; e.g., *waḫnumar* ‹ **waḫnuwar*).

The verbal abstract in *-(ā)tar* with its original all. (= inf. II) in *-anna* belongs to the Ablauting verbs (compare *ed-*/*ad-* "(to) eat" › *adatar* "(the act of) eating" › "*adanna* "to(wards) eat(ing)"). The inf. I (*-wanzi*), the verbal noun (*-war*), and the supinum (*-wan*), on the other hand, originally belong together and are at home with the non-Ablauting verbs. E.g.:

- *walḫ-* "(to) attack" › *walḫuwanzi* "to attack," *walḫuwar* "(the act of) attacking —› attack"
- *tepnu-* "(to) humiliate" › *tepnumanzi* "to humiliate," *tepnumar* "(the act of) humiliating —› humiliation" (for *-uw-* › *-um-*, see Lesson 3.5).

Nevertheless, this distinction has not been systematically upheld; the two systems have partly merged, and many verbs have, for instance, both infinitives: compare Lesson 10.3.1 *danna* next to *dauwanzi*.

For the syntax and semantics of the different members of this system including the special uses of the genitives in *-annaš* (from *-ātar*) and *-uwaš* (from *-war*), see Lesson 10.4.1–3.

We can put together the various forms in the following way:

| | Verbs with Ablaut | Verbs without Ablaut |
|---|---|---|
| verbal noun | -(*a*)*tar* | -(*u*)*war* |
| gen. | -(*a*)*nnaš* | -(*u*)*waš* |
| infinitive I | | -(*u*)*wanzi* |
| infinitive II | -(*a*)*nna* | |
| supinum | | -(*u*)*wan* |

If we take *ed-/ad-* as an example for verbs showing Ablaut and *walḫ-* for those without, we get:

| | *ed-/ad-* | *walḫ-* |
|---|---|---|
| verbal noun | *adatar* | *walḫuwar* |
| gen. | *adannaš* | *walḫuwaš* |
| infinitive I | | *walḫuwanzi* |
| infinitive II | *adanna* | |
| supinum | | *walḫuwan* |

Whereas the forms under "Verbs with Ablaut" are clearly part of the paradigm of the abstract nouns in -(*a*)*tar* and were probably still synchronically felt as such by the Hittites, the forms of the **infinite verb** of "Verbs without Ablaut" are only remnants of what once may have been a complete paradigm. Other forms that might etymologically be linked to the latter do not seem to be available.

## 10.4 Syntax and semantics

### 10.4.1

The semantics of the **verbal noun** in *-tar* or *-war* are best illustrated by its systematic use in the so-called Lexical Lists [GrHL 25.4–9]: this is a well-known and widespread genre of texts in the Ancient Near East, in which people categorized and systematized the world around them in all kinds of lists of words and expressions. Besides lists which only have Sumerian and Akkadian, there are also those adding Hittite and Hurrian. Akkadian verbs appear in these Lexical Lists in the (Akkadian) infinitive which is matched in the Hittite columns with the verbal noun in *-war* (e.g., Akkad. *EREŠU* "to ask, request" = Hitt. *wekuwar* from *wek-*) or *-tar*. In these lists one will *not* find the infinitives I or II corresponding to the Akkadian verbal entries.

### 10.4.2

The genitives of the verbal nouns in *-(u)waš* and *-annaš* are used in constructions to indicate what should be done with the object indicated by the governing noun or what the purpose of that object is [GrHL 25.8]. Compare the following combinations:

- *pedan ḫenkuwaš* "a place of bowing" › "a place where one has to bow"
- *n=aš mān duddunumaš mān=aš kunannaš* "whether he (is one) of pardoning (*duddunu-*) or he (is one) of killing" › "whether he should be pardoned or killed"
- $^{\text{GIŠ}}$GIGIR *ašannaš* vs. $^{\text{GIŠ}}$GIGIR *tiyauwaš* "a cart of sitting" › "a cart to sit on" › "wagon, coach" vs. "a cart to step/stand on" › "chariot."

Borrowing a term from Latin grammar, this genitive has been coined a ***genitivus quasi gerundivalis***.

### 10.4.3

The **infinitive I** in *-wanzi* is mainly final, i.e., it indicates the goal of the action [GrHL 25.10–36]: e.g., *n=ašta* EN.SÍSKUR *warpuwanzi paizzi* "the patient goes (in order) to wash himself." As such it can interchange with a dative of goal (*dativus finalis*): compare the sentences

- *BELI=NI=wa=nnaš* $^{\text{URU}}$*Ḫattuši šāruwauwanzi lē maniyaḫti* "our lord, do not extradite us to (the armies of) Ḫattuša (in order) to plunder" (i.e., to be plundered by Ḫattuša) from the verb *šaruwai-* "to plunder."
- *n=an* $^{\text{URU}}$*Ḫattuši ḫumanti šāraui maniyaḫḫun* "and I extradited it (i.e., a city previously mentioned) to all of Ḫattuša for booty."

In the last sentence the form *šaraui* is a dat. sing. of the noun *šāru-* "booty." Normally, the active finite forms of the verb *šāruwai-* have an active transitive meaning, but the infinitive in the example given here must clearly be translated as a passive; this shows that the infinitives (both I and II) are indifferent to voice. The choice for an active or medio-passive interpretation depends on the context.

That the infinitive could be felt as a verbal form is illustrated by those cases where it has its own dependent accusative object:

- *kue* KARAŠ.ḪI.A *INA* $^{\text{URU}}$*Nuḫašši ḫalki*$^{\text{ḪI.A}}$*-uš* (acc. plur. com.) *ḫarninkuwanzi pēḫudan ḫarta* "the troops which he had brought to Nuḫašše to destroy the grain."

However, a nominal construction can also be found, that is, with the logical object in the genitive depending on the infinitive as if it were a noun; compare the following two phrases from the Hittite Royal Death Ritual:

- MUNUS.MEŠ ... *ḫaštiaš* (gen.) *leššūwanzi pānzi* "the women go to gather the bones (lit. to the gathering of the bones)."
- *nu maḫḫan ḫaštai* (acc.) *leššūwanzi zinnanzi* "when they stop gathering the bones."

## 10.4.4

To make **similes** Hittite mostly uses conjunctions ("just as ...") or postpositions ("like"). The conjunctions are *mān* and *maḫḫan.* Compare the following examples:

- $^{d}$UTU-*uš* $^{d}$IM-*aš mān uktūreš* LUGAL-*uš* MUNUS.LUGAL-*ašš=a* *QĀTAMMA* *uktūreš ašantu* "just as the Sun goddess (and) the Storm god are everlasting, may the king and queen be everlasting in the same way!"
- *kī* $^{NA4}$*pēru māḫḫan uktūri* *BĒLU U* DAM-*ŠU* DUMU.MEŠ-*ŠU* *QĀTAMMA* *uktureš ašandu* "just as this rock is everlasting, may the lord and his wife (and) his children be everlasting in the same way!"

Of course, both conjunctions also have their temporal ("when") and conditional ("if") meanings, but the presence of *QĀTAMMA* in a following or nearby sentence is always a good indicator for their function in a simile.

Both *mān* and *maḫḫan* can also be used as a postposition "like" with a noun; compare:

- *nu=šši=kan* GI-*aš* *IŠTU* $^{GIŠ}$PAN *pariyan* MUŠEN-*iš mān iyattari* "and his (=*šši*=) arrow flies across (*pariyan*) from the bow like a bird."
- *nu=war=uš arḫa dannaruš* $^{DUG}$ÚTUL.ḪI.A *maḫḫan duwarneškeši* "and you will break them like empty vessels."

As opposed to *mān* and *maḫḫan*, the postposition *iwar* governs a case: the preceding word stands in the genitive:

- *nu ammel iwar kuwatqa iyaši* "perhaps you will act like me."

Of course, the gen. can also be expressed by Akkad. *ŠA*:

- *ŠA* LÚ.Ú.ḪUB=*ma=an iwar duddumiyandu* "let them make him deaf like a deaf man!"

In combination with Sumero- and Akkadograms *iwar* can sometimes precede instead of follow the word to which it belongs, but in spoken Hittite it will still have preceded.

### 10.4.5

An adverbial suffix that can also serve to express **comparisons** is *-ili*: e.g., *pittiyantili* "like a fugitive," MUNUS-*li* "like a woman", DUMU-*li* "like a child." Compare the following sentence:

- *nu=wa ḫaranili šākuiškizzi* (describing the Hittite king: "his head is of iron, his teeth are those of a lion, his eyes are those of an eagle,") "he sees like an eagle" (for the noun *ḫaran-*, see Lesson 6.1.1).

The same suffix *-ili* is used in language designations: *nešumnili/nešili/našili* "in Hittite" (i.e., "in the language of the city of Neša," cf. Introduction §2), *luwili* "in Luwian," *babilili* "in Babylonian." Such designations can be preceded by the determinative $^{URU}$.

### 10.4.6

Hittite does not have a morphological category to express a **comparative** or **superlative** [GrHL 17.12–20]. Instead it uses the dative-locative case: "for/to A B is big" › "in comparison to A, B is big" › "B is bigger than A." E.g.:

- *ANA* LUGAL KUR $^{URU}$*Tarḫuntašša* 1-*aš* $^{LÚ}$*tuḫukantiš šalliš ēšdu namma=ma=ši=kan lē kuiški šalliš* "(in comparison) to the king of Tarḫuntašša only the *tuḫukanti* shall be high, but furthermore no one shall be high in comparison to him" › "only the *tuḫukanti* shall rank higher than the king of Tarḫuntašša, but furthermore no one shall rank higher than he."

We can translate a superlative, when Hittite adds *ḫumant-* "all, every" to this construction:

- DINGIR.MEŠ-*naš ḫūmandaš* $^{d}$*Zašḫapunaš šalliš* "(in comparison) to all the gods Zašḫapuna (is) great" › "of all the gods Zašḫapuna is the greatest."

Sometimes the adverb *parā* "forth, further" seems to be used to bring out a comparative notion: e.g., *nu mān* … É $^{d}$UTU $^{URU}$PÚ-*na parā ḫappinešzi* "if … the temple of the Sun goddess of Arinna becomes richer" (lit. "becomes further rich" from *ḫappinešš-* "to become rich"). One also finds *parā* doubled: *IŠTU* DINGIR-*LIM=mu parā parā* SIG$_5$-*iškittari* "through the goddess it became better for me" (lit. "it became more and more good" from SIG$_5$-*eške-* "to become good").

### 10.4.7

In the preceding lessons we have come across adverbs like *anda/andan* "in(to), inside," *katta/kattan* "down, under, next to," *peran* "in front of," and others many times. Here is a more complete list [GrHL 20]:

| | | | | | |
|---|---|---|---|---|---|
| *anda* | into | *andan* | inside, in | *andurza* | in, inside |
| *appa* | to the back, again | *appan* | behind, again | *appanda* | afterwards |
| *arḫa* | out off, away from | | | *araḫza* | outside |
| | | | | *araḫzanda* | around, roundabout |
| *ištarna* | to/in the middle | | | *ištarni-* | in the midst of |
| *katta* | down to, next to | *kattan* | under, next to | *kattanda* | down into |
| | | | | *katti-* | next to |
| *parā* | forth, out of, further | *peran* | in front of, before | *parranda* | over, across |
| | | *pariyan* | over, across | | |
| *šarā* | up(wards), above | *šer* | above, on | | |
| *tapuša* | to the side | | | *tapušza* | on the side |

Originally, these **local** or **dimensional adverbs** were nouns; certain cases gradually evolved into adverbs while the other cases of the paradigm were lost.

- Those in the first column were allatives and generally indicate direction.
- Those in the second column are accusatives and denote the position where somebody or something is.
- In the third column are some original ablatives (*andurza*, *araḫza*, *tapušza*) and compounds with *anda*. The forms *katti-* and *ištarni-* (constructed with the dat.-loc. of the suffixed poss. pron., see Lesson 9.2) are original dat.-locatives: *katti=ti* "with you," *ištarni=šummi* "among ourselves."
- A systematic distinction between the adverbs of direction of the first column and those of the second column, which indicate a static position, is upheld in the older language only.

The original nominal character of the adverbs is only apparent in Old Hittite. Here we find, for instance, cases where the "adverb" has an enclitic possessive pronoun (see Lesson 9.2) attached to it: *peran=met*, *šer=šmet*. E.g.:

- DUMU.É.GAL-*š=a pēra(n)=šet* (written *pé-e-ra-aš-še-et*, cf. already Lesson 9.2) $^{\text{GIŠ}}$*zupāri ḫarzi* "the palace attendant holds the torch in front of himself" (lit. perhaps with an acc. of respect "as to his front side"?)

- $^{\text{MUŠEN}}$*ḫaranan* ÉRIN.MEŠ-*an=a* LUGAL-*aš* MUNUS.LUGAL-*ašš=a šēr=šmet* (*še-e-er-še-me-et*) *waḫnumeni* "we sway the eagle and the troops over the king and queen" (lit. perhaps "as to their, that is the king and queen's, upper side"?)

With *katta* and *ištarna* we find original dative-locatives in this combination: *katti=ti, ištarni=šummi.* E.g.:

- *karūiliyaza=wa=kan* $^{\text{URU}}$*Ḫattušaš* $^{\text{URU}}$*Mizrašš=a ištarni=šummi āššiyanteš ešer* "formerly Ḫattuša and Egypt were on good terms with each other" (lit. "amongst ourselves").

Another hint at the original nominal character of these adverbs is the fact that in Older Hittite they are often construed with a preceding genitive: LUGAL-*aš peran* "in front of the king" (lit. "as to the front side of the king"). In later Hittite these constructions were replaced by a dative of a noun or of the enclitic personal pronoun (Lesson 2.2) and the adverb:

- Instead of *pēran=šet* in the first example we may find *=ši ... peran.*
- Instead of *šēr=šmet* we may see *ANA* LUGAL MUNUS.LUGAL=*ya šēr* or *=šmaš ... šēr, =šmaš ... ištarna.*
- Instead of LUGAL-*aš peran* we see LUGAL-*i peran.*
- Both constructions juxtaposed in the same text are found in the Hittite Amarna letter (first half of the fourteenth century BC): *katti=mi* SIG$_5$-*in* "with me (it is) fine" ... *tukk=a katta ḫūman* SIG$_5$-*in ēštu* "may all be fine with you too!"

Terms often used to describe the function of these local adverbs are postposition, preverb, or adverb. A postposition differs from a preposition only in that it stands after the noun it governs instead of before it: e.g., gen. or dat. + *peran* (*ḫaššaš/ḫašši peran* "in front of the hearth"), abl. + *arḫa* or *parā* (*arunaz arḫa* "out of the sea"). A preverb stands in close relation to the verb and modifies its meaning in a certain way: *pai-* "to go" but *anda pai-* "to go into, enter." As its name indicates, a preverb mostly stands right before the verb, but certain elements may come in between (see below). A local adverb like the ones discussed here differs from a preverb only in its position; it can theoretically stand anywhere in the clause. Other adverbs, of course, (like *mekki* "very, much") can also modify adjectives or other adverbs ("very much").

However, it is often hard to choose between these possibilities. Compare the following clause:

> *uddar=ma=ši kue iššaz parā iyattari*
> "but the words which come out of his (-*ši*, dat. of personal pronoun, Lesson 2.2) mouth."

Is *parā* here a postposition with the immediately preceding abl. *iššaz*? Or is it a preverb with the deponent verb *iya-* "to go out"? If we look at the combination *iššaz parā* with other verbs, we might have an argument in favor of *parā* as postposition here:

> ANA $^{d}$UTU-*ŠI=ya=at=kan* INA $^{URU}$*Zitḫara* INA BURU$_{14}$ *iššaz parā aniyauwen*
> "and for His Majesty we wrote it (i.e., a text) down in the town of Zitḫara in harvest time out of his own mouth" (that is, by dictation or at His Majesty's orders).

This impression becomes even stronger if we look at the following variant of the latter clause:

> *kī=ma=kan tuppi* ANA $^{d}$UTU-*ŠI iššaz parā* $^{m}$*Ḫattušiliš aniyat*
> "this tablet Ḫattušili wrote down for His Majesty out of his own mouth."

Now *iššaz parā* is separated from the verb by the subject ($^{m}$*Ḫattušiliš*) and the possibility of *parā* functioning as preverb seems to be ruled out. This is even more true in yet another variant:

> ANA $^{d}$UTU-*ŠI=at=kan iššaz parā* INA $^{URU}$*Zitḫara* INA BURU$_{14}$ *aniyauwen*
> "for His Majesty we wrote it down out of his own mouth in the town of Zitḫara in harvest time."

Here *iššaz parā* is separated from the verb by the adverbial constituents denoting place ("in Zitḫara") and time ("in harvest time"). However, a final variant overthrows all our previous considerations:

> ANA $^{d}$UTU-*ŠI=ya=at=kan iššaz* $^{URU}$*Zitḫara* INA BURU$_{14}$ *parā aniyauwen*
> "and for His Majesty we wrote it down from his mouth in the town of Zitḫara in harvest time."

This time *iššaz* and *parā* are separated by other constituents, and if we did not have the preceding variants we might have thought of *parā* as a preverb here. Pending further research one should be cautious in using labels like postposition, preverb, or adverb. It seems safer to conclude that the position of the local adverb in the clause is not the sole determining factor for its function and that the same content could be expressed in syntactically different ways.

In most cases the local adverb stands immediately before the verb, but as we saw, certain constituents can separate the two: These are negations (*natta*/UL "not, no," UL *manka* "not at all," prohibitive *lē*), forms of the indefinite pronoun (*kuiški* Lesson 7.2, also combined with negations), and adverbs or adverbial phrases. E.g.: *kūn* UN-*an apez pedaz arḫa* UL=*pat tittanuwanzi* "this man they will certainly (-*pat*) not depose from that office," *n=ašta anda lē kuinki tarnai* "he shall not let anyone in."

## 10.5 Cuneiform signs

rad  gi  nam  pal/BAL 

liš  tàš 

ib  ur 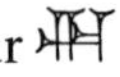 gur 

zu   kiš 

## 10.6 Exercises; KBo 3.4 iii 73–95, iv 22–48

### 10.6.1 Translate:

1. *nu-wa-kán* A-NA ÉRIN.MEŠ-KA ÉRIN.MEŠ-IA *me-ek-ki*
2. *zi-ik-pát* $^{d}$UTU $^{URU}$*A-ri-in-na na-ak-ki-iš šal-le-eš-ša-az zi-ik-pát* $^{d}$UTU $^{URU}$*A-ri-in-na nam-ma-ták-kán da-ma-a-iš* DINGIR-LAM *na-ak-ki-iš šal-li-iš-ša* Ú-UL *e-eš-zi*
3. *nu ku-e-ez* MÁŠ.ANŠE.ḪI.A *ú-e-ši-ia-u-wa-an-zi i-ia-at-ta-ri ša-ku-ru-u-wa-u-wa-an-zi-ia ku-e-ez i-ia-at-ta-ri* $^{d}$*En-ki-du-ša-aš-ma-aš* GAM-*an i-ia-at-ta-ri*
4. $^{m}$*Ma-aš-tu-ri-iš ku-iš* LUGAL KUR $^{ÍD}$*še-e-ḫa e-eš-ta na-an* $^{m}$NIR.GÁL-*iš da-a-aš*
5. SAG.DU-*aš-ma-an-na-aš* $^{LÚ}$BÁḪAR-*aš* $^{GIŠ}$UMBIN GIM-*an ú-e-ḫa-at-ta-ri*
6. (initiation ritual) *nu-uš* (i.e., officers of the Hittite army) MUNUS-*li wa-aš-ša-an-du*
7. *na-aš-kán* A-NA KÁ *an-da ti-ia-zi nu lu-ú-i-li ki-iš-ša-an ḫu-uk-ki-iš-ke-ez-zi*

## Words for Lesson 10

| | | | |
|---|---|---|---|
| *dā-* (IIf) | to take | **GN** | |
| *ḫukkiške-* (Ic) | imperfective of *ḫuek-/ḫuk-* "to cast a spell" | KUR $^{\text{ÍD}}$*Šeḫa* | Šeḫa-Riverland (on the Anatolian west coast) |
| *kuez* | wherever | **DN** | |
| *šakuruwae-* (Ic) | to drink | $^{d}$Enkidu | (companion of Gilgameš) |
| *wešiya-* (Ic) | to graze | **PN** | |
| MAŠ.ANŠE.ḪI.A | animals | $^{m}$Mašduri | |

## 10.6.2 *The Ten-Year Annals* of the Hittite King Muršili II

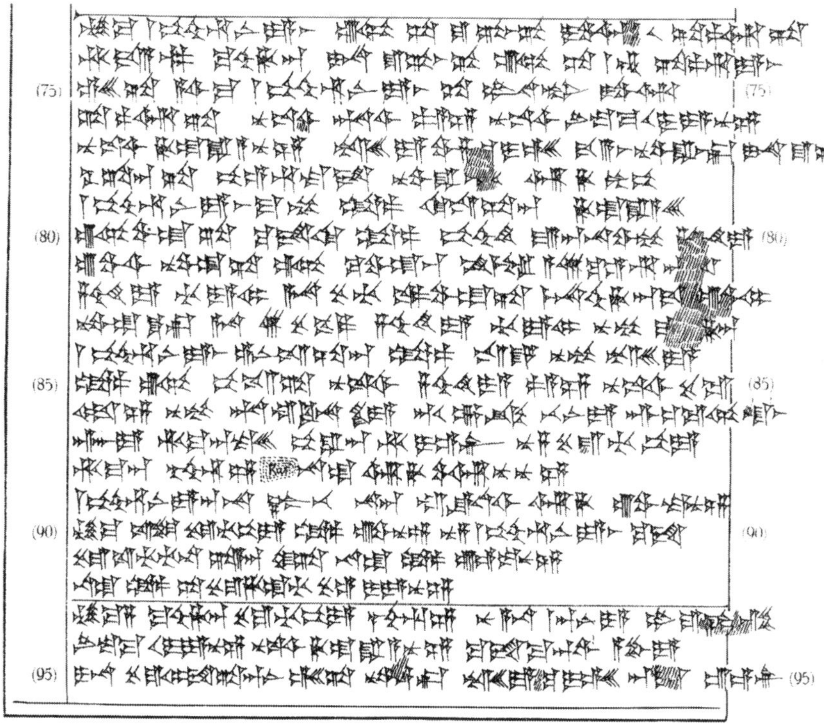

Figure 12

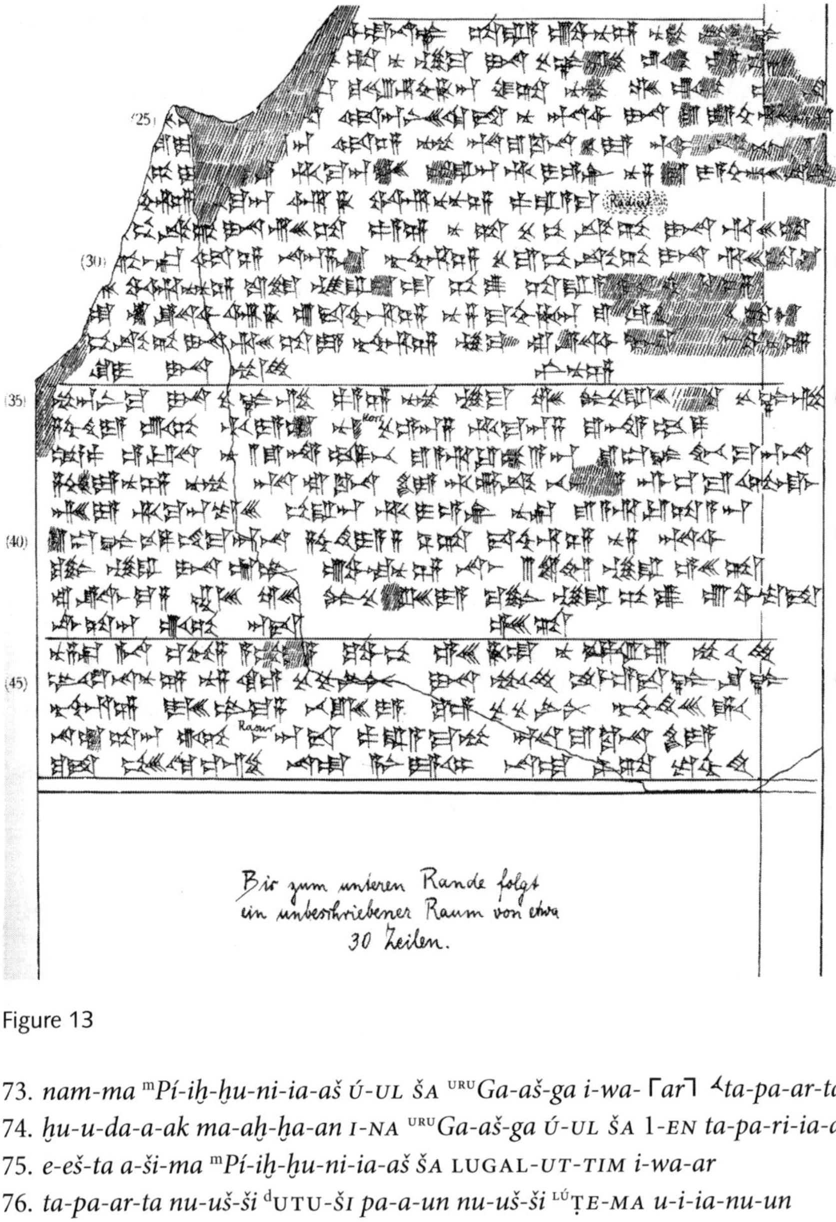


Figure 13

73. *nam-ma* $^{m}$*Pí-iḫ-ḫu-ni-ia-aš* Ú-UL ŠA $^{URU}$*Ga-aš-ga i-wa-*⸢*ar*⸣ <*ta-pa-ar-ta*
74. *ḫu-u-da-a-ak ma-aḫ-ḫa-an* I-NA $^{URU}$*Ga-aš-ga* Ú-UL ŠA 1-EN *ta-pa-ri-ia-aš*
75. *e-eš-ta a-ši-ma* $^{m}$*Pí-iḫ-ḫu-ni-ia-aš* ŠA LUGAL-UT-TIM *i-wa-ar*
76. *ta-pa-ar-ta nu-uš-ši* $^{d}$UTU-ŠI *pa-a-un nu-uš-ši* $^{LÚ}$ṬE-MA *u-i-ia-nu-un*
77. *nu-uš-ši ḫa-at-ra-a-nu-un* ÌR.MEŠ-*ia-wa-za* ⸢*ku*⸣ *-i-e-eš da-a-aš nu-wa-ra-aš-kán* I-NA $^{URU}$*Ga-aš-ga*
78. *kat-ta-an-ta pé-e-ḫu-te-et nu-wa-ra-aš-* ⸢*mu*⸣ *ar-ḫa up-pí*
79. $^{m}$*Pí-iḫ-ḫu-ni-ia-aš-ma-mu* EGIR-*pa ki-iš-ša-an ḫa-at-ra-e-eš*
80. Ú-UL-*wa-at-ta ku-it-ki* EGIR-*pa pé-eḫ-ḫi ma-a-an-na-wa-mu* ⸢*za-aḫ*⸣ *-ḫi-ia*
81. *ú-wa-ši nu-wa-at-ta* Ú-UL *ku-wa-at-qa am-me-el* $^{A.ŠÀ}$*ku-e-ri* ⸢*an*⸣ [-*d*]*a*
82. *za-aḫ-ḫi-ia ti-ia-mi* A-NA KUR-TI-KA-*wa-at-ta me-na-aḫ-ḫa-an-da ú-*⸢*wa*⸣ *-mi*

83. *nu-wa-at-ták-kán* A-*NA* ŠÀ KUR-*KA* *za-aḫ-ḫi-ia ti-ya-mi nu-mu* ⸢*ma*⸣ [-*aḫ*]-*ḫa-an*

84. $^{m}$*Pí-iḫ-ḫu-ni-ia-aš e-ni-iš-ša-an* EGIR-*pa* IŠ-*PUR* *nu-mu* ÌR.MEŠ-*IA*

85. EGIR-*pa* Ú-*UL* *pí-iš-ta nu-uš-ši za-aḫ-ḫi-ia pa-a-un nu-uš-ši* KUR-*ZU*

86. GUL-*un nu-mu* $^{d}$UTU $^{URU}$PÚ-*na* GAŠAN-*IA* $^{d}$U NIR.GÁL *BE*-*LÍ*-*IA* $^{d}$*Me-ez-zu-ul-* ⸢*la*⸣ -*aš*

87. DINGIR.MEŠ-*ia ḫu-u-ma-an-te-eš pé-ra-an ḫu-u-i-e-er nu-za* KUR $^{URU}$*Ti-pí-ia*

88. *ḫu-u-ma-an tar-uḫ-ḫu-un* erasure *na-at ar-ḫa wa-ar-nu-nu-un*

89. $^{m}$*Pí-iḫ-ḫu-ni-ia-an-na* *AṢ*-*BAT* *na-an* $^{URU}$KÙ.BABBAR-*ši ar-ḫa ú-wa-te-nu-un*

90. *nam-ma* IŠ-*TU* KUR $^{URU}$*Ti-pí-ia* EGIR-*pa ú-wa-nu-un nu-za* $^{m}$*Pí-iḫ-ḫu-ni-ia-aš ku-it*

91. KUR $^{URU}$*Iš-ti-ti-na ta-a-an ḫar-ta na-at* EGIR-*pa ú-e-te-nu-un*

92. *na-at* EGIR-*pa* *ŠA* KUR $^{URU}$*Ḫa-at-ti* KUR-*e i-ia-nu-un*

---

93. *nam-ma-za ma-aḫ-ḫa-an* KUR $^{URU}$*Ti-pí-ia tar-uḫ-ḫu-un nu* A-*NA* $^{m}$*An-ni-ia* LUGAL $^{URU}$ ⸢*Az*⸣ -*zi*

94. $^{LÚ}$*ṬE*-*MA* *u-i-ia-nu-un nu-uš-ši ḫa-at-ra-a-nu-un ku-it-ma-an-wa* A-*BU*-*IA*

95. *I*-*NA* KUR $^{URU}$*Mi-it-ta-an-ni e-eš-ta nu-wa-* ⸢*ták*⸣ -*kán* ÌR.MEŠ-*IA* *ku-i-e-eš an-* ⸢*da*⸣ *ú-e-er*

end of column
continuation of iii 95 on beginning of column iv lost

iv

break and then first 21 lines very fragmentarily preserved

22. [GIM-*an-ma-kán* $^{d}$UTU-*ŠI* $^{URU}$*Ki-iz-zu-*]⸢*wa*⸣ -*at-na-az ša-ra-a ú-wa-nu-un nu-* ⸢*mu* MU⸣ .[KAM-*a*]*z*

23. [*te-e-pa-u-e-eš-ša-an-za e-e*]*š-ta nu nam-ma* I-*NA* KUR *Az-* ⸢*zi*⸣ Ú- ⸢UL *pa-a-un*⸣

24. [$^{URU}$*Ia-aḫ-re-eš-ša-aš-ma-mu ku-i*]*t*$^{?}$ *ku-u-ru-ri-aḫ-ḫa-an ḫar-ta nu-* ⸢*mu*⸣ ÉRIN.MEŠ Ú- ⸢UL⸣ *p*[*í-iš-ke-et*]

25. [*na-aš nam-ma*] x x [$^{URU}$ …-*n*]*a* GUL-*an-ni-eš-ke-et nu* $^{d}$UTU-*ŠI* I-*NA* ⸢$^{URU}$*Ia*⸣ -*aḫ-* ⸢*re-eš-ša-an*⸣

26. [*pa-a-un nu*]⸢$^{URU}$⸣*I*[*a-aḫ-re-eš-š*]*a-an* GUL-*un nu-mu* $^{d}$UTU $^{URU}$PÚ-*na* ⸢GAŠAN⸣ -*IA* $^{d}$U ⸢NIR.GÁL *BE*-*LÍ*-*IA*⸣

27. [$^{d}$*Me-ez-zu-u*]*l-l*[*a-aš* DINGIR.MEŠ-] ⸢*ia*⸣ *ḫu-u-ma-an-* ⸢*te*⸣ -*eš pé-ra-an ḫu-u-i-e-er nu-za* ⸢$^{URU}$⸣ *Ia-aḫ-* ⸢*re-eš-ša-an*⸣

28. [URU-*an tar-*]*uḫ-ḫu-un* [*na*]*m-ma-an ar-ḫa wa-ar-nu-nu-un pa-ra-a-ma* erasure

29. [*I-NA* KU]R *Pí-ig-ga-i-na-re-eš-ša pa-a-un nu* *ŠA* KUR *Pí-ig-ga-i-na-re-eš-⸢ša⸣*
30. [LÚ $^{URU}$*G*]*a-aš-kán* GUL-*un na-an-za-⸢kán⸣ tar-uḫ-ḫu-un* KUR $^{URU}$*Pí-ig-ga-i-na-re-eš-⸢ša-ma⸣*
31. [*ar-ḫ*]*a wa-ar-nu-nu-un* *IŠ-TU* NAM.RA-⸢*ma*⸣-*at* GU$_4$ UDU *ša-ra-a ⸢da-aḫ-ḫu-un⸣*
32. [*na-*]*at* ⸢$^{URU}$⸣KÙ.BABBAR-*ši ar-ḫa ú-da-aḫ-ḫu-un nu-za ma-aḫ-ḫa-an* $^{URU}$⸢*Ia*⸣-*a*[*ḫ-re-e*]*š-⸢ša-an⸣*
33. [KUR$^{URU}$]*Pí-ig-ga-i-na-re-eš-ša-ia tar-uḫ-ḫu-un nam-ma* $^{URU}$⸢KÙ⸣.BABBAR-*ši* ⸢EGIR⸣[-*p*]*a* ⸢*ú*⸣-*wa-nu-un*
34. [*nu*] *ki-i* *I-NA* MU.1.KAM DÙ-*nu-un*

---

35. MU-*an-ni-ma* *I-NA* KUR *Az-zi pa-a-un nu-mu nam-ma* ÉRIN.MEŠ ANŠE.KUR.RA.MEŠ [*Š*]*A* KUR *Az-zi*
36. *za-aḫ-ḫi-ia* *Ú-UL* *ti-ia-⸢at⸣ nu* erasure KUR-*e-an-za ḫu-u-ma-an-za* URU.DIDLI.ḪI.A BÀD
37. EGIR-*pa e-ep-per nu* 2 URU.DIDLI.ḪI.A BÀD-*pát* $^{URU}$*A-ri-ip-⸢ša⸣-a-an* $^{URU}$*Du-uk-kam-ma-an-na*
38. *za-aḫ-⸢ḫi⸣-ia-nu-un nu-mu* $^{d}$UTU $^{URU}$PÚ-*na* GAŠAN-*IA* $^{d}$U NIR.GÁL *BE-L*[*Í-I*]*A* $^{d}$*Me-ez-zu-ul-la-aš*
39. DINGIR.MEŠ-*ia ḫu-u-ma-an-te-es pé-ra-an ḫu-u-i-e-er nu-kán* $^{URU}$*A-ri-ip-ša-a-an*
40. $^{URU}$*Du-uk-ka-am-ma-an-na za-aḫ-ḫi-ia-za kat-ta da-aḫ-ḫu-un nu-za* $^{d}$UTU-*ŠI*
41. *ku-in* NAM.RA *I-NA* É.LUGAL *ú-wa-te-nu-un na-aš* 3 *LI-IM* NAM.RA *e-eš-ta*
42. $^{URU}$KÙ.BABBAR-*aš-ma-za* EN.MEŠ ÉRIN.MEŠ ANŠE.KUR.⸢RA⸣.MEŠ-*ia* *ku-in* NAM.RA GU$_4$ UDU *ú-wa-te-et*
43. *na-aš-ša-an* *Ú-UL* *an-da e-eš-ta*

---

44. *nu-za-kán* *A-NA* $^{GIŠ}$GU.ZA *A-⸢BI-IA⸣ ku-wa-pí e-eš-ḫa-at nu ka-ru-ú* MU.10.KAM
45. LUGAL-*u-iz-na-nu-un nu-za ke-e* KUR.KUR LÚ.KÚR *I-NA* MU.10.KAM *am-me-e-da-az* ŠU-*az*
46. *tar-uḫ-ḫu-un* DUMU.MEŠ.LUGAL-*ma-za* *BE-LU*$^{MEŠ}$-*ia ku-e* KUR.KUR LÚ.KÚR *tar-uḫ-ḫe-eš-ker*
47. *na-⸢at⸣-ša-an* *Ú-UL* erasure *an-da pa-ra-a-ma-mu* $^{d}$UTU $^{URU}$PÚ-*na* GAŠAN-*IA*
48. *ku-it pé-eš-ke-ez-zi na-at a-ni-ia-mi na-at kat-ta te-eḫ-ḫi*

---

## Questions

1. Identify in the handcopy the cuneiform signs given in this and the previous Lessons.
2. Translate the text using the notes below.

## Words

| | |
|---|---|
| 73. ⸗*tapar-* (Ia) | to reign (marked as Luwian by *Glossenkeil*, see Introduction §6) |
| 74. *ḫūdāk* (adv.) | immediately, suddenly (to be taken with the sentence that starts with *ašima*) |
| *tapariya-* (Ic) | rule, reign |
| 75. LUGAL-*UTTU*(*M*) | kingship |
| 78. *kattanda* | down into, downwards |
| 81. *kuwatqa* | perhaps |
| 91. *tān* | from *dā-* |

iv

| | |
|---|---|
| 22. URU*Kizzuwatna* | area roughly coinciding with Classical Cilicia |
| MU.KAM | = Hitt. *wet-* year, here nom. sing. /*wet-s*/ spelled with *-az* |
| 23. *tēpaweššant-* | (too) short |
| *namma* … UL | no longer |
| KUR *Azzi* | area in north-west Anatolia towards Armenia |
| 36. KUR-*eant-* | = *utneant-*, see Lesson 9.4.2 |
| URU.BÀD | fortress, fortified settlement |
| 37. *appa ēpp-* (Ib) | to take/seek refuge in |
| 44. *kuwapi* | since |
| *karū* | already; formerly, in the past |
| 47. *anda* | i.e., on this tablet |
| 48. *aniya-* (Ic) | to record, write down |
| *katta dai-/tiya-* | to deposit (in the temple before the deity) |

# APPENDIX 1: Paradigms

## 1. Nouns and adjectives

*Overview of case endings*

| | Older | | Newer |
|---|---|---|---|
| **Sing.** | | | |
| nom. com. | *-š*, Ø | | *-š* |
| voc. | -Ø, *-i* | | -Ø, *-i/e* |
| acc. com. | -V*n*, -C*an* | | -V*n*, -C*an* |
| nom.-acc. neut. | *-n*, -Ø | | *-n*, -Ø |
| gen. | *-aš* (*-š*) | | *-aš* (*-š*) |
| dat. | *-i* | | *-i* (dat., loc., all.) |
| loc. | *-i*, -Ø | | |
| all. | *-a* | | |
| abl. | | *-z*, *-az* | |
| instr. | | *-it*, *-t*(*a*) | |
| **Plur.** | | | |
| nom. com. | *-eš* (*-aš*) | | *-eš*, *-uš* *-aš* |
| acc. com. | *-uš* | | *-uš*, *-aš*, *-eš* |
| nom.-acc. neut. | *-a*, *-i*, -Ø | | *-a*, *-i*, -Ø |
| gen. | *-an*, *-aš* | | *-aš* |
| dat.-loc. | *-aš* | | *-aš* |

*-a-Stems* (1.1.2)

| | | | | |
|---|---|---|---|---|
| **Sing.** | | | | |
| nom. com. | *lalaš* (EME-*aš*) | *arunaš* | | *araḫzenaš* |
| acc. | *lalan* (EME-*an*) | *arunan* | | *araḫzenan* |
| nom.-acc. neut. | | | *pedan* | *araḫzenan* |
| gen. | *lalaš* | *arunaš* | *pedaš* | *araḫzenaš* |
| dat.-loc. | *lali* (EME-*i*) | *aruni* | *pedi/pidi* | *araḫzeni* |
| all. | | *aruna* | | *araḫzena* |
| abl. | *lalaz* (EME-*az/za*) | *arunaz* (A.AB.BA-*az*) | *pedaz* | *araḫzenaz* |
| instr. | *lalit* | | | |

| | | | | |
|---|---|---|---|---|
| **Plur.** | | | | |
| nom. com. | *laleš, laluš* | | | *araḫzeneš/ araḫzenaš* |
| acc. | *laluš* (EME-*uš*) | *arunuš* | | *araḫzenuš/ araḫzenaš* |
| nom.-acc. neut. | | | *peda* | *araḫzena* |
| gen. | | *arunaš* | | *araḫzenaš* |
| dat.-loc. | | | *pedaš* | *araḫzenaš* |

*-i-Stem nouns* (2.1.1)

| | | | |
|---|---|---|---|
| **Sing.** | | | |
| nom. com. | *ḫalkiš* | *luliš* | |
| acc. com. | *ḫalkin* | *lulin* | |
| nom.-acc. neut. | | | *išpanduzzi* |
| gen. | *ḫalkiyaš* | *luliyaš* | *išpanduzziyaš* |
| dat.-loc. | (*ḫalḫaltumari*) | *luli, luliya* | *išpanduzzi* |
| all. | | *luliya* | *išpanduzziya* |
| abl. | *ḫalkiyaz* | *luliyaz* | *išpanduzziyaz* |
| instr. | *ḫalkit* | *lulit* | *išpanduzit* |
| **Plur.** | | | |
| nom. com. | *ḫalkeš* | *luliyaš* | |
| acc. com. | *ḫalkiuš, ḫalkeš* | | |
| nom.-acc. neut. | | | ($^{NA4}$*ḫuwaši*$^{ḪI.A}$) |
| gen., dat.-loc. | (*ḫalḫaltumariyaš*) | | |

*-i-Stem adjectives* (2.1.2)

| | | | |
|---|---|---|---|
| **Sing.** | | | |
| nom. com. | *nakkiš* | *šalliš* | *mekkiš* |
| acc. com. | *nakkin* | *šallin* | (*mekkan*) |
| nom.-acc. neut. | *nakki* | *šalli* | *mekki* |
| gen. | | *šallayaš, šallaš* | |
| dat.-loc. | *nakkiya* | *šallai* | |
| abl. | *nakkiyaz* | *šallayaz* | *mekkayaz* |
| instr. | *nakkit* | (*šuppit*) | |
| **Plur.** | | | |
| nom. com. | *nakkiyaeš* | *šallaeš* (*šuppeš*) | *mekkaeš, mekkauš* |

| | | | |
|---|---|---|---|
| acc. com. | *nakkiuš* | *šallauš* | *mekkauš* |
| nom.-acc. neut. | *nakki* | *šalla, šalli* | *mekkaya* |
| gen., dat.-loc. | *nakkiyaš* | *šallayaš* | *mekkayaš* |

*-u-Stem nouns* (3.1.1)

| | | | |
|---|---|---|---|
| **Sing.** | | | |
| nom. com. | *ḫaššuš* (LUGAL-*uš*) | *ḫeuš* | |
| acc. | LUGAL-*un* | *ḫeun* | |
| nom.-acc. neut. | | | *ḫalentu* |
| gen. | LUGAL-*waš* LUGAL-*i/e* | *ḫeuwaš/ḫeuaš* | *ḫalentuwaš* |
| dat.-loc. | | | *ḫalentūi* |
| all. | | | *ḫalentuwa* |
| abl. | LUGAL-*waz* | | *ḫalentuwaz* |
| instr. | | *ḫeauit* | *išḫaḫruit* |
| **Plur.** | | | |
| nom. com. | LUGAL-*ueš* | *ḫēuēš* | |
| acc. com. | LUGAL-MEŠ | *ḫēmuš, ḫēūš* (*ḫēamuš*) | |
| nom.-acc. neut. | | | *genuwa* |
| gen. | LUGAL-*an* (LUGAL-*wan*)/ LUGAL.MEŠ-*aš* | | |
| dat.-loc. | LUGAL.MEŠ-*aš* | | *genuwaš* |

*irregular*: šiu- *"god, deity"*

| | Sing. | Plur. |
|---|---|---|
| nom. | *šiuš*, DINGIR-(*LIM*-)*uš/iš* | DINGIR.MEŠ-*eš* |
| acc. | *šiun, šiunan*, DINGIR-*LAM-an*/-*LIM-in* | *šimuš*, DINGIR.MEŠ-(*m*)*uš* |
| gen. | *šiunaš*, DINGIR-*LIM*-(*n*)*aš* | *šiunan*, DINGIR.MEŠ-(*n*)*aš* |
| dat.-loc. | *šiuni*, DINGIR-*LIM-ni* | *šiunaš*, DINGIR.MEŠ-(*n*)*aš* |
| abl. | *šiunaz*, DINGIR-*LIM-za* | |
| instr. | *šiunit*, DINGIR-*LIM-it* | |

## *-u-Stem adjectives* (3.1.2)

| | | |
|---|---|---|
| **Sing.** | | |
| nom. com. | *aššuš* | *idaluš* |
| acc. com. | *aššun* | *idalun* |
| nom.-acc. neut. | *aššu* | *idalu* |
| gen. | *aššawaš* | *idalawaš* |
| dat.-loc. | *aššawi* | *idalawi* |
| abl. | *aššawaz* | *idalawaz* |
| instr. | *aššawit* | *idalawit* |
| **Plur.** | | |
| nom. com. | *aššaweš* | *idalaweš* |
| acc. com. | *aššamuš, aššaweš* | *idalamuš* |
| nom.-acc. neut. | *aššawa, aššū* | *idalawa* |
| gen., dat.-loc. | *aššawaš* | *idalawaš* |

## *-ai- and -au-Stems* (4.1)

| | -ai- | -ai- | -au- | -au- |
|---|---|---|---|---|
| **Sing.** | | | | |
| nom. com. | *lingaiš* | | *ḫarnāuš* | |
| acc. com. | *lingain* | | *ḫarnaun* | |
| nom.-acc. neut. | | *ḫaštai* | | *išḫunāu* |
| gen. | *linkiyaš, lingayaš* | *ḫaštiyaš* | *ḫarnuwaš ḫarnauwaš* | *išḫunauwaš* |
| dat.-loc. | *linkiya* (=all.), *linkai* | *ḫaštai* | *ḫarnui ḫarnāuwi* | *išḫunaui* |
| abl. | *linkiyaz* | ($^{GIŠ}$*luttiyaz*) | | |
| instr. | | *ḫaštit* | | |
| **Plur.** | | | | |
| nom. com. | | | *ḫarnaueš* | |
| acc. com. | *lingauš* | | | |
| nom.-acc. neut. | | | | |
| gen., dat.-loc. | | ($^{GIŠ}$*luttiyaš*) | | |

*-nt-Stems* (5.1.1)

| | Subst. | Adj. | Part. |
|---|---|---|---|
| **Sing.** | | | |
| nom. com. | *išpanza* | *ḫumanza* | *walḫanza* |
| acc. com. | *išpantan* | *ḫumantan* | *walḫantan* |
| nom.-acc. neut. | | *ḫuman* | *walḫan* |
| gen. | *išpantaš* | *ḫumantaš* | *walḫantaš* |
| dat.-loc. | *išpanti* | *ḫumanti* | *walḫanti* |
| abl. | *išpantaz* | *ḫumantaz* | *walḫantaz* |
| instr. | | | *walḫantit* |
| **Plur.** | | | |
| nom. com. | | *ḫumanteš* | *walḫanteš* |
| acc. com. | *išpantiuš* | *ḫumantuš* | *walḫantuš* |
| nom.-acc. neut. | | *ḫumanta* | *walḫanta* |
| gen., dat.-loc. | | *ḫumantaš* | *walḫantaš* |

*-tt-Stems* (5.1.2)

| | | | |
|---|---|---|---|
| **Sing.** | | | |
| nom. com. | *naḫšaraz* | UD-*az* | (= *šiwat-š*) |
| acc. com. | *naḫšarattan* | UD-*an*, | (= *šiwattan*) |
| | | UD.KAM-*an* | |
| gen. | *naḫšarattaš* | UD-*aš* | (= *šiwattaš*) |
| dat.-loc. | *naḫšaratti* | *šiwatti*, UD-*ti*, | (= *šiwatti*) |
| | | *šiwat*, UD-*at* | (= *šiwat-Ø*) |
| abl. | *naḫšarataza* | UD.KAM-*az* | (= *šiwattaz*) |
| **Plur.** | | | |
| nom. com. | *naḫšaratteš* | UD.KAM.ḪI.A-*uš* | (= *šiwattuš*) |
| acc. com. | *naḫšaradduš* | UD.KAM.ḪI.A-*uš* | |
| nom.-acc. neut. | | | |
| gen., dat.-loc. | *naḫšarattaš* | UD.KAM.ḪI.A-*aš* | (= *šiwattaš*) |

*-n-Stems* (6.1.1–2)

| | | | | |
|---|---|---|---|---|
| **Sing.** | | | | |
| nom. | | | *ḫaraš* | *išḫimāš* |
| acc. | | | *ḫaranan* | *išḫimanan* |
| nom.-acc. neut. | *tekan* | *laman* | | |
| gen. | *taknaš* | *lamnaš* | *ḫaranaš* | |
| dat.-loc. | *takni* | *lamni* | | |

| | | | | |
|---|---|---|---|---|
| all. | *takna* | | | |
| abl. | *taknaz* | ŠUM-*za*/-*az* | | *išḫimanaz* |
| instr. | | *lamnit* | | *išḫimanta*, *išḫimanit* |
| **Plur.** | | | | |
| nom. | | | *ḫaraneš* | *išḫimaneš* |
| acc. | | | | *išḫimanuš* |
| gen., dat.-loc. | | *lamnaš*, ŠUM.ḪI.A-*aš* | | |

| | Sing. | Plur. |
|---|---|---|
| nom. com. | *memiaš* (INIM-*aš*) | *AWĀTE*$^{\text{MEŠ}}$ |
| acc. com. | *memian* (INIM-*an*) | *memiyanuš* |
| nom.-acc. neut. | *memian* | |
| gen. | *memiyanaš* | *memiyanaš* (INIM.MEŠ-*aš*) |
| dat.-loc. | *memiyani*, *memini* (INIM-*ni*) | *memiyanaš* |
| abl. | *memiyanaz*, *meminaz*, *memiaz* (INIM-*za*) | |
| instr. | *memiyanit*, *meminit* | |

## -*r*-/-*n*-*Stems* (7.1.1–3)

| | A | B | C | D |
|---|---|---|---|---|
| **Sing.** | | | | |
| nom.-acc. | *papratar* | *ḫanneššar* | *partawar* | *ḫilammar* |
| gen. | *paprannaš* | *ḫannešnaš* | *partaunaš* | *ḫilamnaš* |
| dat.-loc. | *papranni* | *ḫannešni* | *partauni* | *ḫilamni* |
| all. | (*adanna*) | | | *ḫilamna* |
| abl. | *paprannaz* | *ḫannešnaz* | *partaunaz* | *ḫilamnaz* |
| instr. | | *ḫannešnit* | *partaunit* | |
| **Plur.** | | | | |
| nom.-acc. | *paprata* *zankilatarri*$^{\text{ḪI.A}}$ | *uppeššar*$^{\text{ḪI.A}}$ | | |
| dat.-loc. | | | *ḫaršaunaš* | |

**Sing.**

| | | | |
|---|---|---|---|
| nom.-acc. | *uddar* | *watar* | *meḫur* |
| gen. | *uddanaš* | *wetenaš* | *meḫunaš* |
| dat.-loc. | *uddani* | *weteni* | *meḫuni, meḫueni* |
| all. | | *wetena* | |
| abl. | *uddanaz* | *wetenaz* | |
| instr. | *uddanit, uddanta* | *wedanda, wetenit* | |
| **Plur.** | | | |
| nom.-acc. | *uddār* | *widār* | *meḫurri*$^{\text{ḪI.A}}$ |
| gen., dat.-loc. | *uddanaš* | A.ḪI.A-*aš* | *meḫunaš* |

## *-r-Stem nouns and adjectives* (8.1.1–2)

| | | | |
|---|---|---|---|
| **Sing.** | | | |
| nom. com. | *ḫupparaš* | | *šakuwaššaraš* |
| acc. com. | *ḫupparan* | | *šakuwaššaran* |
| nom.-acc. neut. | *ḫuppar* | *kurur* | *šakuwaššar* |
| gen. | *ḫupparaš* | *kururaš* | *šakuwaššaraš* |
| dat.-loc. | *ḫuppari* | *kururi* | *šakuwaššari* |
| abl. | *ḫupparaz* | | *šakuwaššaraz* |
| instr. | *ḫupparit* | | *šakuwaššarit* |
| **Plur.** | | | |
| nom. com. | | | *šakuwaššaruš* |
| acc. com. | | | *šakuwaššaruš* |
| nom.-acc. neut. | *ḫuppari*$^{\text{ḪI.A}}$ | *kururi*$^{\text{ḪI.A}}$ | |

| | Sing. | Plur. |
|---|---|---|
| nom. | *keššar, kiššeraš,* ŠU*(-aš)* | |
| acc. | *kiššeran,* ŠU-*an,* ŠU-*šar* | *kiššeruš,* ŠU.MEŠ-*uš* |
| gen. | *kišraš* | *kišraš,* ŠU.ḪI.A-*aš* |
| dat.-loc. | *kiššari,* ŠU-*i* | |
| all. | *kišra* | |
| abl. | *kišraz, kiššaraz,* ŠU-*az* | |
| instr. | *kiššarta, kišše/arit,* ŠU-*ta/it* | |

*-l-Stems* (8.1.3)

| | | | |
|---|---|---|---|
| **Sing.** | | | |
| nom.-acc. | *waštul* | *išḫiul* | *tawal* |
| gen. | *wašdulaš* | *išḫiulaš* | *tawalaš* |
| dat.-loc. | *wašduli* | *išḫiuli* | *tawali* |
| abl. | | *išḫiullaza* | |
| instr. | *wašdulit* | | *tawalit* |
| **Plur.** | | | |
| nom.-acc. | *wašdul*$^{\text{ḪI.A}}$ | *išḫiuli*$^{\text{ḪI.A}}$ | |

*-s-Stems* (9.1)

| | | | |
|---|---|---|---|
| **Sing.** | | | |
| nom.-acc. | *aiš* | *nepiš* | *tunnakiš*, *tunnakeššar* |
| gen. | *iššaš* | *nepišaš* | *tunnakkešnaš* |
| dat.-loc. | *išši* | *nepiši* | |
| all. | *išša* | *nepiša* | *tunnakišna* |
| abl. | *iššaz* | *nepišaz*, *nepišza* | *tunnakkešnaz* |
| instr. | *iššit* | | |
| **Plur.** | | | |
| nom.-acc. | KAXU.ḪI.A | | |
| gen., dat.-loc. | *iššaš* | | |

*Irregular declinations* (10.1)

| | | | |
|---|---|---|---|
| **Sing.** | | | |
| nom.-acc. | *ker*, ŠÀ-*er* | *per*, É-*er* | *utne*, KUR-*e* |
| gen. | *kardiyaš*, ŠÀ-*aš* | *parnaš*, É-*aš* | *utniyaš*, *utneyaš*, KUR-*eaš* |
| dat.-loc. | *kardi*, ŠÀ-*i* | *parni*, É-*ni*, É-*ri* | *utni*, *utniya*, *utneya*, *utne*, KUR-*e* |
| all. | *karta*, ŠÀ-*ta* | *parna*, É-*na* | *utniya* |
| abl. | *kartaz*, ŠÀ-*az/za* | *parnaz*, É-*az/za*, É-*erza* | *utniyaz*, *utneaz*, KUR-*az* |
| instr. | *kardit*, ŠÀ-*it* | | |
| **Plur.** | | | |
| nom.-acc. | *ker* | É-*er* | *utne*, KUR.KUR.ḪI.A |
| gen., dat.-loc. | | *parnaš*, É-*naš* | |

## 2. Pronouns

*Personal pronoun first person, freestanding* (1.2.2)

| | | |
|---|---|---|
| nom. | *ūk, ammuk* | *wēš, anzaš* |
| acc. | *ammuk* | *anzaš* |
| gen. | *ammel* | *anzel* |
| dat.-loc. | *ammuk* | *anzaš* |
| abl. | *ammedaz* | *anzedaz* |

*Personal pronoun second person, freestanding* (3.2.1)

| | | |
|---|---|---|
| nom. | *zik, tuk* | *šumeš* |
| acc. | *tuk* | *šumaš, šumeš* |
| gen. | *tuel* | *šumel, šumenzan* |
| dat.-loc. | *tuk* | *šumaš* |
| abl. | *tuedaz* | *šumedaz* |

*Personal pronoun first and second person, enclitic* (1.2.3, 3.2.2)

| | 1. sing. | 1. plur. | 2. sing. | 2. plur. |
|---|---|---|---|---|
| dat.-loc. | *-mu* | *-naš* | *-ta* (*-du*) | *-šmaš* |
| acc. | *-mu* | *-naš* | *-ta* (*-du*) | *-šmaš* |

*Third person anaphoric pronoun, enclitic* (2.2)

| | Sing. | Plur. |
|---|---|---|
| nom. com. | *-aš* | *-e, -at* |
| acc. com. | *-an* | *-uš, -aš* |
| nom.-acc. neut. | *-at* | *-e, -at* |
| dat.-loc. | *-ši* | *-šmaš* |

*Possessive pronoun, suffixed* (9.2)

| | | Singularis | | Pluralis | |
|---|---|---|---|---|---|
| **Sing.** | **1: -mi/-ma** | **2: -ti/-ta** | **3: -ši/-ša** | **1: -šummi/a-** | **2–3: -šmi/a-** |
| nom. com. | *-miš* | *-tiš* | *-šiš* | *-šummiš* | *-šmiš* |
| acc. com. | *-min/-man* | *-tin* | *-šin/-šan* | *-šummi/an* | *-šman* |
| nom.-acc. neut. | *-mit* | *-tit* | *-šit* | *-šummit* | *-šmit* |
| voc. | *-mi* | | | | |

| | | Singularis | | Pluralis | |
|---|---|---|---|---|---|
| gen. | *-maš* | *-taš* | *-šaš* | | |
| dat.-loc. | *-mi* | *-ti* | *-ši* | | *-šmi* |
| all. | *-ma* | *-ta* | *-ša* | | *-šma* |
| instr. | | *-tit* | *-šit* | | *-šmit* |
| **Plur.** | | | | | |
| nom. com. | *-miš* | *-tiš* | *-šiš* | | |
| acc. com. | *-muš/-miš* | *-tuš* | *-šuš* | *-šummuš* | *-šmuš* |
| nom.-acc. neut. | *-mit* | | *-šit* | | |
| gen. | *-man* | | | | |
| dat.-loc. | | *-taš* | | | *-šmaš* |

*Demonstrative pronoun* (4.2.1)

| | Sing. | Plur. |
|---|---|---|
| nom. com. | *kāš* | *kē, kūš* |
| acc. com. | *kūn* | *kūš, kē* |
| nom.-acc. neut. | *kī* | *kē* |
| gen. | *kēl* | *kenzan, kēl, kedaš* |
| dat.-loc. | *kēdani* | *kedaš* |

| | |
|---|---|
| abl. | *kēz, kezza* |
| instr. | *kēdanda* |

*Demonstrative/anaphoric pronoun* (5.2)

| | Sing. | Plur. |
|---|---|---|
| nom. com. | *apāš* | *apē, apūš* |
| acc. com. | *apūn* | *apūš, apē* |
| nom.-acc. neut. | *apāt* | *apē* |
| gen. | *apēl* | *apenzan, apēl* |
| dat.-loc. | *apēdani* | *apēdaš* |

| | |
|---|---|
| abl. | *apēz, apezza* |
| instr. | *apedanda* |

*Demonstrative/anaphoric pronoun* (10.2)

| | Sing. | Plur. |
|---|---|---|
| nom. com. | *aši* | *uniuš* |
| acc. com. | *uni, unin, aši* | |
| nom.-acc. neut. | *ini, eni* | |
| gen. | *aši, el, uniaš* | |
| dat. | *edani* | *edaš* |
| loc. | *edi* | |
| abl. | *edez* | |

*tamai-* (4.2.2)

| | Sing. | Plur. |
|---|---|---|
| nom. com. | *tamaiš* | *tamaēš* |
| acc. com. | *tamain* | *tamāuš* |
| nom.-acc. neut. | *tamai* | *tamāe* |
| gen. | *damēl* | *damedaš* |
| dat.-loc. | *tamēdani* (*damēte*) | *damedaš* |
| all. | *tameda* | |
| abl. | *tamēdaz* | |

*Relative/interrogative pronoun* (6.2.1)

| | Sing. | Plur. |
|---|---|---|
| nom. com. | *kuiš* | *kuieš, kueuš* |
| acc. com. | *kuin* | *kueuš, kuiuš, kuieš* |
| nom.-acc. neut. | *kuit* | *kue* |
| gen. | *kuel* | |
| dat.-loc. | *kuedani* | *kuedaš* |
| abl. | *kuez* | |

*Indefinite pronoun* (7.2)

| | Sing. | Plur. |
|---|---|---|
| nom. com. | *kuiški* | *kuieška* |
| acc. com. | *kuinki* | *kuiuška* |
| nom.-acc. neut. | *kuitki* | *kueka, kuekki* |

| | Sing. | Plur. |
|---|---|---|
| gen. | *kuelka* | |
| dat.-loc. | *kuedanikki* | *kuedaška* |
| abl. | *kuezka* | |

*Distributive pronoun* (8.2)

| | Sing. | Plur. |
|---|---|---|
| nom. com. | *kuišša* | *kuešša* |
| acc. com. | *kuinna* | *kuiušša* |
| nom.-acc. neut. | *kuitta* | |
| gen. | *kuella* | |
| dat.-loc. | *kuedaniya* | |
| abl. | *kuezziya* | |

## 3. Verb

### *Overview of endings*

*Present indicative active* (1.3.1)

| | -mi (I) | | -ḫi (II) |
|---|---|---|---|
| **Sing.** 1 | *-mi* | | *-ḫi* |
| 2 | *-ši* | | *-ti* |
| 3 | *-zi* | | *-i* |
| **Plur.** 1 | | *-weni, -meni (-wani)* | |
| 2 | | *-teni (-tani)* | *-šteni* |
| 3 | | *-anzi* | |

*Preterite indicative active* (2.3.1)

| | -mi (I) | | -ḫi (II) |
|---|---|---|---|
| **Sing.** ind. pret. 1 | -V*nun*, -C*un* | | *-ḫun* |
| 2 | -V*š*, -C*ta*, *-šta*, -V*t* | | *-ta* |
| 3 | -V*t*, C*ta*, *-šta* | | *-š, -ta, -šta* |
| **Plur.** ind. pret. 1 | | *-wen, -men* | |
| 2 | | *-ten* | *-šten* |
| 3 | | *-er* | |

*Present indicative medio-passive* (3.3.1)

| | | -mi (I) | | -ḫi (II) |
|---|---|---|---|---|
| **Sing.** ind. pres. | 1 | | *-ḫa, -ḫari, -ḫaḫari* | |
| | 2 | | *-ta, -tari (-tati)* | |
| | 3 | *-ta, -tari* | | *-a, -ari* |
| **Plur.** | 1 | | *-wašta, -waštari (-waštati)* | |
| | 2 | | *-duma, -dumari* | |
| | 3 | | *-anta, -antari* | |

*Preterite indicative medio-passive* (3.3.1)

| | | -mi (I) | | -ḫi (II) |
|---|---|---|---|---|
| **Sing.** ind. pret. | 1 | | *-ḫati, -ḫaḫati, -ḫat, -ḫaḫat* | |
| | 2 | | *-tati, -tat* | |
| | 3 | *-tati, -tat* | | *-ati, -at* |
| **Plur.** | 1 | | *-waštati, -waštat* | |
| | 2 | | *-dumati, -dumat* | |
| | 3 | | *-antati, -antat* | |

*Imperative active* (8.3.3)

| | -mi- | | -ḫi- |
|---|---|---|---|
| **Active** | | | |
| **Sing.** 1 | | *-allu, -allut, -lu, -lut, -lit* | |
| 2 | | *-Ø, -t, -i* | |
| 3 | *-tu* | | *-u* |
| **Plur.** 2 | | *-ten* | *-šten* |
| 3 | | *-antu* | |

*Imperative medio-passive* (8.3.3)

| | -mi- | | -ḫi- |
|---|---|---|---|
| **Medio-passive** | | | |
| **Sing.** 1 | | *-ḫaru, -ḫaḫaru* | |
| 2 | | *-ḫut, -ḫuti* | |
| 3 | *-taru* | | *-aru* |

| | -mi- | -ḫi- |
|---|---|---|
| **Plur.** 2 | *-dumat* | |
| 3 | *-antaru* | |

## *I -mi- Conjugation*

### Ia *Verbs of unchanging stem*

Active indicative

| | Present | Preterite |
|---|---|---|
| **Sing.** | | |
| 1 | *walḫmi* | *walḫun*, GUL-*(aḫ) ḫun*, GUL-*un* |
| 2 | *walḫši* | *walḫta* |
| 3 | *walḫzi* | *walḫta*, GUL-*aḫta* |
| **Plur.** | | |
| 1 | *walḫuweni* | *walḫuwen* |
| 2 | *walḫteni* | *walḫten* |
| 3 | *walḫanzi* | *walḫer*, GUL-*(aḫ)ḫer* |

Medio-passive indicatives

| | Present | Preterite |
|---|---|---|
| **Sing.** ind. 1 | *arḫa(ri)* | *arḫat(i)* |
| 2 | *arta(ri), (artati)* | *artat(i)* |
| 3 | *arta(ri)* | *artat(i)* |
| **Plur.** ind. 1 | *arwašta(ri)* | *aruwaštat(i)* |
| 2 | *arduma(ri)* | *ardumat(i)* |
| 3 | *aranta(ri)* | *arantat(i)* |

Imperative, participle, verbum infinitum, and *-ške-*

| | | | | |
|---|---|---|---|---|
| **Part.** | *walḫant-* | **Imperat.** | Sing. | Plur. |
| **Inf. I** | *walḫuwanzi* | 2 | *walḫ* | *walḫten* |
| **Verbal noun** | *walḫuwar* | 3 | *walḫdu* | *walḫandu* |
| **Supinum** | *walḫuwan* | | | |
| *-ške-* | *walḫeške-* | | | |

Ib *Stems with Ablaut -e-/-a-*

Active

| | | | | |
|---|---|---|---|---|
| **Pres. sing.** | 1 | *ēpmi* | *ēšmi* | *ēdmi* |
| | 2 | *ēpši* | *ēšši* | *ēzši, ezzatti* |
| | 3 | *ēpzi* | *ēšzi* | *ezzazzi* |
| **plur.** | 1 | *appuweni, eppuweni* | *ešuwani* | *aduweni, eduweni* |
| | 2 | *apteni, epteni* | | *azzašteni, ezzatteni* |
| | 3 | *appanzi* | *ašanzi* | *adanzi* |
| **Pret. sing.** | 1 | *ēppun* | *ešun* | *edun* |
| | 2 | *ēpta* | *ēšta* | *ezatta* |
| | 3 | *ēpta* | *ēšta* | *ēzta, ezzatta, ezzaš, ezašta* |
| **plur.** | 1 | *ēppuen, appuen* | *ešuwen* | *eduwen* |
| | 2 | *ēpten* | *ēšten* | |
| | 3 | *ēpper* | *ešer* | *eter* |

Medio-passive

| | | | |
|---|---|---|---|
| **Pres. sing.** | 1 | | *weḫaḫḫa* |
| | 3 | | *weḫari, weḫatta(ri)* |
| **plur.** | 3 | | *weḫanta(ri)* |
| **Pret. sing.** | 1 | | *weḫḫaḫat* |
| | 3 | *appattat* | *weḫtat, weḫattat* |
| **plur.** | 3 | *appandat* | *weḫandat* |

Imperative, participle, verbum infinitum, and *-ške-*

| | | | | |
|---|---|---|---|---|
| **Part.** | *appant-* | **Imperat.** | Sing. | Plur. |
| **Inf. I** | *eppuwanzi* | 2 | *ep* | *epten* |
| **II** | *appanna* | 3 | *epdu* | *appandu* |
| **Verb. subst.** | *appatar* | | | |
| *-ške-* | *appeške-* | | | |

## Ic *Thematic verbs*

Active

| | A | B | C |
|---|---|---|---|
| **Present** | | | |
| **Sing.** 1 | *zinnami, zinnaḫḫi* | *iyami, iyemi* | *ḫatrāmi* |
| 2 | *zinniši* | *iaši* | *ḫatrāši* |
| 3 | *zinnizi, zinnai* | *iezzi, iyazzi* | *ḫatrāezzi* |
| **Plur.** 1 | *zinnaweni* | *iyaweni* | *ḫatrāweni* |
| 2 | *zinnatteni* | | *ḫatrātteni* |
| 3 | *zinnanzi* | *iyanzi, ienzi* | *ḫatrānzi* |
| **Preterite** | | | |
| **Sing.** 1 | *zinnaḫḫun* | *iyanun* | *ḫatrānun* |
| 2 | *zinnit* | *iyeš, iyaš* | *ḫatrāeš* |
| 3 | *zinnit, zinnešta* | *iēt, iyat* | *ḫatrāet, ḫatrāeš* |
| **Plur.** 1 | | *iyawen* | |
| 2 | | *iyatten* | |
| 3 | *zinner* | *iēr* | |

Medio-passive

| | A | B | C |
|---|---|---|---|
| **Present** | | | |
| **Sing.** 3 | *zinnattari* | | |
| **Plur.** 3 | *zinnantari* | | |
| **Imperative** | | | |
| **Sing.** 2 | | *iya* | *ḫatrāi* |
| 3 | *zinnešdu, zinnau* | *iyaddu* | |
| **Plur.** 2 | | *iyatten* | |
| 3 | | *iyandu* | |
| **Participle** | *zinnant-* | *iyant-* | *ḫatrānt-* |
| **Supinum** | *zinnauwan* | *iyauwan* | *ḫatrauwan* |

## Ic D

| | Present | Preterite |
|---|---|---|
| **Sing.** 1 | *memiškemi* | *memiškenun* |
| 2 | *memiškeši* | *memiškeš* |
| 3 | *memiškezzi* | *memišket* |

| | Present | Preterite |
|---|---|---|
| **Plur.** 1 | *memiškeuwani* | |
| 2 | *memiškettení* | *memišketten* |
| 3 | *memiškanzi* | *memišker* |

| | Imperative | Participle |
|---|---|---|
| **Sing.** 2 | *memiški* | *memiškant-* |
| 3 | *memiškeddu* | |
| **Plur.** 2 | *memišketten* | |
| | | Supinum |
| 3 | *memiškandu* | *memiškeuwan* |

Id *Stems with Ablaut -e-/Ø*

Ie *Stems with Ablaut -n-/Ø*

Active

| | Id | Id | Ie | Ie |
|---|---|---|---|---|
| **Pres.** | | | | |
| **Sing.** 1 | *ḫuekmi* | *kuemi* | | *šanḫmi* |
| 2 | | *kueši, kuenti* | | *šanḫti* |
| 3 | *ḫuekzi* | *kuenzi* | *likzi, linkzi* | *šaḫzi, šanḫzi* |
| **Plur.** 1 | *ḫuekkueni* | | *linkueni* | *šanḫueni* |
| 2 | | | | *šaḫteni* |
| 3 | *ḫukanzi* | *kunanzi* | *linkanzi* | *šanḫanzi* |
| **Pret.** | | | | |
| **Sing.** 1 | | *kuenun* | *linkun* | *šanḫun* |
| 2 | | | *(ḫarnikta)* | |
| 3 | *ḫuekta* | *kuenta* | *likta, linkta* | *šanḫta* |
| **Plur.** 1 | | *kuewen* | *linkuen, lingawen* | |
| 2 | | | *likten* | |
| 3 | | *kuenner* | *linker* | *šanḫer* |
| **Participle** | *ḫukant-* | *kunant-* | *linkant-* | *šanḫant-* |

Id Imperative, participle, verbum infinitum, and *-ške-*

| | | | | |
|---|---|---|---|---|
| **Part.** | *kunant-* | **Imperat.** | Sing. | Plur. |
| **Inf. I** | *kunanna* | 2 | *kuenni* | *kuenten* |
| **II** | | 3 | *kuendu* | *kunandu* |
| **Verbal noun** | *ḫukatar* | | | |
| *-ške-* | *kuwaške-* | *ḫukiške-* | | |

Ie Imperative, participle, verbum infinitum, and *-ške-*

| | | | | |
|---|---|---|---|---|
| **Part.** | *linkant-* | **Imperat.** | Sing. | Plur. |
| **Inf. I** | | 2 | *lik, link* | *linkten* |
| **II** | *linkuwanzi* | 3 | *linkdu* | *linkandu* |
| **Verbal noun** | *linkuwar* | | | |
| *-ške-* | *linkiške-* | | | |

If *ḫar-/ḫark-*

| | Pres. Sing. | Plur. | Pret. Sing. | Plur. |
|---|---|---|---|---|
| 1 | *ḫarmi* | *ḫarweni* | *ḫarkun* | *ḫarwen* |
| 2 | *ḫarši, ḫarti* | *ḫarteni* | | *ḫarten* |
| 3 | *ḫarzi* | *ḫarkanzi* | *ḫarta* | *ḫarker* |

Imperative, participle, verbum infinitum, and *-ške-*

| | | | | |
|---|---|---|---|---|
| **Part.** | *ḫarkant-* | **Imperat.** | Sing. | Plur. |
| **Inf. I** | | 2 | *ḫark* | *ḫarten* |
| | | 3 | *ḫardu* | *ḫarkandu* |
| **Supinum** | | | | |
| *-ške-* | *ḫarkiške-* | | | |

Ig *damašš-/damešš-*

Active

| | Sing. | Plur. |
|---|---|---|
| **Pres.** 1 | *tamašmi* | |
| 2 | *tamašti* | |
| 3 | *tamašzi, dammešzi* | *dameššanzi, tamaššanzi* |
| **Pret.** 1 | *damaššun* | *tameššuwen* |
| 3 | *damašta, dammešta* | *tameššer, tamaššer* |

| | Sing. | Plur. |
|---|---|---|
| **Medio-passive** | | |
| **Pres.** 3 | *damašta(ri)* | |
| **Pret.** 3 | *tamaštat* | |

Imperative, participle, verbum infinitum, and *-ške-*

| | | | | |
|---|---|---|---|---|
| **Part.** | *damešsant-* | **Imperat.** | Sing. | Plur. |
| **Inf. I** | *damaššuwanzi* | 3 | *tamašdu* | |
| *-ške-* | *dameške-*, *damaške-*, *damaškeške-* | | | |

Ih *pai-* "to go"

| | Present | Preterite |
|---|---|---|
| **Sing.** 1 | *paimi* | *pāun* |
| 2 | *paiši* | *paitta* |
| 3 | *paizzi* | *pait* |
| **Plur.** 1 | *pa(i)weni, paiwani* | *pa(i)wen* |
| 2 | *paitteni* | |
| 3 | *pānzi* | *pāer* |

Imperative, participle, verbum infinitum, and *-ške-*

| | | | | |
|---|---|---|---|---|
| **Part.** | *pānt-* | **Imperat.** | Sing. | Plur. |
| **Inf. I** | *pāuwanzi* | 2 | *(it)* | *paitten* |
| **Verbal noun** | *pāuwar* | 3 | *paiddu* | *pāndu* |
| *-ške-* | *paiške-* | | | |

Ii *uwa-*

| | Present | Preterite |
|---|---|---|
| **Sing.** 1 | *uwami* | *uwanun* |
| 2 | *uwaši* | *ueš, uwaš* |
| 3 | *uezzi* | *uet* |
| **Plur.** 1 | *uwaweni* | *uwawen* |
| 2 | *uwatteni* | *uwatten* |
| 3 | *uwanzi* | *uēr* |

Imperative, participle, verbum infinitum, and -*ške*-

| | | | | |
|---|---|---|---|---|
| **Part.** | *uwant-* | **Imperat.** | Sing. | Plur. |
| **Inf. I** | *uwauwanzi* | 2 | | *uwatten* |
| **Verbal noun** | | 3 | *uiddu* | *uwandu* |
| -*ške*- | *ueške-* | | | |

Ij *te-/tar-*

| | Sing. | Plur. |
|---|---|---|
| **Present** | | |
| 1 | *temi* | *tarweni* |
| 2 | *teši* | *tarteni* |
| 3 | *tezzi* | *taranzi* |
| **Preterite** | | |
| 1 | *tenun* | |
| 2 | *tēš* | |
| 3 | *tet* | *terer* |

Imperative, participle, verbum infinitum, and -*ške*-

| | | | | |
|---|---|---|---|---|
| **Part.** | *tarant-* | **Imperat.** | Sing. | Plur. |
| **Inf. I** | | 2 | *tet* | *teten* |
| **Verbal noun** | | 3 | *teddu* | *tarandu* |
| -*ške*- | *taršike-*, *taraške-* | | | |

## -ḫi- Conjugation

### IIa *Verbs of unchanging stem*

Active

| | Present | Preterite |
|---|---|---|
| **Sing.** 1 | *išpantḫi* | *šipandaḫḫun* |
| 2 | *(maniyaḫti)* | *(maniaḫta)* |
| 3 | *išpanti/šipanti* | *šipandaš, šipanzašta* |
| **Plur.** 1 | *šipanduweni* | |
| 2 | *šipanzašteni (maniyaḫteni)* | |
| 3 | *šipandanzi* | *šipanter* |

Medio-passive

| | Present | Preterite |
|---|---|---|
| **Sing.** ind. 1 | *ešḫa(ri)* | *ešḫaḫat(i)* |
| 2 | *ešta(ri)* | *eštat(i)* |
| 3 | *eša(ri)* | *ešat(i)* |
| **Plur.** ind. 1 | *ešuwašta(ri)* | *ešuwaštat(i)* |
| 2 | *ešduma(ri)* | *ešdumat(i)* |
| 3 | *ešanta(ri)* | *ešantat(i)* |

IIa Imperative, participle, verbum infinitum, and *-ške-*: Active

| | | | | |
|---|---|---|---|---|
| **Part.** | *šipantant-* | **Imperat.** | Sing. | Plur. |
| **Inf. I** | *šipanduwanzi* | 2 | *maniyaḫ* | *maniyaḫten* |
| **Verbal noun** | *šipanduwar* | 3 | *maniyaḫdu* | *maniyaḫḫandu* |
| **Supinum** | | | | |
| *-ške-* | *šipanzake-* | *maniyaḫḫeške-* | | |

IIa Imperative, participle, verbum infinitum, and *-ške-*: Medio-passive

| | | | | |
|---|---|---|---|---|
| **Part.** | *ašant-* | **Imperat.** | Sing. | Plur. |
| **Inf. II** | *ašanna* | 2 | *ešḫut* | *ēšdumat* |
| **Verbal noun** | *ašatar* | 3 | *ešaru* | *ešantaru* |
| *-ške-* | *eške-* | | | |

IIb *Verbs with Ablaut -a-/-e-*

Active

| | | | |
|---|---|---|---|
| **Present** | | | |
| **Sing.** 1 | *šākḫi* | | *ašašḫi* |
| 2 | *šākti* | | *ašašti* |
| 3 | *šākki* | *ḫāši, ḫašzi, ḫešzi* | *ašaši* |
| **Plur.** 1 | | | |
| 2 | *šekteni, šakteni* | | |
| 3 | | *ḫešanzi, ḫaššanzi* | *ašešanzi* |
| **Preterite** | | | |
| **Sing.** 1 | | *ḫašḫun* | *ašašḫun* |
| 3 | *šakkiš* | *ḫašta* | *ašašta, ašešta* |
| **Plur.** 1 | | *ḫešuwen* | |
| 3 | *šekker* | *ḫeser, ḫašer* | *ašešer, ašašer* |

Medio-passive

| | |
|---|---|
| **Preterite 3.** Sing. | *ḫeštat* |

IIb Imperative, participle, verbum infinitum, and *-ške-*

| | | | | |
|---|---|---|---|---|
| **Part.** | *šakkant-*, | **Imperat.** | Sing. | Plur. |
| | *šekkant-* | 1 | *šeggallu* | |
| **Inf. I** | (*ašešuwanzi*) | 2 | *šāk* | *šekten* |
| **Inf. II** | (*ašešanna*) | 3 | *šākku* | *šekkandu* |
| **Verbal noun** | *ḫešuwar* | | | |
| *-ške-* | *ḫešike-*, *ḫaške-*, *ḫeške-* | | | |

IIc Semi-consonant stems

Active

| | Present | Preterite |
|---|---|---|
| **Sing.** 1 | *eššaḫḫi* | *iššaḫḫun* |
| 2 | *eššatti* | |
| 3 | *iššai* | *iššišta (tarnaš)* |
| **Plur.** 1 | *iššuweni* | *iššuwen* |
| 2 | *išteni, iššatteni* | |
| 3 | *iššanzi* | *iššer* |

Medio-passive

| | | |
|---|---|---|
| **Sing.** 3 | *tarnattari* | *tarnattat* |
| **Plur.** 3 | *tarnantari* | |
| **Participle** | *tarnant-* | |

IIc Imperative, participle, verbum infinitum, and *-ške-*

| | | | | |
|---|---|---|---|---|
| **Part.** | *tarnant-* | **Imperat.** | Sing. | Plur. |
| **Inf. I** | *tarnummanzi* | 2 | *tarna* | *tarnatten* |
| **Verbal noun** | *tarnummar* | 3 | *tarnau* | *tarnandu* |
| **Supinum** | *iššuwan* | | | |
| *-ške-* | *taršike-*, *tarške-* | | | |

IId *Verbs with stem in -e/i-, -iya-, and -ai-*

Active

| | | | |
|---|---|---|---|
| **Pres. sing.** 1 | *peḫḫi* | *teḫḫi* | *neḫḫi* |
| 2 | *paiti, paišti* | *daiti* | *naitti* |
| 3 | *pāi* | *dāi* | *nāi* |
| **plur.** 1 | *piweni* | *tiiaweni* | *naiwani* |
| 2 | *pišteni, paišteni* | *taitteni, taišteni* | *naišteni* |
| 3 | *pianzi* | *tianzi* | *neanzi* |
| **Pret. sing.** 1 | *peḫḫun* | *teḫḫun* | *neḫḫun, neyaḫun* |
| 2 | *paitta, paišta* | *daišta* | *naitta* |
| 3 | *pais, paišta* | *daiš* | *naiš, naišta* |
| **plur.** 1 | *piwen* | *daiwen* | *neyawen* |
| 2 | *pišten, paišten* | *daišten* | |
| 3 | *pier* | *daer, tier* | *naer, neier* |

Medio-passive

| | | | |
|---|---|---|---|
| **Pres. sing.** 1 | | *neyaḫḫari* | |
| 2 | | *neyattati, naištari* | |
| 3 | | *nea, neyari* | |
| **plur.** 3 | | *neanda, neantari* | |
| **Pret. sing.** 1 | | *neyaḫḫat* | |
| 3 | | *neat, neyattat* | |
| **plur.** 3 | | *neantati, neyantat* | |

## Imperative, participle, verbum infinitum, and *-ške-*

| | | | |
|---|---|---|---|
| **Imperative** | | | |
| **sing.** 2 | *pai* | *dāi* | *nāi, neya* |
| 3 | *pāu* | *dāu* | *nāu* |
| **plur.** 2 | *pešten, paišten* | *dāišten* | *naišten* |
| 3 | *piyandu* | *tiyandu* | *neyandu* |
| **Part.** | *piyant-* | *tiyant-* | *neyant-* |
| **Inf. I** | *piyauwanzi* | *tiyanna, tiyawanzi* | |
| **Verbal noun** | *piyauwar* | *tiyauwar* | *neyawar, naiwar* |
| *-ške-* | *peške-* | *zikke-* | *naiške-, nieške-* |

IIe *Verbs with stem in -a- and -i-*

| | Pres. | Pret. |
|---|---|---|
| **Sing.** 1 | *memaḫḫi* | *memaḫḫun* |
| 2 | *mematti* | *memišta* |
| 3 | *memai* | *memišta, memaš* |
| **Plur.** 1 | *memiweni, memiaweni* | *memawen, memiawen* |
| 2 | *mematteni, memišteni* | *memišten* |
| 3 | *memianzi, memanzi* | *memer* |

Imperative, participle, verbum infinitum, and -*ške-*

| | | | | |
|---|---|---|---|---|
| **Part.** | *memant-*, | **Imperat.** | Sing. | Plur. |
| | *memiant-* | 1 | *memallu* | |
| **Inf. I** | *memiawanzi* | 2 | *memi* | *memišten* |
| **Verbal noun** | | 3 | *memau* | *memandu* |
| -*ške-* | *memiške-* | | | |

IIf *dā- and lā-*

Active

| | Sing. | Plur. |
|---|---|---|
| **Present** 1 | *dāḫḫi* | *tumeni, dāweni* |
| 2 | *dātti* | *datteni* |
| 3 | *dāi* | *dānzi* |
| **Preterite** 1 | *dāḫḫun* | *dāuen* |
| 2 | *dātta* | *datten* |
| 3 | *dāš, datta* | *dāēr* |

Medio-passive

| | | |
|---|---|---|
| **Present** 3 | *dattari* | |
| **Preterite** 3 | *dattat* | |
| **Imperative** | | |
| 2 | *dā* | *dātten* |
| 3 | *dāu* | *dandu* |
| **Infinitive II and I** | *danna, dauwanzi* | |
| **Participle** | *dānt-* | |

Imperative, participle, verbum infinitum, and *-ške-*

| | | | | |
|---|---|---|---|---|
| **Part.** | *dānt-* | **Imperat.** | Sing. | Plur. |
| **Verbal noun** | *dāuwar* | 2 | *dā* | *dātten* |
| **Inf. I** | *danna* | 3 | *dāu* | *dandu* |
| **Inf. II** | *dāuwanzi* | | | |
| *-ške-* | *daške-* | | | |

III *Irregular* auš-/au-/u-

Active

| | Present | Preterite |
|---|---|---|
| **Sing.** 1 | *ūḫḫi* | *uḫḫun* |
| 2 | *autti* | *aušta* |
| 3 | *aušzi* | *aušta* |
| **Plur.** 1 | *umeni, aumeni* | *aumen* |
| 2 | *ušteni, autteni* | *aušten* |
| 3 | *uwanzi* | *auer* |

Medio-passive

| | |
|---|---|
| **Plur.** 3 | *uwanta* |

| | |
|---|---|
| **Imperative** | |
| **Sing.** 1 | *uwallu* |
| 2 | *au* |
| 3 | *aušdu* |
| **Plur.** 2 | *aušten* |
| 3 | *uwandu* |
| **Participle** | *uwant-* |
| **Verbal noun** | *uwatar* |
| **-ške-** | *uške-, uškiške-* |

# APPENDIX 2: Sources of exercise material

## 1.8.1

1. KUB 26.12 iii 17 2. KBo 13.16, 9 3. KUB 20.87 i 17 4. KBo 13.29 ii 10 5. KUB 8.36 ii 12 6. KUB 27.1 i 1–2 7. HT 1 ii 10–11 8. Bo 86/299 (= Bronze Tablet, abbrev. Brt.) ii 51 9. KBo 4.9 iii 6 10. KUB 30.26 i 1–2 11. KBo 5.11 iv 14 12. KBo 22.178 + KUB 48.109 ii 3 13. KBo 15.10 ii 7 14. KUB 48.119 obv.? 12 15. KBo 5.1 ii 7.

## 2.8

1. KBo 4.4 iii 43–44 2. KBo 19.76 i 26 3. KBo 2.5 i 2–3 4. KBo 3.34 ii 12–13 5. KBo 6.29 ii 19 6. KUB 43.60 i 33–34 7. KBo 5.9 iii 19 8. KBo 3.1 ii 12 9. KUB 20.87 i 5–6, 11–12 10. HKM 58, 9 11. KBo 3.16 iv 16 12. HKM 19, 12–14 13. HKM 10, 36–37 14. KBo 32.14 ii 9–11 15. KBo 22.2 rev.13 16. KBo 32.14 ii 42.

## 3.8

1. KUB 29.1 i 21 2. KUB 23.85, 6 3. IBoT 1.36 ii 16–17 4. KUB 50.79 obv.? 4 5. KBo 25.112 ii 14 6. KBo 5.3+ i 34 7. KUB 17.1 ii 4–5 8. KUB 8.36 iii 9–10 9. KBo 6.2+ ii 12 10. Apol. i 22–24 11. KBo 47.239 iii 13–14 12. KUB 21.29 iii 31 13. KBo 11.44 rev. 4–6 14. KUB 17.21 iv 5–6 15. KBo 11.1 rev. 23 16. KUB 14.15 i 5–6 17. Brt. ii 51–52 18. KUB 13.3 ii 11 19. KBo 3.7 i 11 20. KUB 14.10 i 16–18.

## 4.8

1. KUB 13.4 ii 70 2. KBo 5.3 + KBo 19.43 ii 61–62 3. KUB 17.7 i 6 4. Brt. ii 33–34 5. incipit and colophon of Hittite Royal Death Ritual passim 6. KUB 31.127+ i 35–36 7. KUB 33.83 + KBo 26.74 ii 3 8. KUB 33.67 iv 17 9. HKM 19, 7–8 10. KBo 4.10+ rev. 8 11. KBo 19.112, 8–9 12. KBo 2.3 i 42 13. KBo 13.15, 5–6 14. KBo 17.40 i 3–5.

## 5.8

1. KUB 29.1 ii 50–51 2. KUB 1.1 i 9–11 3. Brt. i 63–64 4. KUB 42.100 iii 38 5. KUB 13.7 iv 3–7 6. KUB 14.106, 48 7. KBo 4.6 obv. 13–14 8. KUB 36.104 i 6–7 9. KUB 17.10 i 19 10. KBo 6.2+ iv 52 11. KUB 13.4 ii 29 12. KUB 7.1+ ii 5–6 13. KBo 10.2 i 25 14. KBo 5.3+ i 6–7.

## 6.8

1. KBo 17.74 iv 33–34 2. KUB 31.124 ii 10–11 3. KBo 2.5 i 15–16 4. KBo 19.128 iv 4–5 5. KBo 15.33 ii 32–33 6. KUB 33.106 + KBo 26.65 i 23 7. KUB 31.127+ i 52–53 8. KUB 21.27 i 13–15 9. Brt. ii 46–47 10. KBo 3.67 ii 2//KBo 3.1 i 56 11. KUB 1.1 i 28–30 12. KBo 16.47 obv. 10 13. KUB 13.4 iii 50–51 14. HKM 26, 9 15. KUB 41.30 iii 8 16. KUB 12.44 iii 10–13 17. KBo 3.4 i 28–29 18. KUB 1.1 iii 69–70.

## 7.8.1

1. KBo 6.3 iii 68 2. KBo 5.6 iv 6 3. KUB 19.29 iv 16 4. KBo 22.2 rev. 12–13 5. KBo 10.2 ii 7 6. KBo 19.128 i 6–8 7. HKM 6, 5–6 8. KUB 10.91 ii 5–6 9. KUB 8.1 iii 12–13 10. KUB 33.106 iv 18 11. KBo 5.1 iv 4 12. KBo 3.1 i 41 13. KBo 3.4 iii 47–49 14. KBo 32.14 ii 6–7.

## 8.8.1

1. KBo 11.43 i 26–27 2. KBo 5.4 rev. 3, 5 3. KUB 8.53, 22–23 (w. dupl. KUB 33.123, 4) 4. IBoT 1.36 i 73 5. KBo 5.8 i 23–25 6. KUB 33.106 ii 9–10 7. KBo 4.14 ii 9 8. KUB 19.7, 8–9 9. HKM 35, 8–9 10. KBo 5.6 ii 6 11. KUB 14.10 iv 17–19 12. VBoT 2, 24–25 13. KUB 13.8 obv. 6 14. KBo 6.2+ iii 63–64 15. KUB 33.106+ ii 17–18 16. KUB 1.1+ ii 70–72 17. KBo 16.97 rev. 7–8.

## 9.7.1

1. HKM 46, 15–17 2. KBo 3.1 i 22 3. IBoT 1.36 iii 61–62 4. KBo 3.22 obv. 41–42 5. KUB 30.10 rev. 17 6. KUB 31.127+ ii 22–23 7. HKM 25, 11–14, 22–23 8. KUB 13.35 iv 45–46 9. KBo 32.14 ii 7–8 10. KBo 16.47 obv. 15 11. HKM 17, 9–11 12. KUB 15.34 iv 14 13. KUB 2.7 i 5–8 14. KUB 1.1 i 5–6 15. KUB 35.148 iii 12–13 16. KUB 33.120+ i 8 17. KUB 43.38 rev. 14 18. KUB 33.106+ iii 52–53.

## 10.6.1

1. KUB 19.29 iv 18–19 2. KUB 24.3 + i 32'–34 3. KBo 10.47c i 9–12 (w. dupl. KUB 17.2, 7–10) 4. KUB 23.1 + ii 16–17 5. KUB 33.103 iii 5–6 6. KBo 6.34 ii 50 7. KUB 9.31 ii 20–21.

# APPENDIX 3: Grammatical Index

# **APPENDIX 4:** Cuneiform sign list

The following list contains all cuneiform signs given at the end of the preceding ten Lessons, as well as all signs contained in the KBo 3.4 exemplar of Muršili II's *Ten-Year Annals*. The signs are listed in the order given in C. Rüster and E. Neu, *Hethitisches Zeichenlexikon* (abbreviated HZL; Wiesbaden 1989), the standard sign inventory in the field. The first column gives the number in HZL. The signs are ordered according to their shape, that is, starting with the simple horizontal wedge and all signs that start with one or more horizontal wedges (𒀸 through [sign]). Then follow the slanted wedges and signs starting with them (𒀹 through [sign]), and the same principle applies to the *Winkelhaken*-signs (𒌋 through [sign]) and vertical wedges (𒁹 through 𒐊).

If a variant shape is given, this is usually a later variant, although the older variant keeps being used alongside the newer one. Normally, a wedge more or less or its position in the overall build-up of a sign is distinctive, and small differences will have important consequences, resulting in a different sign with a different sound value (compare, for instance, the difference between I 𒄿 and DUMU 𒌉, DI 𒁲 and KI 𒆠, or PÁR 𒈦 and QA 𒋡). In other cases, however, small variations have no consequences, like the height of the inscribed vertical in, for instance, ŠA, GA, or TA, either below the upper horizontal or sticking out over it (𒊭 vs. 𒊭). The sign KÁN in its standard form has three inscribed verticals, but one often encounters variants with either two or four. The same is true for MEŠ, which sometimes shows four *Winkelhaken* instead of the regular three. Truth is, that on the tablet itself it is often difficult to see, because the signs usually are small with an average line height of 3–4 mm. The signs LA 𒆷 and AT 𒀜 are often difficult to tell apart. In all these things, experience is the only solution.

The third column gives the sound value. Exclusive Sumero- and Akkadographic sound values are given only if they differ from the Hittite reading (e.g., BABBAR and UTU for *ud/t*), but *ud/t* can also be read Sumerographically as UD. Hittite sound values containing an *i* can also be read with *e*: *šir* but also *šer*, *im* but also *em*, *di* but also *de*, etc. But when given with an *e*, they only have an *e*-value (*me*, but there is a separate sign *mi*). For this, compare the Introduction §7 and Lesson 1.5.2.

Vowel-consonant signs (AT, IK, etc.) are given ending in a voiceless stop, but they can also be read with their voiced counterpart (AD, IG, etc.), if a following CV (e.g., DA, GA) so requires; for this, see Introduction §7 and Lesson 1.5.4.

The fourth column refers to the Lesson in which the sign was given for the first time. Some signs appear without introduction in the cuneiform copy of Muršili's *Ten-Year Annals*. They are marked as "Murš."

| HZL | Sign form | Variant | Sound value | Lesson |
|---|---|---|---|---|
| 1 | | | aš, RÙ (AŠ.AŠ = DIDLI) | 1 |
| 2 | | | ḫal | 3 |
| 4 | | | pal, BAL | 10 |
| 5 | | | šir | 9 |
| 7 | | | tar | 1 |
| 8 | | | an, DINGIR; det. divine names | 1 |
| 11 | | | nu | 1 |
| 13 | | | pát, BE, ÚŠ | 1 |
| 15 | | | na | 2 |
| 16 | | | ÌR, ARAD | 2 |
| 17 | | | mu | 9 |
| 20 | | | pár, maš | 2 |
| 21 | | | $ka_4$, qa | 2 |
| 24 | | | ḫu, MUŠEN | 5, 7 |
| 27 | | | $ŠE_{12}$ | Murš. |
| 29 | | | rat | 10 |
| 30 | | | gi | 4, 10 |
| 32 | | | ri | 7 |
| 33 | | | zi | 5 |
| 37 | | | ti | 2 |
| 39 | | | nam | 10 |
| 40 | | | en, EN | 2 |
| 43 | | | ru | 8 |
| 44 | | | ip | 10 |
| 51 | | | ur | 10 |
| 57 | | | AMA | Murš. |
| 61 | | | kán | 7 |
| 65 | | | SÍG | 3 |
| 67 | | | ik, GÁL | 9 |
| 68 | | | šu | 9 |
| 68 | | | GÉŠPU | Murš. |
| 69 | | | KÙ | Murš. |
| 72 | | | ni, LÍ | 2 |
| 73 | | | $NA_4$ | 2 |
| 75 | | | DÙ | 2 |

| HZL | Sign form | Variant | Sound value | Lesson |
|---|---|---|---|---|
| 77 | | | ir | 2 |
| 78 | | | LÚ | 1, 3 |
| 79 | | | ŠEŠ | 3 |
| 81 | | | ak | 9 |
| 82 | | | MÈ | Murš. |
| 92 | | | az, *AṢ* | 9 |
| 93 | | | uk | 9 |
| 95 | | | la | 3 |
| 97 | | | ap | 3 |
| 105 | | | at | 3 |
| 107 | | | EZEN$_4$ | Murš. |
| 108 | | | zé | 9 |
| 109 | | | URUDU | 2 |
| 113 | | | ḫé | 9 |
| 114 | | | BÀD | Murš. |
| 115 | | | LUGAL | 1, 3 |
| 120 | | | kum | 8 |
| 126 | | | EGIR | Murš. |
| 128 | | | du | 7 |
| 131 | | | wi$_5$, GEŠTIN | Murš. |
| 132 | | | uš | 7 |
| 133 | | | ka | 8 |
| 151 | | | iš | 7 |
| 152 | | | up | 3 |
| 153 | | | pí, kaš | 3 |
| 157 | | | GU$_4$ (GUD) | 3 |
| 158 | | | ša | 3 |
| 159 | | | ga | 3 |
| 160 | | | ta | 3 |
| 162 | | | DUG | 2, 3 |
| 165 | | | GIM | Murš. |
| 168 | | | am | 4 |
| 169 | | | ne | 4 |
| 173 | | | kat, GADA | 3, 9 |
| 174 | | | pa, ḫat | 2 |
| 178 | | | iz, GIŠ; det. wood | 2 |
| 180 | | | PÚ | 2 |
| 183 | | | al | 8 |
| 185 | | | gur | 10 |
| 187 | | | e | 1, 4 |

| HZL | Sign form | Variant | Sound value | Lesson |
|---|---|---|---|---|
| 191 | | | mar | 9 |
| 192 | | | SAG | 2 |
| 195 | | | ú | 1, 4 |
| 196 | | | kal, dan | 4 |
| 197 | | | un | 4 |
| 199 | | | É; det. houses | 1 |
| 202 | | | dur | Murš. |
| 203 | | | UZU | 4 |
| 204 | | | NIR | Murš. |
| 205 | | | ba | 4 |
| 206 | | | ku | 4 |
| 208 | | | ma | 4 |
| 209 | | | zu | 10 |
| 210 | | | lu, UDU | 9 |
| 212 | | | TÚG | 3 |
| 213 | | | KUŠ | 3 |
| 214 | | | da | 7 |
| 215 | | | it | 7 |
| 217 | | | i | 1, 4 |
| 218 | | | ia | 4 |
| 229 | | | URU | 1, 4 |
| 233 | | | ra | 8 |
| 237 | | | DUMU | Murš. |
| 238 | | | ZAG | Murš. |
| 239 | | | $SIG_7$ | Murš. |
| 241 | | | tàš | 10 |
| 242 | | | GAL | Murš. |
| 245 | | | pur | Murš. |
| 247 | | | GAM | 5 |
| 248 | | | *Glossenkeile* (gloss wedges) | Murš. |
| 249 | | | te | 6 |
| 250 | | | kar | Murš. |
| 256 | | | KÚR | Murš. |
| 259 | | | KASKAL | Murš. |
| 261 | | | u, 10 | 1 |
| 267 | | | mi, $GE_6$ | 9 |
| 269 | | | GIG | Murš. |
| 271 | | | gul | Murš. |
| 272 | | | UGU | Murš. |
| 273 | | | kiš | 10 |

| HZL | Sign form | Variant | Sound value | Lesson |
|---|---|---|---|---|
| 275 | | | ul | 8 |
| 286 | | | liš | 10 |
| 288 | | | ši | 8 |
| 289 | | | ar | 7 |
| 294 | | | ŠÀ | Murš. |
| 297 | | | šal, MUNUS; f: det. female names | 1 |
| 298 | | | dam | 9 |
| 301 | | | GÌR | Murš. |
| 302 | | | ANŠE | Murš. |
| 304 | | | gu | Murš. |
| 306 | | | lam | 9 |
| 310 | | | lum | 9 |
| 312 | | | di | 8 |
| 313 | | | ki | 5, 8 |
| 313 | | | KARAŠ | Murš. |
| 316 | | | ut, pir, tam, BABBAR, UTU | 8 |
| 317 | | | wa | 8 |
| 327 | | | ÉRIN | Murš. |
| 329 | | | KUR; det. geographical names | 1 |
| 330 | | | tén, DIN | 5 |
| 331 | | | eš | 5 |
| 332 | | | aḫ, eḫ, iḫ, uḫ | 5 |
| 333 | | | ḫar, ḫur, mur | 2, 5 |
| 335 | | | ḫi | 5 |
| 336 | | | GAŠAN | Murš. |
| 337 | | | im | 3, 5 |
| 338 | | | še | 5 |
| 339 | | | pu | 5 |
| 340 | | | uz | 5 |
| 343 | | | li | 6 |
| 346 | | | tu | 6 |
| 350 | | | SUM | Murš. |
| 353 | | | šar, SAR | 5, 6 |
| 354 | | | in | 6 |
| 355 | | | kam; $TU_7$ | 4, 5 |
| 356 | | | m: det. male names; diš, 1 | 1, 7 |
| 357 | | | me | 6 |
| 360 | | | MEŠ | 6 |

| HZL | Sign form | Variant | Sound value | Lesson |
|---|---|---|---|---|
| 361 |  | | 2 | 7 |
| 364 |  | | a | 1, 6 |
| 365 |  | | ÍD | 2 |
| 366 |  | | za | 6 |
| 367 |  |  | ḫa | 6 |
| 368 |  | | 3 | 7 |
| 369 |  | | NINDA | 4 |
| 370 |  | | 4 | 8 |
| 371 |  | | 5 | 8 |
| 372 |  | | 6 | 8 |
| 373 |  | | 7 | 8 |
| 374 |  | | 8 | 8 |
| 375 |  | | 9 | 8 |

# APPENDIX 5: Glossary

This Glossary contains all Hittite (1) words as well as Sumero- (2) and Akkadograms (3) that are used in the Exercises and in the *Ten-Year Annals* of Muršili II. At the end follow all names (divine, personal, and geographical) encountered in the sentences of the Exercises.

Hittite words are alphabetized in the following order: *a e ḫ i k/g l m n p/b r š t/d u w z*. Word internally *e* and *i* are not distinguished. The sounds *y* and *w* as glides are ignored in alphabetizing (*iya-* comes before *imma*).

Compound Sumerograms are alphabetized after the first sign (A.ŠÀ comes before AB).

## 1. Hittite

| | |
|---|---|
| *-a/-ya* | and, too, even |
| *akk-* (IIa) | to die |
| *aku-* | see *eku-* |
| *alwanzaḫḫ-* (IIa) | to bewitch |
| *-an* | (sentence particle) |
| *anišiwat* (adv.) | today |
| *anna-*, com. | mother |
| *annalla/i-* | old, former |
| *annišan*, adv. | formerly, already |
| *anš-* (Ia) | to wash, wipe, clean |
| *anda(n)* | in, into, inside |
| *antuḫ(š)a-*, com. (UN) | man, human being |
| *anturiya-* | inner, inside- |
| *-apa* | (sentence particle) |
| *apā-* | that, he, she, it |
| *apiya*, adv. | there, then |
| *apeniššan*, adv. | thus, in that way |
| *apezzi-* | last, youngest, lowest in rank |
| *appa(n)* (EGIR-*pa/an*) | behind, after, back, again |
| *appanda* (EGIR-*anda*) | after(wards) |
| *ar-/er-* (IIb) | to reach, arrive |
| *ar-* (Ia, dep.) | to stand |
| LÚ*ara-* | friend, comrade |
| *araḫzena-* | neighboring, surrounding, foreign |

| | |
|---|---|
| *arawa-* | free |
| *arḫa*, adv. | away (from), off; in compounds also reinforcing |
| *arnu-* (Ia) | to bring, deport |
| *arš-/aršiya-* (Ia/c) | to flow |
| *ardala-*, neut. | saw |
| *aruna-*, com. | sea |
| *ašandula-*, com. | garrison |
| *ašandulae-* (Ic) | to garrison |
| *ašš-* (Ia) | to remain, belong to |
| *aššanuwant-* | provided with |
| *ašaš-/ašeš-* (IIb) | to settle, seat |
| *aši* | (demonstrative and anaphoric pronoun) |
| *aška-* | door, gate |
| *ašnu-* (Ia) | to provide, prepare |
| *ašnuwant-* | provided with |
| *-ašta* | (sentence particle) |
| *aššu-* | beloved (to), good |
| *aššul*, neut. | well-being, benevolence |
| *atta-* | father |
| *auš-/au-/u-* (III) | to see, watch |

| | |
|---|---|
| *eku-/aku-* (Ib) | to drink |
| *eni* | see *aši* |
| *eniššan* | thus, in that way |
| *epp-/app-* (Ib) | to take, hold |
| *eš-/aš-* (Ib) | to be |
| *eš-* (IIa, dep.) | to sit down, occupy |
| *ešḫar*, neut. | blood |
| *ešša-* (IIc) | to do, make |
| *ed-/ad-* (Ib) | to eat |

| | |
|---|---|
| *ḫalentu(wa)-*, neut. | palace complex |
| *ḫaliya-* (Ic) | to kneel (also in med.-pass.) |
| *ḫalki-*, com. | grain |
| *ḫaluga-*, com. | message |
| *ḫalzae-* (Ic) | to call, invoke |
| *ḫalzešša-* (IIc) | (imperfective of preceding) |
| *ḫamešḫant-*, com. | spring |
| *ḫanna-* (IIc) | to judge, decide a lawsuit |
| *ḫanda*, adv. | towards |

| | |
|---|---|
| *ḫandae-* (Ic) | to ascertain, determine |
| (*parā*) *ḫandandatar*, neut. | (divine) guidance, providence |
| *ḫantezzi-* | first, foremost |
| *ḫapa-*, com. | river |
| *ḫappina-*, com. | flame, fire |
| *ḫapuš-* (Ia) | to catch up, resume |
| *ḫar-/ḫark-* (If) | to have, hold |
| *ḫark-* (Ia) | to perish |
| *ḫarga-*, com. | (threat of) death, destruction |
| *ḫarki-* | white |
| *ḫarni(n)k-* (Ie) | to destroy |
| *ḫarninkuwar*, neut. | destruction |
| *ḫarrant-* | damaged, broken |
| *ḫaš-/ḫeš-* (IIb) | to open |
| *ḫašš-* (IIa) | to engender, give birth |
| *ḫašp-* (Ia) | to destroy, tear down |
| *ḫašša-*, com. | hearth |
| *ḫaššu-*, com. (LUGAL) | king |
| *ḫatk-* (Ia) | to close |
| *ḫatkešnu-* (Ia) | to close off, isolate |
| *ḫatrae-* (Ic) | to write, send |
| *ḫeu-*, com. | rain, shower |
| *ḫila-*, com. | courtyard |
| *ḫuwae-* (Ic) | (variant of *ḫuiya-*) |
| *ḫuiya-* (Ic) | to run, march |
| *ḫuitar-*, neut. | fauna, animals |
| *ḫuittiya-* (Ic) | to draw, let march |
| $^{\text{GIŠ}}$*ḫuluganni-*, com. | wagon, cart |
| *ḫumant-* | all, every, each |
| *ḫurnae-* (Ic) | to hunt |
| *ḫudak* | suddenly |
| $^{\text{NA}_4}$*ḫuwaši-*, neut. | stela, monument |
| | |
| *iya-* (Ic, dep.) | to go, march, walk |
| *iya-* (Ic) | to do, make |
| *iyannae-* (Ic) | (imperfective of *iya-* dep.) |
| *imma*, adv. | (gives emphasis) |
| *irma-*, com. | illness |
| *irmala-* | ill |
| *irmaliya-* (Ic) | to fall ill |
| *išḫa-*, com. | lord, master |

| | |
|---|---|
| *išša-/ešša-* (IIc) | to do, make |
| *išḫaḫru-* neut. | tear |
| *išḫiya-* (Ic) | to bind, impose |
| *išḫunau-* neut. | upper arm, power |
| (DUG)*išnura-*, com. | bowl |
| *išpant-*, com. | evening, night |
| (DUG)*išpanduzzi-*, neut. | libation (vessel) |
| *išpart-* (Ia) | to escape |
| *ištaman(a)-*, com. | ear |
| *ištamašš-* (Ia) | to hear, listen |
| *ištanana-*, com. | table, altar |
| *ištandae-* (Ic) | to wait, tarry, be held up |
| *ištanzan(a)-*, com. | soul |
| *ištap-* (IIa) | to close, shut |
| *ištark-* (Ia) | to fall ill |
| *idalawaḫḫ-* (IIa) | to do evil, harm |
| *idalawešš-* (Ia) | to become evil |
| *idalu-*, *idalawant-* | evil, bad |
| *iwar* | just as (postposition with gen.) |
| | |
| *kā-* | this |
| *kakkapa-*, com. | (an animal) |
| *kallešš-* (Ia) | to call, invite, choose |
| (GIŠ)*kalmišana-*, com. | ember, meteorite |
| *-kan* | (sentence particle) |
| *kanint-*, com. | thirst |
| *kanešš-* (Ia) | to recognize |
| *kappuwa(e)-* (Ie) | to count, take care of |
| *kappuwauwar*, neut. | count(ing) |
| *karat-*, com. | innards |
| *kari* | (see *tiya-*) |
| *kariya-* (Ic) | to cover |
| *karp-* (Ia) | to lift, pick up |
| *karš-* (Ia) | to cut |
| *kartimmiyawant-* | angry |
| *karū*, adv. | formerly, already |
| *karuili-* | old, primeval |
| *kāša/kašma*, adv. | behold!, just now |
| *kašt-*, com. | hunger |
| *katta(n)* | down, under, next to |
| *kattanda* | down into |

| | |
|---|---|
| *ki-* (dep.) | to lie down, be laid |
| *gimmant-*, com. | winter |
| *gimmantariya-* (ŠE$_{12}$; Ic) | to hibernate |
| *genu-*, neut. | knee |
| *ginuššuš* | to/on his knees |
| *kinun*, adv. | now, at that moment |
| *ker/kard(i)-*, neut. | heart |
| *kiš-* (IIa, dep.) | to become, happen |
| *kiššan* (adv.) | thus, in this way |
| *kiššar(a)-*, com. | hand |
| *kitpantalaz*, adv. | from now on |
| *kui-* | (relative pronoun) |
| *kuen-/kun-* (Id) | to kill |
| *kuer-* (Id) | to cut |
| $^{(A.ŠÀ)}$*kuera-*, com. | field |
| *kuiški* | (indefinite pronoun) |
| *kuit*, conj. | since, that |
| *kuitman*, conj. | as long as, when, until |
| *kuitman nawi/nawi kuitman* | before |
| *gulš-* (Ia) | to carve, draw |
| $^{NA_4}$*kunkunuzzi-*, com. | (a stone) |
| *kurimma-*, com. | orphane(d) |
| ⟨ *guršauwana-*, neut. | island |
| *kurur*, neut. | hostility, hostile |
| *kururiyaḫḫ-* (Ia) | to be(come) hostile, wage war |
| *kuwapi* | when, ever |
| *kuwapikki* | somewhere |
| *kuwat* | why, where |
| | |
| *laḫḫa-*, com. | (military) campaign |
| *laḫḫiyaneške-* (Ic) | to campaign |
| *laḫlaḫḫima-*, com. | anguish, worry |
| *laḫu-* (Ia) | to pour, cast |
| *lag-* (IIa) | to knock out, fall |
| *lala-*, com. | tongue |
| *laman-* neut. | name |
| *link-/lik-* (Ie) | to swear (an oath) |
| *lingai-*, com. | oath |
| *linganu-* (Ia) | to make swear |
| *lip-* (Ia) | to lick |
| *luk-* (act. and med.-pass.) | to become light |

| | |
|---|---|
| *lukke-*(Ic) | to set fire to |
| *lukatti/a* | at dawn, the next day |
| *luli-*, com. | pond, basin |
| $^{\text{GIŠ}}$*luttai-*, com. | window |
| *luzzi-*, neut. | corvée |
| | |
| *-ma* | but, while |
| *maḫḫan*, conj. | 1. just as, like<br>2. when |
| *man* | (modality particle cf. 7.4.4) |
| *mān*, conj. | 1. just as, like<br>2. when |
| *mān … mān* | whether … or |
| *maniyaḫḫ-* (IIa) | to govern, assign |
| *mar-/mer-* (IIb) | to disappear |
| *mark-* (Ia) | to cut up |
| *marša-* | profane, treacherous |
| *mad-* (Ia) | to resist |
| *mauš-* (Ia) | to fall |
| *meḫur*, neut. | time, moment |
| *mekki-* | many, numerous |
| *mekki*, adv. | very, much |
| *mema-/memi(a)-* (IIe) | to say, speak |
| *memiya(n)-*, com./neut. | word, matter, deed |
| *menaḫḫanda*, adv. | against, facing |
| *mer-/mar-* (Ib) | to disappear |
| *militešš-* (Ia) | to become sweet |
| *mišriwant-* | shining, beautiful |
| *miu-/meu-* | four |
| *-mu* | me (acc., dat.-loc) |
| *munna(e)-* (Ic) | to hide |
| *munnanda*, adv. | furtively |
| | |
| *naḫḫ- (Ia)* | to be afraid, respect |
| *naḫšaratt-*, com. | fear, awe |
| *naḫšariya-* (Ic) | to fear, be(come) afraid |
| *naḫšarnu-* (Ia) | to make fear, respect |
| *nai-* (IId) | to turn |
| *parā nai-* | to dispatch, send out |
| *nakki-* | important, heavy |

| | |
|---|---|
| *nakkit*, adv. | with might |
| *namma*, adv. | then, subsequently |
| *namma* UL/UL *namma* | no longer |
| *-naš* | us (acc., dat.-loc) |
| *našma* | or, either … or |
| *naššu* | or, either … or |
| *natta* (UL) | not, no |
| *nawi* | not yet |
| *nepiš-*, neut. | heaven |
| *ninink-* (Ie) | to bring into motion, mobilize |
| *nešumnili/nešili*, adv. | in Hittite |
| *newaḫḫ-* (IIa) | to renew |
| *nu* | (connective, 1.4.2) |
| *numan* | (modal negation) |
| | |
| *paḫḫuenant-*, com. | fire |
| *paḫḫur*, neut. | fire |
| *paḫš-* (I/IIa) | to protect, be careful |
| *pai-* (Ih) | to go |
| *pai-/piya-* (IId) | to give |
| *palša-*, com. (KASKAL) | way, journey, time |
| *panku-* (noun) | council |
| *panku-* (adj.) | all, entire |
| *parā* | 1. out of, forth<br>2. further |
| *parā ḫandandatar* | (see *ḫandandatar*) |
| *parḫ-* (Ia) | to chase (away) |
| *parḫeššar*, neut. | hurry, haste |
| *parkui-* | clean, pure |
| *parkunu-* (Ia) | to cleanse, purify |
| *parranda*, adv. | across, over |
| *parš-* (Ia) | to escape |
| *-pat* | (particle expressing emphasis, 3.4.2) |
| *piya-* (Ic) | to send |
| *peḫute-* (Ia) | to bring, lead off |
| *pippa-* (IIc) | to destroy, topple |
| *per/parn-*, neut. | house, domain |
| *peran*, adv. | before, in front of |
| *peda-*, neut. | place, position |
| *peda-* (IIc) | to bring, carry (off) |

| | |
|---|---|
| *piddae-* (Ic) | to run (also in med.-pass.) |
| *pittenu-* (Ia) | to make run |
| *pittuliya-*, com. | anxiety, anguish |
| *punuš-* (Ia) | to question |
| | |
| *šae-/šiya-* (Ic) | to shoot, hurl, press |
| *šaḫḫan*, neut. | tax(es) (based on land property) |
| *šakk-/šekk-* (IIb) | to know |
| *šakuwandariya-* (Ic) | to leave uncelebrated |
| *šakuruwae-* (Ic) | to water, drink |
| $^{\text{LÚ}}$*šalašḫa-*, com. | groom, stable boy |
| *šallanu-* (Ia) | to make big, raise |
| *šalli-* | big, large |
| *-šan* | (sentence particle) |
| *šanezzi-* | sweet, friendly |
| *šanḫ-/šaḫ-* (Ie) | 1. to search, seek 2. to sweep |
| *šannapili-* | empty (-handed) |
| *šarā*, adv. | up, above, on top of |
| *šaramnaz*, adv. | from above, from the top |
| *šarni(n)k-* (Ie) | to compensate |
| *šarra-* (IIc) | to split (up), divide |
| *šašt(a)-*, com. | bed |
| *-ši* | him/her (dat.-loc.) |
| *šiya-* | (see *šae-*) |
| *šipant-* (IIa) | to offer, dedicate |
| *šer*, adv. | up, because of +dat. |
| *šeš-/šaš-* (IIb) | to sleep |
| *šiu(na)-*, com. | god |
| *šiwatt-* (UD.KAM), com. | day |
| *-šmaš* | you (plur. acc., dat.-loc.) |
| | them (dat.-loc.) |
| *šu* | (connective, 1.4.2) |
| *šuḫḫa-*, com. | roof |
| *šuḫḫa-* (IIc) | to pour |
| *šumeš* | you (pl.) |
| *šuppala-*, neut. | cattle |
| *šuppiyaḫḫ-* (IIa) | to cleanse |
| | |
| *ta* | (connective, 1.4.2) |
| *-ta* | you (acc., dat.-loc) |

| | |
|---|---|
| *dā-* (IIf) | to take, seize |
| *šarā dā-* | to capture, seize |
| *dai-/tiya-* (IId) | to put, place |
| *katta dai-* | to deposit |
| *takku*, conj. | when, if |
| *takš-* (Ia) | to fix, put together |
| *dalae-/daliya-* (Ic) | abandon, leave |
| *tamai-* | other |
| *tamašš-/tamešš-* (Ig) | to oppress |
| *dammešḫae-* (Ic) | to damage, punish |
| *tān* | for the second time |
| *taninu-* (Ia) | to bring into order |
| *dannatta-* | empty, unsettled |
| *dannattaḫḫ-* (IIa) | to empty, lay waste |
| (‹)*tapar-* (Ia) | to reign, rule |
| *tapariya-* (Ic) | rule, reign |
| *tarna-* (IIc) | to let go, release |
| *taruḫ-* (Ia) | to conquer |
| *tarupp-* (Ia) | to gather |
| *daššu-* | mighty, strong |
| *dašuwaḫḫ-* (IIa) | to make blind |
| *te-/tar-* (Ij) | to speak, say |
| *tiya-* (Ic) | to step, (take a) stand |
| *appan tiya-* | to take care of, support |
| *kari tiya-* | to yield, be lenient, show leniency |
| *tekan/takn-*, neut. | earth |
| *tekkuššanu-* (Ia) | to show |
| *tepawešš-* (Ia) | to become small |
| *tepaweššant-* | (too) short |
| *tepnu-* (Ia) | to belittle, humiliate (with *-za*) |
| *tepu-* | little, small, few |
| *tešḫa-*, com. | dream, sleep |
| *teššummi-*, com. | cup |
| *tittanu-* (Ia) | to put, install |
| *tu(e)kka-*, com. | body |
| *tuḫkanti-*, com. | second in command |
| *tuliya-*, com. | meeting |
| *tuppi-*, neut. | tablet |
| *tuppiyant-*, com. | tablet |
| *turiya-* (Ic) | to harness |

| | |
|---|---|
| *duwarne-* | to break |
| *tuzzi-*, com. | army, troops |
| | |
| *uiya-* (Ic) | to send |
| *uk* | I (1.2) |
| *unna-* (Ic) | to ride, drive |
| *up-* (Ia) | to rise |
| *uppa-* (IIc) | to send |
| *uške-* (Ic) | (imperfective of *auš-/au/u-*) |
| *uda-* (IIc) | to bring |
| *uddar*, neut. | word, thing, deed |
| *utne-*, neut. | land |
| *utneyant-*, com. | population |
| *uwa-* (Ii) | to come |
| *uwatar*, neut. | inspection |
| *uwate-* (Ia) | to bring, lead towards |
| | |
| *-wa(r-)* | (particle of direct speech) |
| *wah̯nu-* (Ia) | to (make) turn |
| *walh̯-* (Ia) | to attack, strike |
| *walh̯annae-* (Ic) | (imperfective of *walh̯-*) |
| *warrešša-* (IIc) | to help |
| *warnu-* (Ia) | to put on fire, burn |
| *warš-* (Ia) | to wipe, cleanse |
| *waštai-*, com. | sin, error |
| *watar, witen-*, neut. | water |
| *watarnah̯h̯-* (IIa) | to command, order |
| *watku-* (Ia) | to jump |
| *weh̯-/wah̯-* (Ib) | to turn |
| *wellu-*, com. | meadow |
| *wemiya-* (Ie B) | to find |
| *weriya-* (Ie B) | to call, invoke |
| *wēš* | we (1.2) |
| *wešiya-* (Ic) | to graze |
| *wet(ant)-*, com. | year |
| *wete-* (Ia) | to build |
| *wewakk-* (Ia) | to request, demand |
| | |
| *-z(a)/-(a)z* | (reflexive particle) |
| *zah̯h̯-* (IIa) | to beat |
| *zah̯h̯ai-*, com. (MÈ) | battle |

| | |
|---|---|
| *zanu-* | to cook, boil |
| *zeri-*, neut. | cup |
| *zik* | you (3.2) |
| *zinne-/zinna-* (Ie A) | to stop, finish |

## 2. Sumerograms

| | |
|---|---|
| A | = *watar* |
| A.AB.BA | = *aruna-* |
| À.ŠÀA.GÀR | field |
| A.ŠÀ | field |
| GIŠAB | = *luttai-* |
| AMA | mother |
| AN | = *nepiš* |
| ANŠE.GÌR.NUN.NA | mule, donkey |
| ANŠE.KUR.RA | horse, equid |
| ANŠE.KUR.RA. ḪI.A | horses, chariots |
| BA.ÚŠ | he/she died |
| BABBAR | white |
| BÀD | fortress |
| LÚBÁḪAR | potter |
| GIŠBANŠUR | table |
| $BURU_5$ | locust |
| DAM | wife |
| DINGIR(-*LIM*-*i*-) | god(dess) |
| DÙ | = *iya-* (act.) |
| DUB | = *tuppi-* |
| DUMU(-*la*-) | child, son |
| DUMU.DUMU | grandchild |
| DUMU.É.GAL | palace attendant |
| DUMU.LUGAL | prince |
| DUMU.MUNUS | daughter |
| DUMU.(NAM.)LÚ.$U_{19}$.LU | mortal |
| É | = *per* |
| É.DINGIR(-*LIM*) | temple |
| É.GAL | palace |
| EGIR-*anda* | = *appanda* |
| EGIR-*izzi-* | = *appezzi-* |
| EGIR(-*pa/an*) | = *appa*(*n*) |
| EME | tongue, mouth, curse |
| EN | lord, master |

| | |
|---|---|
| ÉRIN.MEŠ | army, troops |
| $EZEN_4$ | festival, celebration |
| GADA | cloth |
| GAL | 1. big (= *šalli-*) 2. chief |
| GAL | cup |
| GAL.GEŠTIN | chief of staff |
| GAL *MEŠEDI* | chief bodyguard |
| GAM(*-an*) | = *katta*(*n*) |
| (d)GAŠAN | lady |
| $GE_6$(.KAM) | evening, night |
| GÉŠPU | fist, violence, force |
| GEŠTIN | wine |
| GIŠGIDRU | staff, stick |
| GIG(*-ant-*, com.) | illness |
| GIG (verb) | to fall ill |
| GIŠGIGIR | wagon, cart |
| GIM-*an* | = *maḫḫan* |
| GÌR | foot, knee |
| GIŠGU.ZA | throne, chair |
| $GU_4$ | ox |
| GUB | = *ar-* dep. |
| GÙB(*-la-*) | left (side) |
| GUL | = *walḫ-* |
| (LÚ)GURUŠ | young man |
| ḪUL-*aḫḫ-* (IIa) | to hurt, maltreat |
| ḪUR.SAG | mountain |
| LÚI.$DU_8$ | gateman |
| ÍD | river, stream |
| dIM | Storm god |
| ÌR | servant, subject, slave |
| ÌR-*atar*, neut. | servitude |
| ÌR-(*n*)*aḫḫ-* (Ia) | to subject |
| ITU(.KAM) | month |
| IZI | = *paḫḫur* |
| KÁ.GAL | gate |
| KARAŠ | army |
| KASKAL | way, road, journey |
| KAŠ | beer |
| KUR | = *utne* |
| (LÚ)KÚR | enemy, hostile |
| LÚ | man, person |

| | |
|---|---|
| LUGAL | king |
| LUGAL-*izziya-* (Ie) | to be(come) king |
| LUGAL-*UTTU(M)* | kingship |
| LUGAL-*weznae-* | to be king, rule as king |
| LUGAL.GAL | Great King |
| MÁŠ.ANŠE.ḪI.A | animals of the field |
| ME | 100 |
| MÈ | = *zaḫḫai-* |
| MU(.KAM) | = *wet-* |
| MU(.KAM)-*anni* | in the following year |
| $^{\text{LÚ}}$MUḪALDIM | cook |
| MUNUS | woman |
| MUNUS.LUGAL | queen |
| NAM.RA | inhabitant, deportee |
| NÍ.TE | body |
| NIN | sister |
| NINDA | bread |
| NIR.GÁL | mighty |
| PA$_5$ | canal, stream |
| SAG.DU | head |
| SAG.UŠ | regular |
| $^{\text{LÚ}}$SANGA(*šankunni-*) | priest |
| SIG$_5$(-*ešš-*) | to become good |
| SIG$_7$ | 10,000 |
| SILA$_4$ | lamb |
| $^{\text{LÚ}}$SIMUG | smith |
| SISKUR | offer, ritual |
| $^{\text{MUNUS}}$SUḪUR.LÁ | temple servant |
| ŠÀ | 1. heart 2. in midst of |
| ŠAḪ(.TUR) | pig(let), swine |
| ŠE$_{12}$-*yanu-* (Ia) | = *gimmandariyanu-* |
| ŠEŠ | brother |
| ŠU | hand |
| ŠU.GI | old, elderly |
| $^{\text{GIŠ}}$ŠUKUR | spear |
| TA | by, through |
| TI-*nu-* (Ia) | to save |
| $^{\text{GIŠ}}$TUKUL | weapon, tool |
| $^{\text{d}}$U | Storm god |
| $^{\text{LÚ}}$U.ḪUB | deaf (man) |
| UD(.KAM) | = *šiwatt-* |

| | |
|---|---|
| UDU | sheep |
| UGU | = *šarā*, *šer* |
| UGULA | chief, overseer |
| GIŠUMBIN | wheel |
| UN | = *antuḫša-* |
| UR.BAR.RA | wolf |
| URU | town, city |
| ZAG | border, territory |
| ZI (*ištanzan*(*a*)-) | soul |

## 3. Akkadian

| | |
|---|---|
| *ABU* | father |
| *ADDIN* | I gave |
| *ANA* | to, for (= Hitt. dat.) |
| *ANA PANI* | to, for, facing (= Hitt. dat.-loc.) |
| *AQBI* | I said |
| *AṢBAT* | I took, seized |
| *AŠRU* | = *peda-* |
| *BĒLTU* | lady |
| *BĒLU* | lord, master, chief |
| *ELLU* | free |
| *ḪALZU* | fortress |
| *IDDIN* | he/she gave |
| *IMUR* | he/she saw |
| *INA* | in(to), to |
| *IQBI* | he/she said |
| *IŠME* | he/she listened, heard |
| *IŠPUR* | he/she wrote |
| *IŠTU* | 1. out, from 2. by, through |
| *IŠṬUR* | he/she wrote, sent |
| *ITTI* | together with |
| *LIM* | 1,000 |
| *MĀMĪTU* | oath |
| LÚ*MEŠEDI* | bodyguard |
| *NARARU* | auxiliary |
| *NĪŠ* DINGIR-*LIM* | oath, oath deity |
| *QADU* | together with |
| *QATAMMA* | likewise, just so, thus |
| *QIBI* | speak! |
| *ŠA* | of (= Hitt. gen.) |

| | |
|---|---|
| *ŠARRATU* | queen |
| *ŠARRU* | king |
| *ŠUMU* | name |
| $^{\text{LÚ}}$*ṬEMU* | envoy, messenger |
| *ṬUPPU* | tablet |
| *U* | and |
| *UL* | not, no |
| *UMMA* | thus, as follows |
| *UMMĀNU* | army, troops |

## 4. Names (of Exercises only)

### *Divine*

| | |
|---|---|
| Enkidu | |
| Ḫašamili | |
| Ḫepadu | |
| $^{\text{MUŠ}}$Illuyanka | |
| IM | = Storm god (see also U) |
| Išḫara | |
| *IŠTAR* | |
| Ištuštaya | |
| Gulša- | |
| Kumarbi | |
| Malliyanneš | |
| Papaya | |
| *SÎN* | = Moon god |
| Šiušummi- | |
| U | = Storm god (see also IM) |
| U.GUR | = Nergal, god of the Netherworld |
| UTU | = Sun god(dess) |

### *Personal* (women marked by $^{\text{f}}$)

Anitta
$^{\text{f}}$DINGIR.MEŠ.IR-i-
Ḫalpašulupi
Ḫalwa-LÚ (Ḫalwazidi)
Ḫattušili
Ḫulla
Kallu
Gilgameš
Kupanta-$^{\text{d}}$LAMMA

Maḫḫuzzi
Mašduri
Muršili
Muwatalli
Pišeni
Telipinu
Duda

## *Geographical*

Arauwanna
Arinna (PÚ-na)
Ḫapara
Ḫatti (KÙ.BABBAR-ti)
Ḫattuša (KÙ.BABBAR-ša-)
Ḫayaša
Kašepura
Gašga
Katḫaidduwa
Kiššiya
KÙ.BABBAR (Ḫatti/Ḫattuša)
Mizri = Egypt
Nerik
Niḫiriya
Palḫuišsa
Parḫa
PÚ-na (Arinna)
Šeḫa
Taḫurpa
Taggašta
$^{d}$U-tašša/$^{d}$U-ašša (Tarḫuntašsa)
Zalpuwa

28304883R00124

Made in the USA
Middletown, DE
09 January 2016